Search Engine

Finding Meaning in Jewish Texts
Volume 2: Jewish Leadership

Rabbi Gil Student

KODESH PRESS

Search Engine Volume 2

© Gil Student, 2018
ISBN: 978-1-947857-08-7
Paperback Edition

All rights reserved. Except for brief quotations in printed reviews, no part of this publication may be reproduced, stored in a retrieval system, or transmitted in any form or by any means (printed, written, photocopied, visual electronic, audio, or otherwise) without the prior permission of the publisher.

Letters for the Previous Volume

Letter from Rav Menachem Genack, CEO of OU Kosher, for Previous Volume

Union of Orthodox Jewish Congregations of America • איחוד קהילות האורתודוקסים באמריקה
Eleven Broadway • New York, NY 10004-1303 • Tel: 212-563-4000 • Fax: 212-564-9058 • www.ou.org

KASHRUTH DIVISION

MOISHE BANE
President

Gary Torgow
Chairman

Rabbi Yitzchak Fund
Vice Chairman

RABBI MENACHEM GENACK
Rabbinic Administrator, CEO

RABBI ALEXANDER S. ROSENBERG
Rabbinic Administrator (1950-1972)

Letter from Rav Shlomo Aviner,
Rosh Yeshiva of Yeshivat Ateret Kohanim, for Previous Volume

Letter from Rav Yitzchak Breitowitz, Rav of Kehillat Ohr Somayach, for Previous Volume

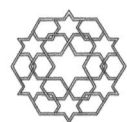

ק״ק אהבת תורה
Woodside Synagogue Ahavas Torah
9001 Georgia Avenue
Silver Spring, MD 20910

4 Kislev 5778
21 November 2017

Rabbi Emeritus
Yitzchak Breitowitz

Rabbi
Moshe Walter

President
Richard Sassoon

Vice President for Administration
Chanoch Kanovsky

Vice President for Programming
Adina Gewirtz

Vice President for Membership and Community Relations
Alida Friedrich

Treasurer
Jerry Saunders

Secretary
Daniel Friedman

For almost 15 years, first in Hirhurim and now in Torah Musings, Rabbi Gil Student has educated, inspired and entertained thousands of people with his perceptive and comprehensive essays on halacha, Jewish thought and Jewish history. He is one of the true pioneers in harnessing the power of the internet to convey the timeless and eternal truths of the Torah and it is no accident that his blogs have been consistently recognized for their excellence.

For the second time, he has collected many of these pieces in book form. In almost 300 pages, R. Gil covers a wide variety of topics—marriage, Shabbat and holidays, prayer, food, recreation, death. All of the essays, as brief as many are (a concession to the diminished attention span of the online generation!), are well-thought out, organized and cogent. He addresses his topics with clarity and roots his conclusions in authoritative Torah sources. Moreover, his tone towards rabbonim and poskim, even those that he may disagree with, is consistently respectful. He debates ideas, not personalities. As such, both in style and substance, his work is a pleasure to read and is of real benefit not only to beginners but even to accomplished Torah scholars.

May R. Gil continue to spread the Dvar Hashem in his "Yeshiva without walls."

Yitzchak A. Breitowitz
Rav, Kehillat Ohr Somayach
Jerusalem, Israel

Letter from Rav Aharon Rakeffet, Rosh Yeshiva at RIETS, for Previous Volume

ישיבה יוניברסיטי בישראל ע"ר
Yeshiva University in Israel
RIETS Kollel - Aaron Rakeffet
Caroline and Joseph S. Gruss Institute
40 Rechov Duvdevani,
Bayit Vegan, Jerusalem ISRAEL 9641423
Tel: 972-2-531-3000 Fax: 531-3021

בס"ד

The bon mot that contemporary rabbis often cited was about the question that the Orthodox rabbi received. It concerned the appropriate bracha when one obtains a new Lamborghini. The rabbi responds "What is a Lamborghini?" The same question was then asked of a Reform clergyman. He answered, "What is a *bracha*?" When I went over Rabbi Gil Student's new volume I felt like the Orthodox rabbi in this lark.

What are Combat Exoskeletons, Instagram, Kosher switches, Powerball, Soundcloud and many other phrases in this publication? Rabbi Student has admirably brought Jewish Law into the twenty-first century in this volume. He exhibits a wide range of knowledge and cites many sources of both contemporary and classic rabbinical literature. While many issues that are discussed have still not reached a rabbinical consensus, this work will provide much data for future dialogue.

I have known Rabbi Gil Student for many years now. He is a true example of the best in the Torah world who attempt to strive in contemporary civilization.

May I express my blessings to the author
שיזכה להוציא את חידושיו הנכונים על פני תבל מתוך בריות גופא ונהורא מעליא, ורוב נחת מבנים ובני בנים העוסקים בתורה ובמצוות.

Aaron Rakeffet

Letter from Rav Arie Folger, Chief Rabbi of Vienna, for Previous Volume

ISRAELITISCHE KULTUSGEMEINDE WIEN

ARIE FOLGER, MBA
OBERRABBINER · CHIEF RABBI

אריה פאלגער
הרב הראשי דק"ק וויען יצ"ו

Approbation for the sefer "Search Engine" by Rabbi Gil Student

Vienna, the 15ᵗʰ of Kislev 5778

To readers of the Sefer "Search Engine,"

For many years, Rabbi Gil Student has been concerned with matters pertaining to the klal and has applied his ability to handle the written word in order to educate and elucidate. He has done so with essays he published into book form some fifteen years ago, has done so through a publishing label he had launched, with which he published a variety of thought provoking books, and most importantly, was ahead of the curve in understanding the internet's potential to spread Torah, particularly addressing timely topics. Through his Hirhurim - Torah Musings web site, initially a blog, which later became a full fledged internet periodical in which numerous authors teach Torah, Rabbi Gil Student has consistently aimed to present Torah responses to contemporary issues, as well as to sift the wheat from the shaft regarding what one might, using the Rashbam's idiom, term *hapeshatim hamitchadshot bekhol yom*.

As Rabbi Student notes in his introduction, we do not suffer from too few books. Books are readily available. If anything, we suffer from information overload. Through well researched halakhic essays and well founded book reviews, Rabbi Student helps us sift through this humongous pile of information, finding the gems while disregarding - at times subjecting to critical inquiry - some of the less solid material out there. But his isn't just a scholarly undertaking. Reacting to a phenomenon Rabbi Alfred Cohen once labeled presenting "The Torah in a Brown Paper Bag," Rabbi Student goes out of his way to do the opposite and show the reader how compelling Torah is.

Rabbi Student's commitment to halakha is profound. Following in the footsteps of the Rov, Rabbi J. B. Solovitchik, he stresses that halakha is not distinct from Jewish theology, but is rather applied Jewish theology. It is surely in this spirit that we find him addressing both philosophical and halakhic issues, at times blending both in a

A-1010 WIEN · SEITENSTETTENGASSE 4 · TEL. +43/1/531 04-111 · FAX +43/1/531 04-155
rabbinat@ikg-wien.at · www.ikg-wien.at

manner that injures neither one nor the other, but rather allows our understanding of each to enrich the other. One example is found in the book review he includes in the present volume of Rabbi Eliezer Melammed's sefer on marriage and marital intimacy. Seeing the unity of halakha and hashkafa is what sets that sefer and its approach apart, and allows it to stay clear of some pitfalls of other approaches.

Though I must admit to only having read some of the essays in the present volume, I can confidently say, based on the essays I have seen, as well as numerous other writings of Rabbi Student, that they are well researched, compellingly written, and infused with yirat shamayim, coming from a solid commitment and also of a realistic understanding of society, in the spirit of educating a student ba'asher hu sham. I therefore much appreciate the appearance of the present volume and am eager to see the appearance of the other two forthcoming volumes he announced in the introduction of the present volume.

May he succeed in drawing more people to more intense Torah learning, and even draw readers to delve into the sources included in his footnotes. May be we'll even develop a somewhat longer attention span. I wish this volume much success.

Arie Folger

Table of Contents

Preface 13
Introduction 15

Chapter 1: Authority and Leadership 30
A Rabbi's Role 32
Rabbinic Qualifications 36
What is Ordination? 42
Gradations of Authority 47
Who Can Be Called "Rabbi"? 51
Revoking Ordination 57
Revoking Ordination II 61
Undermining a Rabbi 66
The Repentant Rabbi 71

Chapter 2: Studies in Leadership 78
Learning from Moshe 79
Growth into A Rabbi 86
The President's Rabbi 90
The Elected Official 95
How Should Jews Vote? 98
Religious Liberty 101
Religious Politicians 104
Is A Politician Allowed To Retire From Public Office? . . . 111
Finding Inspiration In Politics 115

Chapter 3: Using Authority 119
A Rabbi's Obligation 120
A Rabbi's Method 127
A Rabbi's Approach 133
Religious Law and Change 137
Religious Law and Historical Context 141
Contemporary Changes 144
Proposed Changes 148
Communal Impact of Strict Standards 153
Threatening *Halakhah* 161
Losing the Next Generation 164
The Israeli Chief Rabbinate: Why? 168
Determination of Jewish Status 175
The Decline and Fall of Local Rabbinic Authority 180

Chapter 4: Followership 207
The Need For A Rabbi 208
Communal Cynicism 214
Challenging Your Rabbi 217
Rating Your Rabbi 221
Retreating From Community: House *Minyanim* *226*
Conversion Guidelines, Transparency, and Accountability . 232
Conversion Control In Israel 237

Chapter 5: Community 242
Why Are There Jewish Denominations? 243
Secession 247
Crossing Denominational Lines 252
Will Charedi Ideology Change? 257
Why We Fight 260
The *Agunah* Debate Continues 264
The Convert Problem 270

Why Orthodoxy Needs Its Left Wing 273
Leaving Modern Orthodoxy 278
How Orthodox Is Open Orthodoxy? 282
All the Lonely People on Social Media 287
A Turkish Community's Tax Revolt 291

Chapter 6: Values 298
Gender Roles 299
What Does Modern Orthodoxy Stand For? 305
How Much Does Unity Cost? 308
Tzelofchad's Daughters and Open Orthodoxy 312
Judaism and Women's Changed Status 317
Clemency in the Jewish Tradition 320
Biblical Defamation in Divorce and Politics 324
EpiPen Pricing and Jewish Law 334
Officiating At A Gay Marriage 338
May A Jew Register in a National Muslim Registry . . . 338
Counting for a Minyan 344
Women Rabbis 350
Women Leaders 361

Afterword 365

Preface

I thank God for allowing me to complete the second volume in this three-volume series. I pray that He allows me to finish volume three and to continue learning and teaching.

Many of these essays appeared originally on my website, *Torah Musings*. Where indicated, essays appeared elsewhere first. Regarding *Torah Musings*, I thank the members of the editorial board: R. Basil Herring and R. Moshe Schapiro. Efraim Vaynman does a lot of work on the website behind the scenes, often going above and beyond the call of duty. Regular contributors to the magazine include R. Gidon Rothstein, R. Daniel Mann, and Joel Rich. R. Micha Berger served as an invaluable early source of advice and editorial assistance during the transition to *Torah Musings*. I thank them all for their continued efforts to spread Torah. This book emerges from my contributions to *Torah Musings* over the past four years. Some of the essays were part of major communal controversies, as readers will see. On such issues, I benefit from the wise counsel of many different thinkers and communal leaders. My policy is to maintain the secrecy of people who offer me advice and halakhic guidance. I thank all those anonymous wise people for their assistance.

R. Alec Goldstein of Kodesh Press served as the impetus for this series. In addition to being a good friend, he is an excellent editor. His tireless work and precision has made this process a pleasure.

It would be difficult for me to name every teacher who has influenced me or taught me, and I certainly do not want to imply that they agree with everything that I say or write. However, I would be negligent if I did not acknowledge their contributions to my education. What follows is a list of synagogue and school rabbis from whom I have learned: R. David M. Feldman, R. Ephraim Kanarfogel, R. Feivel Cohen, R. Mordechai Marcus, R. Yisroel Hirsch, R. Baruch Pesach Mendelson, R. Shalom Z. Berger, R. Yitzchak Goodman, R. Shlomo Stochel, R. Menachem Meier, R. Benzion Scheinfeld, R. Mordechai Willig, R. Hershel Schachter, and in particular R. Mayer Twersky. I also highlight the influence of R. Aharon Rakeffet and R. Menachem Genack. I thank them all for inspiring and educating me in the path of Torah. My lifelong friends, R. Daniel Z. Feldman and R. Benjamin G. Kelsen, have been constant sources of support and advice. I thank them for always being there for me.

I would not be where I am, for better or for worse, without the dedication of two people who have set me on my current path: my mother and father. Their devotion to our family and Jewish education, and their encouragement for each of their children to grow in their own ways, serves as an inspiration to me and my children.

And, of course, nothing in my life would have been possible without the loving patience and support of my wife, Miriam. She is a true partner in everything that I do. I thank her every day for bringing joy to my life. Our four children—Deena, Shea, Shmuly, and Tzaly—have always been blessings and sources of pride. Our family was recently joined by our son-in-law Dovid, and even more recently by our granddaughter, Ayala. We have so many blessings for which to be thankful. We pray for all their continued success in a Torah-infused life.

Gil Student
Gil.student@gmail.com
5 Elul 5778
August 16, 2018

Introduction

Torah Authority in the Internet Age

A famous saying has it that Jews in America are just like everyone else, only more so.[1] Perhaps when it comes to the Internet, Jews are like everyone else, only less so. The following thoughts are admittedly impressionistic due to a lack of data. Moreover, I am not a sociologist. However, I am very much involved in the use of the Internet for Orthodox communal purposes. Likely because of that role, I have been observing the Orthodox community's interaction with the Internet, particularly since the focus on its dangers was raised in broad communal terms in the Asifah anti-Internet gathering of 2012, which I strongly opposed for reasons I will explain below.[2]

The Internet's impact on general society has certainly seeped into the Orthodox Jewish community, but to a lesser degree for us than for others because of our unique communal and cultural traits. For example, Shabbos observance forces us offline for approximately 25 hours a week. On occasion, throughout the year, we have prolonged electronic "fasts" due to holidays, sometimes

---

1. An earlier version of this essay appeared in *Klal Perspectives* (Fall 2015).
2. In 2012, tens of thousands of Charedi Jews attended a gathering (*asifah*) at Citi Field to hear about the dangers of the Internet. I was vocally critical of this event, which failed to address the real problems people are facing. See "Haredi Event On Internet Dangers Draws Thousands Of Participants," *The Jewish Press*, May 23, 2012.

lasting as long as three consecutive days. Forced to live in the pre-Internet era for these short periods, we exercise the skills that the Internet tends to suppress, such as holding conversations without electronic interruptions and reading without interrupting to check emails. Similarly, though our schools' policies limiting Internet use are generally observed only in the breach, the concerned attitude toward Internet use conveyed by our *yeshivos* and rabbis force us to at least construe Internet use as an option, rather than an unquestioned necessity. Nevertheless, just as the Internet has dramatically changed general society, it has had a substantial impact on our community as well.

The Orthodox community has captured many opportunities afforded by the Internet, but also has experienced significant challenges. Some of the more obvious and seemingly pressing issues generated by the Internet are, from a historical perspective, not particularly concerning. There is, however, another issue that is historic as well as theologically urgent, threatening to undermine our entire communal order and tradition. That issue will be discussed in the second half of this introduction. While I believe that, unfortunately, there is no simple solution for these problems, the old approach, exemplified by the aforementioned Asifah, is doomed to failure.

Section I: The Internet and the Individual

I. Facilitating Increased Torah Learning

Probably the most significant contribution of the Internet has been its dramatic expansion of the sheer volume of Torah that is available to be learned. The immense storehouses of Torah articles, books and audio lectures posted online, and thereby accessible to all, are astounding. A simple personal device can store more information, study tools, and resources than the ancient library in Alexandria. This new technology allows yeshiva graduates to listen to, and learn from, their *rabbeim* (religious teachers) for years after leaving the yeshiva, something that was but a rare treat in earlier times. Perhaps the even greater innovation is its enabling of graduates of one yeshiva to learn from *rabbeim* of another yeshiva. The Gemara (*Avodah Zarah* 19a) encourages Torah learning from more than one teacher, since such practice broadens one's understanding of Torah. As never before, the Internet allows mature students to learn from the widest selection of leading Torah scholars and lecturers.

Different people gain in different ways from the access to their earlier *rabbeim,* as well as to others. For some, an ongoing connection to the *rabbeim* of their younger years expands the teachers' influence into the student's adult years. Others, who never really connected to their *rabbeim* while in yeshiva, find new *rabbeim* better suited to their disposition or learning interests. Yet others may have had excellent relationships while in yeshiva, but discover on the Internet new *rabbeim* who are better suited to their needs as an adult, and to their more mature emotional and intellectual orientation. They now have many more options to find a *derekh* in learning that matches their proclivities. But this opportunity also highlights a danger.

II. Whose *Derekh*?

Although most men leave yeshiva while in their twenties, they never stop growing and changing in adulthood.[3] Such continuing development is both natural and wonderful. On the one hand, the Internet allows *rabbeim* and others with traditional Torah voices to play an integral role in this maturation process. On the other hand, the Internet makes it easier than ever for fully committed

---

3. The Internet's impact on women's Torah study requires separate study. In some ways, it is a more profound change.

and believing Orthodox Jews to find themselves attracted to different streams of thought and practice. Rather than going "off the *derekh* (path)," they are going "off their *derekh*." This tendency is particularly pervasive among those intellectually inclined, and in my experience is actually far more common than the more-frequently-discussed phenomenon of individuals going "off the *derekh*" completely.

Perhaps for social and family reasons, and perhaps because it makes them more comfortable, most people who change beliefs, whether off the *derekh* or off their *derekh*, do not actually leave their community. They keep their new attitudes more or less to themselves and alter little in their outward behavior; they certainly do not change the schools to which they send their children. This absence of social expression greatly diminishes the impact of Internet-induced *derekh* issues. It is true that some young people are leaving the community, but that was also the case in the 1950's, 60's, 70's, 80's and 90's. One should not minimize the pain and concern related to any individual leaving the community, or to the spiritual damage of any individual abandoning traditional beliefs. But, the Internet does not appear to be causing any sort of mass exodus from our communities.

III. More Learning Opportunities, Yet Less Time Learning

Greater than its impact on the Orthodox Jew's theological views is the Internet's consumption of a colossal amount of time. The *frum* Jew has no shortage of demands on his or her time, yet technology is unquestionably diverting time from other far more important and productive uses. This diversion desperately requires corrective action.

The onslaught of e-mails, many demanding immediate attention, is a normative part of everyone's day. Rabbis report that they spend huge parts of their day responding to e-mails and texts from their congregants. On the one hand, this expanded contact between rabbi and congregant is wonderful because increased accessibility strengthens the trust and relationship between them. On the other, it detracts from other activities the rabbi had otherwise committed to be doing, such as spending time with his family, planning communal events, and learning Torah. Rabbis are not the only ones who carry this new burden. Leaving an office at day's end no longer allows one to enter into an alternative restricted zone of family, Torah study, and other activities. E-mails, texts, and cell phones allow the office to be an intrusive and demanding part of life, at any time and in any place. Moreover, social media and many websites are intentionally designed to capture the viewer's attention for extended periods of time. People read innocuous status updates and watch mildly interesting videos, despite recognizing that they are wasting time. But the intrusion into time otherwise more wisely allocated is only one dimension of the issue. A second dimension is the resulting compromised ability to focus.

A personal device may contain a plethora of Torah texts — *Tanakh*, *Shas*, and several hundred *sefarim*, including *rishonim* and *poskim* and almost everything else. When learning this Torah on a device, it is hard not to take an occasional peek at e-mail. In fact, simply having the device accessible creates this urge. Similarly, someone typing on a smartphone could be writing a *devar Torah* one minute and texting the next. While these functional overlaps can theoretically be conquered with self-control, self-control is a trait that has always suffered an imbalance of supply and demand.

The distractive nature of devices is recognized by the technology industry. In fact, apps and programs have been introduced to force users to focus; alas for a variety of reasons they inevitably fail. Ultimately, the most effective strategy to manage this challenge is by employing a time log, which is a daily or weekly estimate of the time spent online. After keeping such a log for a few weeks, and seeing the shocking amount of time spent unproductively online, conscientious people will inevitably take action to reduce their usage.

IV. Inattention Span
Many have written, with varying degrees of alarm, about the widespread decrease in the attention span of the Sesame Street, and now Internet, generations. I find myself struggling to read long articles and, *le-havdil*, occasionally skipping to the end of long responsa. There is even a trend among Religious Zionist rabbis to include a summary at the end of each responsum or article. I am not sure how that started, but it is quite a reflection of the needs of the current generation.

Teachers and rabbis must adjust their styles to accommodate the realities of their less attentive listeners. The days are long gone when Rav Joseph B. Soloveitchik could capture an audience's attention for a four-hour lecture. To maintain students' attention, we must intersperse stories and surprising insights into our adult education classes. To a degree, this practice, though necessary, has watered down some of the learning in our community. It has also given higher profiles to rabbis who excel in infotainment, which sometimes comes with the risks attendant to a charismatic personality (*ve-ha-meivin yavin*). Writers, too, need to entertain. Articles need cliffhangers and teasers to get people to read to the end.

But the implications of the Internet to our community are even more ominous and profound.

V. *Shmutz*
I mentioned above the well-publicized 2012 Asifah. The Asifah focused almost exclusively on preventing access to the inappropriate

material available online. Similarly, ongoing discussions abound in shuls and by rabbis concerning the allegedly rampant infidelity caused by the Internet. I suggest that this narrow focus is misplaced.

By its nature, the *yetzer hara*—the impulse to sin—finds opportunities to wreak havoc. The Internet did not introduce marital cheating, nor is looking at inappropriate things a new concern or practice. For centuries, even prior to the Internet, the *yetzer hara* enjoyed much tragic success. Even in more recent times, summer bungalow colonies have, arguably, been a far bigger source of infidelity than the Internet. Certainly, those engaged in extramarital affairs use any technology available, including cellphones and social media. These technologies may be tools of choice, but eliminating them will not hinder cheating spouses. Admittedly, this perspective is premised on anecdotes alone, but so is the view that the Internet is the primary inducer of misbehavior.

That is not to suggest that the Internet is not rampantly abused and that it need not be assiduously controlled. However, the tone and rhetoric regarding its dangers must be appropriately measured lest the damage of the rebuke be more devastating than the improper behavior being addressed.

For example, we are often warned that Internet users can lose their souls, or entire afterlife, with the click of a link. This declaration is incredibly unhelpful. We believe that people can do *teshuvah* until their last breathing moment. It is horribly inappropriate to employ language that effectively writes off those who have sinned—whether by viewing online pornography or otherwise—by asserting that those people are a lost cause. People make mistakes; in moments of weakness they make bad choices. We must vociferously discourage inappropriate behavior but the wholesale and absolute marginalization of those who succumb to temptation is counter-productive. In fact, some people are addicted to pornography and they need professional help. If their behavior is simply characterized as evil, they probably will not seek the necessary assistance. Others can stop their inappropriate behavior, and should be effectively motivated to do so. Rather than loud clamoring, the most effective method to motivate the ceasing of hidden behavior is to promote the threat of discovery (see *Berakhos* 28b).

Internet filters are necessary, but filters alone are insufficient, particularly on mobile devices. Image and ad blockers are also very important. But more powerful are stories of men losing their families and livelihoods because of accessing pornography. If people realize that they are likely to get caught and are truly scared of what will happen to them when they are caught—what their children, friends and bosses will think of them—they will stop if they can. Sadly, we do not lack for many true stories that can bring this message home. The stories must be utilized to scare people away from pornography and infidelity. Imposing the requisite fear of discovery does not require fire and brimstone rhetoric. Every rabbi and educator, in their own style, should repeatedly remind people that no one is truly anonymous online; every search can be traced and every user unmasked; and thus, eventually, misdeeds will be disclosed.

However, the language and tactics were not the primary failing of the Asifah. Rather, something more fundamental was missing, the discussion of which requires us to look from a communal perspective and take a brief historical and theological detour to see the truly historic change generated by the Internet.

Section II: The Internet and the Community

I. Mockery and A Weakened Communal Leadership

Online mockery and derision are ubiquitous. Their pervasiveness imbues readers with a diminished sensitivity to improper language and to attitudes that are fundamentally anathema to religious life. More than that, however, is the impact of anonymous frontal attacks on communal leadership. In the face of unbridled and unabashed anonymous bomb throwing, many community leaders simply choose to avoid the heat by saying nothing publicly. Whether or not this intimidation is the very goal of the derision, the community suffers immeasurably from the silencing of at least some of its leadership. Because of the widespread mockery and uncharitable reading of the media, particularly on the Internet, the community is being deprived of invaluable guidance and a sorely needed counterbalance to the rather loud and incessant voices that are unsympathetic to Torah tradition.

This is all in addition to the traditional damage caused by ever-present mockery, cynicism, and frivolity. They destroy faith in—and respect for—others, and diminish the inclination to accept rebuke. The Internet has raised the impact of mockery to new heights, thereby decreasing *teshuvah* in the world.

None of these evil challenges, however, are new. Mockery is denounced in *Tanakh*, indicating that it has been a problem for millennia. In our own lifetimes, we recall how Israeli reporters would attend the speeches of Rav Elazar Shach and Rav Ovadiah Yosef, waiting breathlessly to mock their teachings. The Communists in the early twentieth century mercilessly mocked rabbis and Judaism in newspapers, theater, and other media. Even our forefather Avraham Avinu faced the *leitzanei ha-dor*, the scorners of the generation, who would mock him.[4]

---

4. See Rashi, Gen. 25:19.

The impact, as well, is not unprecedented. In the past, mockery has won impressive victories. A century and a half ago, yeshiva benches were emptied to the halls of Communism and Socialism, largely due to a campaign of mockery against traditional Judaism. Compared to the spiritual devastation wrought in such eras, twenty-first century Internet challenges pale in comparison. Perhaps Heaven has mercy on our unprepared community.

The unique challenge of Internet mockery, however, is the Internet's unparalleled penetration into our communities, our schools and our homes. In other situations, however uncomfortable the mockery, we can tolerate the unpleasantness by avoiding it. The intrusion of the Internet, however, has diminished the ability to avoid it, even for those in the most insular of communities.

The only effective defense to mockery is sophistication. Rabbis need to become PR mavens, savvy in the judicial use of media to convey a message. The current generation of *gedolim* grew up in a different era and cannot be expected to master new technologies. The next generation, however, must become expert. An excellent example is Rav Shlomo Aviner in Israel, who has developed relationships with the media and publishes with such frequency and ferocity that his views cannot be easily distorted. He is well-known for answering all text message questions, affording him a radical availability, allowing anyone to directly ask his opinion on almost any subject. We cannot defeat mockery outright, but we can wage a good fight. That effort, however, requires a willingness to use the right tools. Leading rabbis need to follow basic PR ideas like staying positive, learning what your opponents are saying, and trying to convince bystanders and not your opponent.

Mockery is a clear Internet challenge to Torah leadership but the very culture of the Internet poses a more subtle and pervasive challenge to the Torah tradition.

II. Democratization of Torah

Though Torah study is a universal Jewish obligation, mastery of Torah is a prized and limited achievement. Prior to the publication of the Talmud, when the Torah was primarily transmitted orally, only those who studied in the controlled environment of a yeshiva academy could ever gain access to the "texts." And only those with phenomenal memories could actually master the material. Everyone else recognized their own limitations in scholarship and, to a great degree, had no choice but to defer to the wisdom and guidance of their rabbis. Their only alternative, if we can call it that, was to reject the oral tradition outright and adopt the more accessible text of the Bible as the sole source of religious truth.

This wish to minimize rabbinic influence could likely have been the allure of the Sadducee, and later Karaite, ideology. These were paths that allowed for Torah expertise without the prerequisite of mastering the oral Torah. In this sense, the Sadducees were religious populists, democrats of the religious spirit. They sought to wrench religious authority away from the rabbis and allow everyone to participate equally. Rather than spreading greater knowledge, they reduced the knowledge requirement and merely distributed authority more arbitrarily. We can sense a rebirth of this strategy in the Internet era.

The Torah, however, does not encourage populist authority, but rather places authority on the shoulders of the contemporary, scholarly experts. The "priest and the judge who shall be in that day" serve as the highest religious decision-making body, from whose rulings we must not "deviate right or left" (Deut. 17:11). Through the teachings of the oral tradition, the Sages taught that Torah mastery and guidance require true, substantive expertise. Absent both intellectual and moral mastery, the Torah's lessons are vulnerable to distortion, whether deliberate or otherwise. Therefore, rabbis must shepherd their flocks and nurture a connection to Torah in the proper measures, as befitting their spiritual readiness. Sometimes, restricting access to certain types of information is appropriate.

III. Torah for Scholars

There is a concept of "*halakhah ve-ein morin ken*," which translates as "this is the law but we do not teach it this way." This principle reflects the fact that the law occasionally includes dimensions that create opportunities for abuse. The ruling is only appropriate for Torah scholars who are equipped to appreciate these legal dimensions within a fuller context.

This attitude can be criticized as paternalistic and condescending. Who are the rabbis to decide who is ready to learn certain things, and who is not? Who are they to restrict access to dimensions of the Torah; after all, is not Torah the inheritance of the entire nation?

On the other hand, if it is true that certain knowledge will be abused if shared, or be wholly misunderstood and then misapplied, is a degree of restriction not appropriate? For example, is it appropriate to teach an entire community how to delay divorce proceedings through legal technicalities? Are there not topics that should be broached only with those who are sufficiently mature or sophisticated to understand and utilize them appropriately? Of course not all information is ripe to be shared with everyone. Yet this seemingly elitist attitude is certainly being challenged by contemporary societal attitudes.

One might have thought that the centralized influence of the rabbis would diminish when, out of necessity, the Oral Torah was committed to writing. The recording and resulting text of the Oral Torah, however, was so confusing and voluminous, and its manuscripts so rare, that few could claim to master it. Torah remained within the exclusive purview of the experts, and the rabbis remained the sole source of Jewish information. During that period, rabbis could and frequently did challenge each other, often heatedly. Rabbinic assertions were checked against original sources, and compilations of arguments were tested against other views. Yet due to its complexity, the discussion remained closed to those without sufficient training. The barrier to entry was years of textual study and apprenticeship.

The exclusive access to views and arguments then began to diminish. Certainly the introduction of the printing press played a significant role in the democratization of Judaism, but another culprit demands notice. Not only were texts made readily accessible, but summary works, like *Ba'eir Heitev*, condensed complex textual debates into manageable digests. These books allowed proficiency to masquerade as expertise. To the uninitiated, someone able to skim the summaries could appear to be a master, a lamentable situation in any field. Being familiar with the *Mishnah Berurah*'s position on a particular law cannot compare to having extensively studied the underlying texts, commentaries, and codes.

IV. Torah in a Democratic Age

Halakhic Judaism may have now truly entered its democratic age. Electronic databases, and the Internet in particular, produce an ever greater democratization of knowledge. Those who do not even know Hebrew can Google their way to proficiency, on some level. The clever yeshiva graduate, who is familiar with the ways of the Talmud and codes, but has certainly not yet mastered them, can use Google and databases to amass impressive arguments and even produce seemingly informed articles. The Internet is a magnification of the once minor threat of democratization of Torah.

In this age, can the traditional respect of, and deference to, expertise survive? Does "*halakhah ve-ein morin ken*" have any meaning in the electronic age?

One strategy for Torah leaders is to bemoan this democratization by standing their ground and denouncing the non-experts who overstate their competence for the intellectual frauds that they are. Unfortunately, however, calling out frauds generally alienates more than it attracts. The authentic scholar appears self-serving and uncharitable, even when correct. Similarly, debate will fail, since the audience lacks the requisite sophistication and training to evaluate the credibility and strength of competing arguments. Consequently, such debates are won through rhetoric and slogan, usually the province of the fraud, and not authenticity and truth, the province of the scholar.

Authority has been transferred to the people. The Asifah failed to recognize this and therefore proposed solutions to the Internet that immediately failed. Respected communal leaders attempted to impose strict limitations on Internet use. Among the proposals were communal requirements of "kosher" devices or mandatory expulsion from school of students whose families access the Internet at home. Even the subsequent Flatbush Asifah, which was more moderate in its tone, attempted to impose communal guidelines that limited Internet use. This approach will continue to fail because the Internet is about democracy and autonomy, which is in direct contradiction to externally imposed limits. Today, even insular Chasidic groups struggle to maintain Internet limits; more open communities have no chance for success. In a contemporary Western society, a direct fight against autonomy and freedom will lose.

Since the times of Korach, Torah leadership has faced challenges to its authority. Each generation needs its own way of protecting our sacred tradition and community against what Rav Joseph Soloveitchik aptly called a "common-sense rebellion" against Torah expertise.[5] To address the unique dangers of the Internet, particularly its challenge to authority, we need an approach that is appropriate for today.

---

5. Rav Abraham Besdin, *Reflections of the Rav* (Hoboken, NJ, 1993), p. 139ff.

V. Exploring Leadership

This book attempts to explore the issues of authority and autonomy in the twenty-first century. The Jewish community cannot continue without tradition and authority. Its future depends on its consistency with its past, even while adjusting for new situations. The texts and beliefs of the past must guide us in the present and beyond.

We first attempt to understand the elusive nature of authority and leadership according to Jewish tradition. We then explore concepts and applications of leadership and authority. Leaders cannot exist without followers and a community. Perhaps most importantly, we engage with the Jewish values that must serve as the basis of authentic Jewish leadership.

The introduction to volume 1 explains the unconventional writing style of this series. In this volume, I take some controversial stands on communally sensitive issues, which may offend some readers on the left and right wings of Judaism. I do not apologize for staking out positions on important issues. The great traditions of Judaism demand that we take an honest and confident path forward, treasuring our heritage while acknowledging the realities in which we live. I do so with one eye to the past, alert to the nuanced approaches of our predecessors, and another eye to the future, to the challenges that lie just a few years ahead.

CHAPTER 1:
AUTHORITY AND LEADERSHIP

Leadership manifests in two ways, emerging from opposite impulses. Authority is imposed on us. An authority figure exerts control over our lives, binding us with his decisions. A police officer is an authority who protects and serves us, but also commands us. In contrast, influence convinces us, inspires us, draws us in. Authority pushes down on us while influence draws us up.

In the pre-Modern world, religious leaders acted with top-down authority, often enjoying government sanction to compel obedience. When the Jews became emancipated citizens in the eighteenth and nineteenth centuries, religious authorities lost this power. Today, religious authority is voluntary—people choose to listen to a rabbi. They might submit to that authority because they believe their religion requires it or due to social pressure. Regardless, when we speak today of religious authority, we mean a position almost devoid of actual authority. Instead, it is a theological authority imposed by religion on those who accept it on their own—often diminished—terms. Some people listen to a rabbi only when convenient. Others change the most intimate aspects of their lives based on rabbinic decisions.

Because public opinion defines leadership, influencers have the upper hand. Influence commands allegiance when it is freely given. Since media plays such an oversized role in our world, we risk missing the prominent place of influence in our lives due to its prevalence. Often, the rabbis who lead are entertainers, inspiring us to join rather than commanding us to follow. Celebrity rabbis comprise an important part of religious leadership today.

Influencers are important because they create a compelling reason for leading a religious life. However, the Torah sees *halakhah*—Jewish law—as authoritative, a binding, all-encompassing life guide that commands us to follow religious authority. A rabbi's halakhic decisions are similarly authoritative.

"*Pasken*" is a Yiddish term for issuing a halakhic ruling, a "*pesak*." The act of paskening is an expression of rabbinic authority. It establishes law for an inquirer and obligates a community. Wielding this authority requires responsibility, including empathy, knowledge, experience, wisdom, and fear of the Lord as expressed in thought and action. Not everyone shares these traits equally.

This chapter explores the requirements for rabbinic authority—who qualifies and who does not. As always, there is much more to say on this subject.

A Rabbi's Role

What does a rabbi do? What is his role in the community? In a 2011 article,[6] Rav Hershel Schachter (contemporary, U.S.) quotes Prof. Saul Lieberman's (20th century, U.S.) responsum demonstrating that ordination includes permission to serve as a rabbinic judge (*dayan*). We can look at other evaluations and see similar sentiments.

Not long ago, I discovered a book by Rav Moshe Lowenthal (contemporary, Israel) titled *Serarah She-Hi Avdus: Sugyos Be-Rabbanus Ha-Kehillah*.[7] In a compelling style, freely mixing *halakhah*, history, advice, and personal experience, Rav Lowenthal explores at length the roles, responsibilities, and opportunities of a community rabbi. In section 2 chapter 1, he quotes historians and halakhists who discuss the primary functions of a community rabbi. Everything I quote here is from his book, but I cannot quote everything. Note that these are just brief lists of a rabbi's main tasks. It is not surprising that scholars disagree about which are considered "main."

Many like to cite Rav Joseph B. Soloveitchik's (20th century, U.S.) quote from his famous grandfather, Rav Chaim (19th-20th century, Russia), that the main job of a rabbi is to look after the underprivileged.[8] This is certainly true, but does not represent Rav Soloveitchik's full view. Rav Lowenthal quotes an important

---

6. "Women Rabbis?," *Hakirah*, vol. 11 (Spring 2011).
7. Jerusalem, 2007.
8. *Halakhic Man* (Philadelphia, PA, 1984), pp. 91-92.

footnote in Rav Soloveitchik's *Chamesh Derashos* that I present here in the translation found in *The Rav Speaks*:[9]

> If the position of the Rav [community rabbi] were connected solely with halakhah, Din Torah and the spreading of Torah knowledge, then the halakhah that one may not appoint a leader without first consulting the community would not apply. Rabbinic appointment would in that case be in the category of the appointment of a Sanhedrin or a Judge, which is effected from above…
>
> If, however, the Rabbinate finds expression in socio-political functions (care for general welfare, kindness, charity, representation and the like), then he is not only a *Moreh Hora'ah* and *Dayyan* but also a leader and his appointment requires the sanction of the community. It is unnecessary to stress that the history of the Rabbinate endorses the second definition. The Rav has never been only the *Moreh Tzedek*, but also the faithful shepherd of his flock…

Rav Soloveitchik directly addresses the important point that rabbis today function in many spheres. Some are more social workers than judges. Rav Soloveitchik concludes that rabbis are both and have always been. Perhaps today the balance has shifted more toward administrator and pastor, but that is a change in emphasis, not a historical break. Note, also, that Rav Soloveitchik uses the category of a judge to evaluate the legal side of a rabbi's function. In contrast to Rav Soloveitchik's vision of a dual role, Rav Moshe Sternbuch (contemporary, Israel; *Teshuvos Ve-Hanhagos* 2:722)

---

9. Lakewood, NJ, 2002, p. 189 n. 6.

rules that many rabbis serve only as social workers and therefore lose all tenure rights reserved for halakhic leaders.[10]

Rav Samson Raphael Hirsch (19th century, Germany), quoted by Rav Lowenthal (ibid.), describes the following primary tasks of a rabbi in a letter to a student:

1. Fearless devotion
2. Studying Torah
3. Dedicated leader
4. Role model
5. Education of children

Rav Yitzchak Shmelkes[11] (19th century, Galicia) lists the following functions in two separate places, which explains the slight overlap:

1. Studying and teaching Torah
2. Defending the faith
3. Supporting the poor
4. Arousing love of the nation
5. Encouraging fear and love of God
6. Teaching Torah and judging cases
7. Encouraging peace and mutual support

Rav Chaim Ozer Grodzenski[12] (19th-20th century, Lithuania) requires three things of a rabbi:

1. Teaching Torah and *halakhah*
2. Establishing Jewish education, availability of kosher food, an *eruv* and a *mikveh*
3. Caring for the underprivileged

---

10. Generally speaking, a rabbi cannot be fired as long as he continues to fulfill his job requirements (Rema, *Yoreh De'ah* 245:22).
11. *Beis Yitzchak*, end of *Orach Chaim*, *Tzela'os Ha-Bayis* 4; *Divrei Yitzchak*, end of vol. 1.
12. Quoted in *Teshuvos Ve-Hanhagos* 1:844.

Rav Yechiel Ya'akov Weinberg[13] (20th century, Germany-Switzerland) writes that a rabbi's job consists of:

1. Teaching Torah
2. Ruling on Jewish law, both as a *posek* (decisor) and as a *dayan* (judge)
3. Preaching and imbuing religious spirit
4. Caring for the underprivileged

Rav Meir Bar-Ilan[14] (19th-20th century, Russia-Israel) asked Rav Chaim Soloveitchik and Rav Yechiel Michel Epstein (19th century, Lithuania; Rav Bar-Ilan's grandfather) what a rabbi's job is. Rav Soloveitchik responded: Ensuring that the city's religious institutions function properly. Rav Epstein replied: Answering halakhic questions and judging civil cases. (Rav Bar-Ilan also asked Rav Raphael Shapiro, who responded in silence.)

Rav Lowenthal quotes Rav Mordechai Auerbach (contemporary, Israel), the rabbi of central Tel Aviv, who explained the above disagreement between Rav Soloveitchik and Rav Epstein. Each emphasized the area in which they excelled. They certainly agreed that a rabbi must do many things but each focused on his personal area of expertise.

Elsewhere in the book (section 2, chapter 6), Rav Lowenthal quotes Rav Yechiel Ya'akov Weinberg in the name of Rav Azriel Hildesheimer (19th century, Germany) that, in the latter's time (mid to late nineteenth century Germany), it was insufficient for a rabbi to only know Jewish texts; he also had to know how to reach out to the public and teach them about Judaism. Rav Shlomo Dichovski (contemporary, Israel) quipped that in our day, the issues are reversed. It is not enough for a rabbi to know how to influence the community; he also has to know how to decide matters of Jewish law. As Rav Joseph B. Soloveitchik said, both areas are important rabbinic roles.

---

13. *Lifrakim*, pp. 287-292.
14. *Mi-Volozhin Ad Yerushalayim*, p. 297.

Rabbinic Qualifications

Since a rabbi's responsibility includes deciding on issues of Jewish law, we must ask what qualifies someone to make such decisions. In 2014, an "Open Orthodox" rabbi published an online critique of a responsum by Rav Hershel Schachter (contemporary, U.S.). In this critique, the author attempts to expand the ability to decide Jewish law by offering a limited explanation of Rashi's (11th century, France) view on rabbinic qualifications. According to this view, any rabbi with minimal qualifications may rule on any halakhic issue, regardless of complexity. A further investigation reveals a very different approach that fully supports Rav Schachter's position. What I undertake here is not a comprehensive review of either Rav Schachter's views or the critique of his views. I am merely exploring one issue raised in the discussion.

I. Pious Fool

The Gemara (*Sotah* 21b) asks who is a *chasid shoteh*, literally, "a pious fool," and provides numerous answers from different scholars. One answer is a man who refuses to save a drowning woman for reasons of modesty. Another answer is someone who gives a poor man enough money so that the poor man is now disqualified from receiving other charity, thereby harming him.

The sage Ulla defines a *chasid shoteh* as someone who learned texts but did not serve under established scholars (*kara ve-shanah ve-lo shimesh talmidei chakhamim*). Rashi (22a) explains that this refers to someone who studied the texts but failed to adequately master their underlying meaning. He knows the basic laws but fails to fully grasp them and will therefore misapply them. He thinks he knows how to *pasken*, to issue halakhic rulings, but his learning is actually limited. Such a person, the Gemara later says, is an *am ha-aretz*, an ignoramus. His little knowledge is dangerous when put into practice.

The Gemara later quotes a similar saying: those who teach Tannaitic sayings destroy the world. How so? Ravina explains that they issue halakhic rulings based on those sayings. Rashi (s.v. *she-shonin*) further explains that they did not serve under scholars and therefore do not adequately understand the laws they learned. *Paskening*, issuing halakhic rulings, requires a profound understanding of the underlying principles and an ability to apply them properly to practical questions. Only someone who has studied under a master, who truly understands the laws, may rule on practical matters.

II. Who is a *Rebbe*?

Rashi similarly explains the varying definitions of a *rebbe*, a Torah mentor. The Mishnah (*Bava Metzi'a* 33a) discusses the priority given to a *rebbe* over a father. Even though respect for one's father is an important biblical commandment, the respect for one's Torah teacher is an even more important biblical commandment. Both deserve your respect, but when faced with an unavoidable conflict, one that cannot be creatively satisfied without choosing, you must assist your *rebbe* first.

Who is this *rebbe*? The Gemara quotes a three-way dispute. According to R. Meir, someone who taught you wisdom. According to R. Yehudah, the teacher from whom you learned most of your knowledge. And according to R. Yosi, anyone who explained to you even one law. Rashi (s.v. *she-limdo*) divides Torah knowledge into three categories: Bible, laws, and explanations. R. Meir considers your *rebbe* only the teacher who guided you in explanations, who taught you the underlying reasons for the laws so you can properly apply them. Similarly, R. Yosi also defines a *rebbe* as the one who taught you explanations but even just one explanation. While R. Yehudah considers your *rebbe* anyone who taught you anything from any of the categories of Torah.

According to Rashi, a deep understanding of Torah, an ability to distinguish and apply the laws, comes from intensive study of the explanations. It is not enough to merely know the laws. You have to understand them, know their reasons and how to differentiate between similar cases. But according to Rashi, understanding alone is insufficient.

III. Torah Battles

The Gemara (*Sanhedrin* 42a) quotes R. Yochanan as saying that the Torah battle (*milchamtah shel Torah*), the thrust and parry of proof and counterproof, can only be found with someone who has "packages" of Mishnah. Rashi (s.v. *milchamtah*) explains that someone who merely speculates about explanations is not truly reaching the depths of Torah. You need breadth in order to reach depth. You need a balanced understanding of a wide span of Torah in order to truly understand a single law. Speculation, attempting to explain a law, cannot be confirmed without further proofs and counterproofs. You cannot test a theory without additional evidence. Only someone with a breadth of knowledge, with packages full of Mishnah from which to cull evidence, can arrive at a sustainable understanding.

According to Rashi, a Torah scholar needs balance. He must have breadth of knowledge throughout the Torah's many areas and a depth of understanding. Someone lacking that expertise must have humility, must recognize that he is, at least in some respects, an *am ha-aretz*. If he fails to maintain adequate humility, if he oversteps his abilities, he may even be a *chasid shoteh*.

IV. Who Can *Pasken*?

The Maharsha (16th-17th century, Germany; *Sotah* 22a, *aggados* s.v. *yerei*), writing just decades after the publication of the *Shulchan Arukh*, strongly opposed those who issue halakhic rulings directly from the legal code. They are like someone who knows the laws but not the explanations, who lacks *shimush talmidei chakhamim*. As such, they are essentially ignoramuses. The Maharsha was later joined by other luminaries, such as the Maharal and the Bach. They follow Rashi in insisting that a rabbi must understand the underlying reasons for a law before *paskening* on it.

The *Pischei Teshuvah* (19th century, Lithuania; *Yoreh De'ah* 242:8) suggests—only as a possibility (*ve-efshar*)—that this problem was eliminated by the publication of commentaries on the *Shulchan Arukh* that explain the laws. According to this approach, it is possible to avoid the problem of failing to understand the laws by studying and understanding the commentaries. This should solve the problem. However, there are times when someone with insufficient breadth or depth will fail to completely understand the issues. Secondary knowledge, especially when studied from a book, is inferior to mastery of the primary sources. Note that the *Arukh Ha-Shulchan* (*Yoreh De'ah* 242:36) rejects this entire approach that does not require study of primary sources.

Regardless of whether we follow the *Pischei Teshuvah* or *Arukh Ha-Shulchan*, someone with breadth and depth has more of a right to *pasken* than someone who merely learns explanations from the commentaries. The person with the overflowing packages of Mishnah, who has undergone a true battle of Torah, has a much more profound and well-rounded understanding of the Torah.

The student of secondary sources may very well miss an important issue because the case he is facing is different than that discussed in the commentaries.

V. Rashi and Maharsha

In Rav Hershel Schachter's responsum on Partnership Minyanim,[15] among the many things he states is that not everyone who went to yeshiva, not even everyone with rabbinic ordination, is a well-rounded Torah scholar. Indeed, rabbis have usually passed tests on a limited amount of material, for at least some parts of which they probably studied only secondary sources. It is the rare rabbi who has mastered the Talmud, gaining both breadth and depth. These rabbis are the people who have the ability to truly *pasken*. Lower rabbis may be able to apply the codes and commentaries, but we often fail to recognize unusual circumstances that are not addressed by the commentaries. We defer when greater rabbis disagree, and we bring any but the obvious questions to those with more knowledge and experience. Most local rabbis and yeshiva teachers lack the mastery of sources necessary to qualify for the breadth and depth Rashi requires.

The "Open Orthodox" critic responded to Rav Schachter on a number of issues. His first point is on the question of who may *pasken*. He suggests that while the Maharsha insists that only a "great" Torah scholar may *pasken*, Rashi believes that any qualified rabbi not only may but must issue halakhic rulings.

This inference from a single Rashi is questionable. The Gemara learns from a verse that uses the word "*atzumim*" that a Torah scholar who is capable of issuing a halakhic ruling (*higi'ah le-hora'ah*) is obligated to do so. According to Rashi, "*atzumim*" is a form of a word that means "to close," as in a scholar closing his mouth and refusing to issue a halakhic ruling. The critic infers

---

15. http://www.rcarabbis.org/pdf/Rabbi_Schachter_new_letter.pdf

from this that Rashi does not require great Torah scholarship to rule on halakhic matters, an inference that is at best weak. In contrast, Maharsha explains "*atzumim*" to mean greatness and importance. The critic infers from this that Maharsha requires greatness in order to rule.

As we have already seen from many comments in multiple tractates, Rashi's view is in consonance with Maharsha's. The Gemara is discussing a Torah scholar who is qualified to issue a ruling. According to Rashi, that means he has both breadth and depth, he has packages of Mishnah about which he has learned the underlying explanations. This is precisely the person Maharsha has in mind. Indeed, Rav Schachter's position is supported by both Rashi and Maharsha, which states that only someone with breadth and depth should issue halakhic rulings, particularly on complex issues.

What is Ordination?

I. Original Ordination

Originally, ordination was passed down from teacher to student, beginning with Moshe and continuing throughout the generations. This original ordination had a number of rules, as described by the Rambam (12th century, Egypt; *Mishneh Torah*, *Hilkhos* Sanhedrin, ch. 4).

One important rule is that ordination can be given for ruling on specific areas of Jewish law and need not be given for everything (par. 8). However, a candidate must be qualified for all areas in order to receive even limited ordination. Someone halakhically unqualified to rule in all areas may not receive any ordination. Thus, for example, a blind person cannot be a *dayan* (*Hilkhos Sanhedrin* 2:9) and therefore may not receive even limited ordination (ibid. 8:10).

This chain of ordination ended sometime in the talmudic era, after Hillel II established a fixed calendar (cf. Ramban's glosses to *Sefer Ha-Mitzvos*, *aseh* 153). The question remains what kind of ordination remains beyond that point. More importantly, what does it mean today?[16]

16. Rav Yisrael Ariel (*Sanhedrin Ha-Gedolah*, Jerusalem, 2015, pp. 357-362) suggests that Rashi does not recognize the need for a chain of ordination. According to this interpretation of Rashi, any court of three today can ordain a rabbi with biblical ordination. However, we

II. Two Views of Later Ordination

Rav Moshe Isserles (Rema; 16th century, Poland) writes in a responsum (no. 24) that we should still follow the rules of ordination even if they do not technically apply. In other words, the ordination we have today is essentially a replica of the original ordination, continued as a memorial. Similarly, Rav Moshe Sofer (*Chasam Sofer*; 19th century, Hungary; Responsa, *Even Ha-Ezer* vol. 2 no. 94) rules, based on the Rema's responsum, that we cannot give limited ordination to someone halakhically unqualified for everything (although he understands the definition of "limited ordination" differently).

However, the Rema follows a different view in *Darkhei Moshe* and his glosses to *Shulchan Arukh* (*Yoreh De'ah* 242:14). He rules like the Rivash (14th century, Algeria; Responsa, no. 271) that ordination today is totally unrelated to the original type of ordination. Rather, it is permission from a teacher to a student to issue halakhic rulings. Therefore, rules such as that against limited ordination to someone halakhically unqualified for full ordination do not apply.

While the *Chasam Sofer* seems to assume that the Rema's responsum is definitive, Rav Meshulam Rothe (20th century, Israel; *Kol Mevaser*, vol. 1 no. 12) argues that the ruling in *Darkhei Moshe* and *Shulchan Arukh* were written later and represent the Rema's final view. Despite this, R. Rothe prefers the former view and recommends convening a rabbinic gathering in Israel to institute a rule that limited ordination not be given.

Rav Yechiel Michel Epstein (19th century, Russia; *Arukh Ha-Shulchan, Yoreh De'ah* 242:29) accepts the Rema's view in *Shulchan Arukh* that ordination is permission to issue a halakhic ruling. However, he adds that in his time ordination took on a slightly

---

will focus on the modern discussion which is based almost exclusively on Rambam's view.

different meaning. Rather than just being permission to rule on halakhic matters, it is certification to serve as a communal rabbi ("this is the primary function of ordination today").

This is a subtle but crucial distinction. According to the Rema (in *Shulchan Arukh*), anyone qualified to issue halakhic rulings can be ordained. According to the *Arukh Ha-Shulchan*, only someone qualified to be a community rabbi can be ordained. Even if limited ordination for someone halakhically unqualified for everything is possible, someone unable to fulfill the primary role of ordination cannot be ordained.

III. Permission

Within the second view—that ordination constitutes permission to rule on *halakhah*—is ordination (1) permission to rule on halakhic matters (and serve as a rabbi) or (2) a testimony to its bearer's qualifications? According to (1), ordination is the act of obtaining permission from one's teacher. It is a function of respect for one's teacher. According to (2), it is a public declaration that the ordained is qualified to rule (and serve as a rabbi).

What is the difference?

1. If your mentor is dead. According to (1), you do not need ordination because there is no longer an issue of respect. According to (2), you still need ordination because the public requires official testimony that you are qualified.
2. If you are a famous rabbi. According to (1), you still need permission from your teacher, out of respect. According to (2), everyone already knows that you are famous so you don't need the testimony.
3. Can a rabbi who isn't your mentor ordain you? According to (1), no. You need permission from your teacher. According to (2), yes. Anyone can testify to your qualifications.

How do the authorities who take this general approach rule? Rivash (14th century, Algeria) writes in a responsum (no. 271) that ordination is a matter of permission out of respect. Rav David Cohen (Radakh; 15th-16th century, Greece) writes in a responsum (no. 12) that it is testimony to both qualifications and permission. Both of these views are quoted by the Rema in *Darkhei Moshe* (*Yoreh De'ah* 242:14).

In *Shulchan Arukh* (ibid.), Rema seems to follow neither Rivash nor Radakh. He writes that ordination nowadays is "so that the people will know that he reached [the ability to] rule and that what he rules is with the permission of his teacher who ordained him." In other words, ordination is a testimony that you are qualified to rule and you have permission from your mentor (who ordains you). This implies that you need ordination even if your teacher is dead because people still need to know that you are qualified. Additionally, a famous rabbi does not need ordination because people can assume that he is qualified and has permission. This also implies that anyone can ordain a rabbi, regardless of jurisdiction.

However, Rema continues in that same paragraph that if your mentor has died you do not need ordination. I don't understand the Rema. Why not? He just finished stating that ordination is so that people will know that you are qualified to serve as a rabbi!

Interestingly, *Otzar Yisrael* (vol. 7 p. 223) quotes a 1651 responsum from Rav Yitzchak Halevi, grandson of Rav Leon de Modena (17th century, Italy), about whether the rabbi of a city can ordain someone living in a different city without the permission of the rabbi of that other city. Rav Halevi ruled that ordination is a testimony of the person's qualifications and therefore anyone who is capable of giving such testimony is allowed to do so. If it was permission, though, there would be room to argue that he could not do so.

IV. Ordination Today

What is ordination today, over a hundred years after the publication of *Arukh Ha-Shulchan*? It seems clear to me that ordination today implies three things that an ordainee is qualified to:

1. Rule on halakhic matters,
2. Serve as a synagogue rabbi,
3. Serve as a *dayan*, a religious judge.[17]

I do not believe that ordination implies a qualification to teach Torah because we regularly find people who are not rabbis teaching Torah. This all seems to me to be a sociological reality that is consistent with the *Arukh Ha-Shulchan*'s approach.

If that is, indeed, what ordination implies, then someone who cannot serve as a *dayan* or synagogue rabbi cannot be ordained as a rabbi. This is within the view of the Rema (in *Shulchan Arukh*) and the *Arukh Ha-Shulchan*. According to the Rema's responsum and the *Chasam Sofer*, there can be no limited ordination to someone halakhically unqualified for full ordination.

What is the current custom regarding ordination? In practice, do we follow the *Arukh Ha-Shulchan* or *Chasam Sofer*? We ordain converts. This is problematic according to the *Arukh Ha-Shulchan* because converts cannot serve as synagogue rabbis.[18] However, according to the *Nesivos Ha-Mishpat* (7:1), there is no problem of limited ordination, because a convert can serve as a *dayan* for other converts. Therefore, it would seem that the custom is to follow the view of the Rema's responsum and the *Chasam Sofer*.

---

17. The *yadin yadin* degree, which certifies someone as a judge, is rarely required, and even plain rabbis serve as *dayanim*.
18. See my *Posts Along the Way* (Brooklyn, 2010), p. 89ff.

Gradations of Authority

I. Mistaken Permission

Not all scholars in any specific discipline have equal expertise, and not all rabbis have equal authority. Complex or consequential questions must be taken to rabbis with sufficient expertise and experience to answer them properly. This idea is so self-evident that one who ignores it faces potential halakhic ramifications.

Rav Meir of Rothenburg (the Maharam, 13th century, Germany), in a responsum published in standard editions of the *Mishneh Torah* (after *Nashim*, no. 11), answers the following question: A woman's husband drowned in a body of water that qualifies as "endless" (*mayim she-ein lahem sof*). What happens if she remarries?

The law is that she may not—according to rabbinic decree—remarry, since the husband may have survived and resurfaced far away. However, if she remarries she need not get divorced (*Shulchan Arukh, Even Ha-Ezer* 17:34). In other words, *lechatchilah* she is not allowed to remarry but *bedi'eved*, after the fact, she may.

Maharam qualifies this. If the rule was really that any such woman who marries may remain married, then this rabbinic decree would be ineffective and meaningless. Rather, the rule must be that if such a woman receives mistaken permission from a rabbi to remarry, she need not divorce her husband. Because she did the right thing by asking a rabbi, she is in a state of *bedi'eved*. However, if she failed to ask a rabbi, her intentional disregard places her in a state of *lechatchilah* and she must divorce. She is not considered an accidental sinner in the category of *shogeg* but an intentional sinner in the category of *meizid*.

Maharam writes that she needs to ask "a scholar who issues rulings like Rav Nachman and Rav Shila in their generations." In other words, she must ask a rabbi who is sufficiently expert to rule on such a complex question. Anything less renders her negligent, for which she must suffer halakhic consequences.

II. Insufficient Consultation

Rav Menachem Mendel Krochmal (17th century, Moravia; *Responsa Tzemach Tzedek*, no. 44) addresses a similar question. During a time of war and displacement, a widower married his former father-in-law's widow. Because of the turbulent situation, they could not ask a rabbi but found a learned man who permitted the marriage. Rav Krochmal, however, held that such a marriage is *lechatchilah* forbidden but *bedi'eved* permitted (see *Shulchan Arukh, Even Ha-Ezer* 15:24 and commentaries).

Presumably, this couple should be allowed to remain married because they had already entered into their union accidentally, under the category of *shogeg*. They had even asked a Torah scholar! However, Rav Krochmal ruled that since they asked a scholar who was not qualified to answer this difficult question, they are considered intentional (*meizid*) rather than accidental initiators of this situation. If not for the other mitigating factors in this situation, Rav Krochmal would have insisted that this couple dissolve their marriage.

The implication of these responsa[19] is both obvious and significant. The title "rabbi" is substantive but does not confer onto its holder unlimited legal authority. Only proficient scholars

---

19. These responsa are quoted in *Pischei Teshuvah, Yoreh De'ah* 99:5.

may rule on any given area. Not only must a rabbi turn away or redirect a question he cannot answer, a questioner must carefully consider whether the rabbi he is asking is sufficiently experienced and expert to respond to his inquiry. Even with this in mind, there are times when seemingly lesser issues grow in significance.

III. Big Issues

The Mishnah (*Sanhedrin* 32a) states that when a court adjudicates a capital case, a junior member of the court must begin the discussion. He must offer his opinion first because if the most senior member gives his opinion first, there is a danger that those more junior will automatically defer to him without fully discussing the various sides of the case. In a civil or ritual case, however, we are not as concerned and allow the senior member to begin the discussion.

The Gemara (*Gittin* 59a, *Sanhedrin* 36a) says that every time Rav Yehudah Ha-Nasi would institute an enactment, even regarding civil matters, he would insist that a junior member begin the discussion. Rashi (*Gittin* 36a s.v. *de-kulhu*) explains that Rav Yehudah Ha-Nasi disagreed with the Mishnah's distinction and held that discussion of all cases—not just capital cases—must begin with a junior member. Tosafos (*Gittin* 36a s.v. *de-kulhu*) suggest that there was no dispute of law and Rav Yehudah Ha-Nasi had an idiosyncratic practice due to his extreme humility.

Rav Reuven Margoliyos (20th century, Israel; *Margoliyos Ha-Yam* 36a:2) offers an explanation with broader application. Even though civil and ritual cases are normally less severe than capital cases, that is when dealing with specific cases. However, when the *halakhah* is being established for generations to come, such as in Rav Yehudah Ha-Nasi's deliberation, the issue is much more serious and has such broad impact that it reaches the level of a capital case and requires the stricter treatment.

This is an important principle to consider. True, we no longer have such rabbinical courts. But we still have to recognize that wide-reaching changes to practice affect the entire nation for generations to come. These are not matters to be taken lightly. While less established scholars are certainly allowed to voice their opinions and make their arguments known, the final decisions must be reached by the leading scholars of the generation. A local rabbi is allowed to rule on local matters, but global issues with long-range impact fall on broader shoulders.

Whose shoulders? Reasonable people can disagree on who is the right choice, but there can still be widespread agreement that those with limited expertise should not be issuing decisions on Jewish law that will reverberate for generations.

Who Can Be Called "Rabbi"?

I. Respecting Torah Scholars

Calling someone by a title is a public display of respect, a conferral of authority, which is why it raises so many complex issues. Who is unworthy of that authority and who, even if he once deserved that title, has lost the right to that level of respect? Convention varies by community and culture, some valuing titles more than others. However, in a culture where a title conveys authority, its proper use becomes even more important.

In the letters section of volume 13 of the journal *Hakirah*, writers discuss whether Conservative rabbi and scholar Elliot Dorff should have been mentioned with the title "rabbi." I do not have a final opinion on the matter but can begin a discussion of the various issues.

The Bible commands us to respect Torah scholars: "Rise before the aged and honor an elder" (Lev. 19:32). The Talmud (*Kiddushin* 32b) understands "elder" in this verse to refer to a Torah scholar. There are four types of Torah scholars for whom you must show respect:

1. your mentor(s) (*rebbe muvhak*),
2. world-class Torah scholars (*gedolei ha-dor*),
3. someone who taught you a little Torah,
4. regular Torah scholars who have not taught you anything.

II. Respecting Your Teachers

You must show extra respect to your mentor, such as rising from the moment he enters a room (as opposed to when he approaches your immediate vicinity; *Shulchan Arukh, Yoreh De'ah* 242:16). Among the obligations to your mentor is refraining from calling him by his name (ibid., 15). The Rema adds that you may call him by his name if you preface his name with the title "rabbi" (or another title of respect). The *Shakh* (17th century, Moravia; no. 24) says that this is only when he is not there but if he is there you must call him simply "*rebbe*." Rav Akiva Eiger (18th-19th centuries, Poland) and the *Pischei Teshuvah* (19th century, Lithuania; no. 10) quote some who disagree.[20]

We see that you must use the title "rabbi" when referring to your mentor. Tosafos (*Berakhos* 31b s.v. *moreh*, as understood by *Terumas Ha-Deshen* 1:138) explain that the rule that you may not issue a halakhic ruling in front of your mentor also applies to a *gadol ha-dor*. This is generally understood as meaning that you must apply the extra level of respect reserved for your mentor to the great Torah scholars of the generation. For example, the *Shulchan Arukh* (*Yoreh De'ah* 244:10), in the context of the distinction between when you must rise for a Torah scholar (mentioned above), states that you must treat a *gadol ha-dor* like your mentor. Similarly, the *Shulchan Arukh* (*Orach Chaim* 472:5) rules that you need not lean at the Passover *seder* in the presence of a *gadol ha-dor*, just like in the presence of your mentor. Therefore, you must also refer to a *gadol ha-dor* with the title "rabbi."

You must also respect someone who taught you a little Torah—even just one word. However, the respect you must show him is less than what you must show your mentor (*Shulchan Arukh, Yoreh De'ah* 242:30). The *Sedei Chemed* (19th century, Turkey-Russia;

---

20. Note that par. 30 in the *Shulchan Arukh* clarifies that this is all referring specifically to your mentor and not just any teacher.

Ma'arekhes Khaf, no. 104) quotes the *Tzapichis Bi-Dvash* who argues that you may call such a teacher by name, without a title, while the *Tzelach* (*Berakhos* 4a s.v. *va-ani*) holds that you must use a title although you need not call him just "*rebbe*." The *Tiferes Yisrael* (18th century, Germany; *Avos* 6:3 no. 50) also contends that you are obligated to call him by a title.

III. Respecting Torah Scholars

The *Sifra* (Lev. 19:32, quoted by Rashi, ad loc.) posits that the obligation to honor the elderly also applies to all Torah scholars, even if they never taught you anything. Quite surprisingly, no subsequent Medieval or early Modern source repeats that obligation. The *Shulchan Arukh* (*Yoreh De'ah* 243:6, 244:1) follows the unanimous precedent and states that your only obligation to respect Torah scholars consists of rising when they enter your vicinity and refraining from insulting them. The *Birkei Yosef* (18th century, Israel; *Yoreh De'ah* 244:6) notes that the *Sifra*'s extensive list of mandatory respectful practices was disputed and concludes that the law requires nothing more than rising and refraining from insulting. However, the *Chafetz Chaim* (19th-20th century, Russia; *Asin*, n. 8 in asterisk) assumes that the law follows the *Sifra* and leaves as an open question why the codes omit this obligation.

Apparently, according to the *Birkei Yosef*, you need not refer to a rabbi with the title "rabbi" unless he is your mentor or a world-class Torah scholar. Failing to use the title hardly classifies as an insult for which someone can be sued in a religious court because it is only an implied insult by omission. However, according to the *Chafetz Chaim* you must refer to any Torah scholar with the appropriate respectful title. In my experience, widespread practice follows the *Chafetz Chaim*—we reserve extra respect for Torah scholars beyond the standard respect shown to all people.

Who is a Torah scholar? The Rema (*Yoreh De'ah* 244:2) defines a Torah scholar for whom one must rise as someone who is more knowledgeable than you and worthy of learning from. The *Shakh* (ad loc., no. 2) adds that he must be an exceptional scholar who is greater than most others (*muflag be-chokhmah yoser mi-sh'ar ha-am*).

IV. Sinful Scholars

The Gemara (*Kiddushin* 32b) states that we need not show respect for an ignorant elder (*zaken ashmai*). I translate this as "ignorant elder" rather than "wicked elder" following Tosafos (ad loc., s.v. *zaken*; see *Arukh Ha-Shulchan, Yoreh De'ah* 244:2, who argues that Rashi agrees) because we are specifically forbidden to show respect to a sinful but knowledgeable individual, even a rabbi. Presumably, we must distinguish between his improper actions and the Torah for which he would otherwise deserve respect. The *Shulchan Arukh* (*Yoreh De'ah* 243:3), as understood by *Arukh Ha-Shulchan* (ibid.), rules that we are prohibited from showing respect to a Torah scholar who lacks care for the commandments (*mezalzel be-mitzvos*) and lacks fear of God, but must rather treat him like a lowly member of the community (*kal she-ba-tzibbur*).

This vague definition allows for a certain amount of flexibility to specific circumstances and seems to me to include those who unambiguously deny fundamental beliefs of Judaism. It would certainly include rabbis who permit blatant halakhic violations, although we must be careful to distinguish between disregard for Jewish law and legitimate leniencies that emerge from within the halakhic process. Someone who is convicted of a serious crime, or has otherwise caused serious injury contrary to *halakhah*, cannot be called "rabbi."

My working assumption is that most Reform and Conservative Jews serving professionally as rabbis fail to meet Orthodox religious standards, and some Orthodox Jews serving as rabbis do as well. Based on the above, it would seem that we should withhold the title "rabbi" from them. We need not (but may) call "rabbi" those Jews who do not reach the definition of a Torah scholar and may not call "rabbi" those who fail religious standards even if they are Torah scholars. However, other issues complicate the matter.

V. Other Considerations

To many people, "rabbi" is a professional title. Failing to use that title confuses people and, to a small degree, hurts the individual's livelihood. Is it proper, in such a circumstance, to withhold the title "rabbi" from someone who fails the religious standards mentioned above but serves in that professional capacity?

Additionally, failing to refer to a community's leader with the title its members believe he deserves will be considered insulting. Is this offense to an entire community, even though only by omission, acceptable? And what about the personal offense when we distinguish between individuals we believe sufficiently knowledgeable or observant to merit the title "rabbi" and those not?

Furthermore, the right to refuse the title can be easily distorted into the "right" to insult rabbis we do not like. Many will withhold the title based on rumor or unproven allegation, thereby perpetuating a questionable accusation. And some will blow out of proportion the acceptance of leniencies they don't like, such as accepting a particular *eruv*, and consider that lenient attitude to constitute lacking care for commandments. The ease of abuse argues for a liberal application of the title.

All these potential offenses are aggravated if the convention in general society is to refer as "rabbi" to people who have achieved some sort of sanctioned ordination, regardless of actual qualifications. When nearly everyone calls a person "rabbi," failing to do so is even more offensive.

On the other hand, the title "rabbi" has long been understood as implying that its bearer is qualified to rule on halakhic matters and serve on a religious court. In reference to someone who lacks those qualifications, do we have license to use the title colloquially and imprecisely?

Additionally, calling someone "rabbi" who fails to meet basic Torah standards can be seen as admission that Torah observance is subject to compromise. How can we honor an unrepentant sinner, whether affiliated with Orthodoxy or not, with the title "rabbi"?

VI. Inconclusion

As I mentioned above, I have no conclusion to this question. I have seen three general attempts to delicately navigate this minefield:

1. Praise those from whom you are withholding the title "rabbi" or use another respectful title, to eliminate or reduce the offense.
2. Use "rabbi" as a professional description rather than title.
3. Refer even to those undeserving with the title "rabbi" and reserve the title "rav" for those deserving.[21]

I don't know what is halakhically proper in every situation. However, while I personally feel profoundly uncomfortable withholding a professional title someone regularly uses, I feel even more uncomfortable conferring the title "rabbi" on someone who eats non-kosher food and violates Shabbos.

---

21. My esteemed high school teacher, Rav Yisrael Goodman, suggested this approach.

Revoking Ordination

Earlier, we offered three possible reasons for contemporary ordination: (1) a replica of the original Mosaic ordination, (2) permission from one's mentor to issue halakhic rulings or (3) testimony that the rabbi is worthy of the title. According to the first approach, only someone who qualifies for the original ordination can obtain ordination today. According to the second approach, you need not obtain ordination if your mentor is deceased. According to the third approach, someone already famous as a Torah scholar need not obtain ordination. As we showed, authorities differ over which theory is correct.

I. Theories of Ordination

1. Replica

According to the first approach, ordination can be revoked. The Rambam (12th century, Egypt; *Mishneh Torah, Hilkhos Sanhedrin* 4:15) writes:

> Someone who is unfit to serve as a judge due to lack of knowledge or suitability but was improperly given permission by the exilarch or accidentally given permission by a court, the permission is ineffective until he becomes worthy.

A rabbi who acts improperly is not a rabbi; his ordination is invalid. While his mentor can formally declare this by revoking his ordination, that is merely a formality. His ordination automatically becomes invalid even before the public revocation. That is based on the model of the original Mosaic ordination.

2. Permission

If ordination is permission, then certainly it can be revoked just like any other permission. The rabbi serves at the pleasure of his mentor and must take care to live up to his standards. However, if ordination is testimony to its bearer's worthiness, then we run afoul of the rule that testimony can never be rescinded. As the Talmud (*Sanhedrin* 44b) puts it, *keivan she-higgid, shuv eino chozer u-magdid*, "once he spoke (testified), he cannnot return and speak." Presumably, then, a rabbi who ordains another and thereby testifies to his worthiness cannot retract this testimony. However, that depends on the reason for the rule against retracting testimony.

3. Testimony

Is testimony permanent because a retraction is inherently unbelievable or as a procedural matter in court? Rashi (11th century, France; *Sanhedrin* 44b s.v. *keivan*) implies the former reason, that the retraction is implausible. However, the Ritva (12th-13th century, Spain; *Kesubos* 18b) and others seem to accept the latter reason. Rav Aryeh Leib Heller (18th-19 century, Galicia; *Shev Shemat'sa* 6:8) accepts the latter, as well. If it is a procedural matter, the rule only applies when two witnesses testify before a court. In other cases, such as when a single witness testifies in cases in which he is believed, the rule does not apply (see the above *Shev Shemat'sa*).

Ordination does not consist of the testimony of two witnesses before a court. It is the written testimony of one or more witnesses. Therefore, even if ordination serves as a rabbi's testimony that his student is worthy of being called a rabbi, the mentor may retract his earlier testimony if new information or new behavior arise.

II. Historical Cases

A. Rav David Tzvi Hoffman

Ordination has been revoked in the past. Rav David Tzvi Hoffmann (19th-20th century, Germany; *Melamed Le-Ho'il, Orach Chaim* no. 16), the rector of what is commonly called the Hildesheimer Seminary in Berlin, writes that he would not revoke a student's ordination merely for permitting use of an organ in a wedding during the week, implying that he would revoke it over other organ use. However, his case is different because the Hildesheimer Seminary issued ordination specifically on condition that the rabbi not serve in a synagogue with an organ, making such revocation a simple matter.[22] The codicil with the condition served as a warning to rabbis but does not inform our current discussion of ordination without an explicit condition.

B. Rav Bernard Revel

Rav Aharon Rakeffet (contemporary, Israel) records that Rav Bernard Revel revoked a RIETS graduate's ordination (*Bernard Revel*,[23] pp. 165-166):

> When a Yeshiva graduate refused Revel's request to leave a position which had both mixed pews and a mixed choir,

---

22. See David Ellenson, *After Emancipation: Jewish Religious Responses to Modernity* (2004), p. 184ff.
23. New York, 2013.

his ordination was revoked. Revel wrote to a graduate on September 19, 1933: "It grieves me to inform you that since you refuse to leave Temple… where the sacred laws of traditional Judaism are violated, I urgently request that you return the conditional document of ordination that you received from the Yeshiva. The basic purpose of the Yeshiva is to guard the sanctity of Jewish Law in this land. If you will not return the document of ordination, I will be obligated to publish newspaper announcements declaring the nullification of your ordination." The rabbi did not heed Rabbi Revel's request, and the Yeshiva publicly announced the cancellation of his ordination and proclaimed that "one can no longer rely on his answers to inquiries of Jewish Law."

C. Rav Yehudah Aszod

Similarly, Rav Yehudah Aszod (19th century, Hungary) published in a newspaper the revocation of ordination from one of his students (*Responsa Yehudah Ya'aleh, Orach Chaim* no. 37). This is certainly possible and, according to the above, understandable.

Revoking Ordination II

What do you do when a rabbi is shown to be incompetent in Torah matters, perhaps even adopting heretical views? We discussed above the revocation of ordination based on the theories underlying ordination in the modern era. However, this approach cannot explain the Alexandersohn affair of 1834.

I. One Rabbi Giveth, Another Taketh Away

Jonathan Alexandersohn, the rabbi of Csaba in Hungary, was accused by some of his townspeople of improper personal conduct, incorrect halakhic rulings, heretical views, and having arranged an improper *get*. This last issue is as follows. A *get* must include the name (in Hebrew letters) of the town in which it is written. Many European town names are very difficult to spell in Hebrew. However, if the town's name is misspelled, the *get* is invalid. Therefore, rabbis arrange a *get* in a town in which a *get* has never been written only after consultation with, and consensus among, colleagues. Alexandersohn arranged a *get* in Csaba, where none had previously been performed, after asking a senior neighboring rabbi who told him not to. This deviation from established practice and setting of a precedent for future potentially problematic *gittin* was considered severe and intentional halakhic misconduct.

After a rabbinical court investigated and concluded that the accusations against Alexandersohn were correct (although he refused to participate in the proceedings), leading regional rabbis denounced him. Additionally, Rav Moshe Sofer, commonly known as the *Chasam Sofer*, declared—based primarily on the *get* issue but also on reports of his improper behavior—that Alexandersohn may no longer use the title "rabbi" or issue halakhic rulings. The *Chasam Sofer* explicitly revoked Alexanderson's rabbinic ordination:

> They should entirely remove from him the title of rabbi and take from him the permission to rule with which he was crowned by rabbis before his actions and ways were known.

Rav Sofer remained reluctantly involved in this matter over the course of a few years, issuing at least four letters.[24]

The difficulty is that the *Chasam Sofer* had not ordained Alexandersohn. How could he revoke ordination that he had not given? Our previous theories only allowed the ordainer to revoke ordination he had given. The *Chasam Sofer* went beyond that and revoked ordination given by someone else. What halakhic basis did the *Chasam Sofer* utilize? He did not explain, but I suggest the following as a possibility.

II. Worthy of Respect

I see two issues here, related but distinct. The first is removal of the title "rabbi." That title is a form of respect for a Torah scholar.

---

24. Alexandersohn published a book in his defense titled *Tomekh Kavod* (Frankfurt a.M., 1847). The *Chasam Sofer*'s letters appear in the Hebrew section, parts 21, 31, 48, 58. Two of these letters are also published in *Responsa Chasam Sofer*, *Choshen Mishpat* 162 and 207. Note that Rav Moshe Teitelbaum, the *Yismach Moshe*, also explicitly revoked Alexandersohn's ordination, in a letter appearing in *Tomekh Kavod*, part 27.

The Gemara (*Kiddushin* 32b) says that one need not show respect for a *zaken ashmai*, an ignorant elder (as per Tosafos, ad loc., sv. *zaken*). Showing respect to such a person is optional. However, you are forbidden to show respect to a Torah scholar who lacks care for the commandments (*Shulchan Arukh, Yoreh De'ah* 243:3; cf. *Arukh Ha-Shulchan*, ad loc.). If a rabbi shows that he lacks care for the commandments, people are prohibited from calling him by the respectful title "rabbi."

I am not aware of a specific definition for this category. It seems to be left to the best judgment of the halakhic decisor. However, when invoked, it effectively revokes the title "rabbi" from anyone who listens to the halakhic decisor. Perhaps the *Chasam Sofer* was using this *halakhah* in stating that Alexandersohn should not be called rabbi. Maybe he considered Alexandersohn's disregard for the rules of *gittin* to be lack of care for the commandments.

III. Unqualified Rabbi

Additionally, someone who is unqualified to rule on halakhic issues is forbidden to do so:

> A student who has not reached [the qualifications for ruling] but rules is a fool, a wicked person and a haughty man (*Shulchan Arukh, Yoreh De'ah* 242:13).

When invoked, this rule declares someone unfit to issue a halakhic ruling. It is possible, today even likely, that someone can acquire rabbinic ordination but still be unqualified to rule. Perhaps he was not tested thoroughly or his capacity diminished over time. Either way, by declaring someone currently unqualified to rule, a halakhic decisor effectively removes this person's permission to rule. He revokes the man's ordination.

Perhaps the *Chasam Sofer* was also invoking this rule when revoking Alexandersohn's ordination. The *Chasam Sofer* indicated that Alexandersohn was serving as a stumbling block, presumably by arranging questionable *gittin* and setting a problematic precedent that could lead to many improper *gittin* in the future. By ignoring a basic rule of rabbinic conduct—consultation on such an important communal matter—Alexandersohn demonstrated that he was unfit to serve as a rabbi. The *Chasam Sofer* removed this stumbling block by revoking his ordination, declaring him unfit to rule.

IV. Who Cares?
This episode provides an example of revoking ordination. Even a halakhic decisor who did not give the ordination may revoke it. However, it is not immediately clear what effect this revocation will have. The rabbi whose ordination was revoked will likely ignore it and claim that it was all based on a misunderstanding or politics. Alexandersohn even published a book in German and Hebrew defending himself against the accusations.

The communal value of the revocation of ordination is twofold. Primarily, the *Chasam Sofer* gave the townspeople of Csaba license to remove Alexandersohn from his position as rabbi and instructed them to look elsewhere for halakhic guidance. It is no small matter to undermine a rabbi's authority and damage his career, but sometimes extreme measures are necessary. The *Chasam Sofer*, in a letter Alexandersohn published in his book (part 58), says that he had asked Alexandersohn in person to remove himself from the rabbinate for a year or two to return to yeshiva to study until the controversy died down. Clearly, the *Chasam Sofer* recognized the huge personal impact on Alexandersohn of this action. When a figure of the *Chasam Sofer*'s towering prominence declares a man unfit to be a rabbi, people listen.

Additionally, the *Chasam Sofer*'s revocation of ordination over the *get* impropriety sent a loud message about the importance of care in proper rabbinic conduct in halakhic matters. He took a stand on an issue he felt was critical, even though it meant destroying a man's career over it. Clearly, the *Chasam Sofer* felt his stance was warranted. But his message—that this issue was very serious—could not be missed. Revoking ordination—of course only when warranted—sends an important message about halakhic standards of consultation and ruling.

Undermining a Rabbi

I. Tolerance and Boundaries

Recurring news stories about rabbis convicted of crimes raise questions of when rabbinic behavior becomes unacceptable. Even the most tolerant of people recognize that at some point they must object to deviant behavior. Wherever you draw your red line, there is some person or group who lies beyond it. Engaging in that tricky business of rejection is a necessary part of tolerating those within the bounds. If every group is acceptable, even cults and criminals, then inclusion is meaningless.

A little over ten years ago, Rav Shlomo Aviner (contemporary, Israel) published a collection of his letters against a cult rabbinic figure in the book *Bein Or Le-Choshekh: Bein Chakhamim Amitiyim Le-Admorim Mezuyafim*.[25] Without naming anyone (in the book), Rav Aviner reproduces his attempts to convince adherents that their charismatic leader is a fraud. Watching Rav Aviner walk this tightrope of opposition is a profound lesson in the limits of tolerance.

II. Special Powers

The specific leader claimed paranormal powers, the ability to see into people's lives, tell the future, and communicate with the dead, which he attributed to prophecy and messianic claims. I would

---

25. Jerusalem, 2000.

have objected that he is merely tricking people, but this response would probably have proven unsuccessful. Rav Aviner, instead, accepts that he performs these amazing feats. However, he argues, it is all irrelevant because it proves nothing.

Paranormal powers are documented among many different people, including those who are non-religious and non-Jewish. Police investigators sometimes even consult with such psychics. This man's abilities only demonstrate a rare gift, not prophetic power. Rav Aviner quotes two incidents of apparent prophets, one from Vilna and the other Kovna, about which Rav Chaim Volozhiner (18th-19th century, Russia) testified that the Vilna Gaon (18th century, Lithuania) denounced as non-prophetic activities (introduction to *Sifra De-Tzeni'usa*; *Keser Rosh*, nos. 6-8). Similarly, a student of Rav Tzvi Yehudah Kook (20th century, Israel) was amazed by someone who could tell him intimate details of his private matters. Rav Kook dismissed the entire matter.

Additionally, communicating with the dead is halakhically forbidden. Rav Avraham Yitzchak Kook was asked by a Romanian rabbi whether he may influence wayward Jews to return to the fold by impressing them through communicating with the dead. Rav Kook (*Da'as Kohen* 29) responded that the ends do not justify the unholy means.

III. Religious Leaders Must Be Torah Scholars

What prompted Rav Aviner to speak out publicly against this fraud? Rav Aviner witnessed the many people who suffered from his bad advice. Like many rebbes and kabbalists, this man freely offered his advice on a variety of subjects—marital harmony, business ventures, medical problems, and more. However, unlike many such advisors, this man lacked the Torah knowledge to offer religious guidance. Instead, his advice often led to disastrous consequences, including many destroyed marriages that Rav Aviner saw collapse.

Rav Aviner's outspoken opposition to this religious fraud was in response to the human damage he witnessed.

Rav Aviner repeatedly charges this man with ignorance of Torah. His bluntness is sometimes painful but necessary. You cannot claim the mantle of Torah leadership without excelling in Torah knowledge. Its wisdom can only enter your judgment if you master it. This man was not a Torah scholar, despite his other remarkable abilities. This disqualified him from Torah leadership and certainly from the status of a prophet, for which Torah scholarship is a basic requirement.

His advice was not based on Torah wisdom or any other wisdom. And here we find a tension in Rav Aviner's position. On the one hand, he upholds the guidance of true Torah scholars, who often offer advice on a wide variety of life issues. On the other, he insists that you only obtain medical guidance from doctors and educational advice from educators. You look for a spouse through natural means, not based on kabbalistic concerns. And you never pay for Torah advice. Real rabbis don't give easy paths to success; they demand spiritual work. They don't take money from the needy but distribute it to them.

Yet this latter set of advice, which I wholeheartedly advocate, seems to me to contradict the common practice among many acknowledged Torah scholars who advise on a wide variety of technical issues, often for a fee. Rav Aviner deflects their precedents by pointing out that the target of his criticism is not a Torah scholar like they are. However, I wonder whether their scholarship frees them entirely from criticism.

IV. Tricks of the Trade

Rav Aviner demonstrates the danger of this cult by revealing their devious tricks. They invite recognized Torah scholars to speak with their leader and then publicize these meetings as endorsements.

Very few great rabbis will take the time and effort to publicize their opposition to some ignorant man whom they see as an obvious fraud. And those who do will be explained away as manipulated by handlers or swayed by politics.

The followers speak in two languages. To outsiders, they speak of their leader's greatness with vague terms that can be interpreted innocently. But internally, as Rav Aviner learned from defectors, they use specific terms of prophecy and messianism. This two-facedness is a blatant attempt to deceive the world about their deviant beliefs.

They also speak in apocalyptic terms, about how terrible the world is and how redemption must be around the corner. Their cynicism about the present and pessimism about the future are self-serving and unrealistic. In truth, we live in wonderful times. Any troubles we experience are less than those in past years. Yet they use this apocalyptic pessimism to intimidate questioning members, telling them that they will be "left behind" in the redemption if they fail to follow their leader.

V. The End, Or Is It?

In the end, this leader's messianic predictions failed to materialize, and many of his followers finally recognized his failures and abandoned him. He took Rav Aviner to a rabbinical court which forbade him to declare himself the messiah or offer marital advice. He disappeared for a number of years and, after his return, was rejected by his followers.

Rav Aviner's criticisms show how to argue forcefully against ideas without, or with minimal, attacks on the person. He exhibits courage in the face of intimidation and uncompromising devotion to consistent principles. He loves his fellow Jew but not every manifestation of Judaism.

While the specific cult against which Rav Aviner campaigned disappeared, I wonder whether his arguments have wider application. Does the increasingly common cultic devotion to purported kabbalists and charismatic rabbis deserve condemnation? Should we be denouncing rabbis with limited training who offer medical, business, and marital advice for large fees?

The Repentant Rabbi

I. When Leaders Sin

Like all others, our community has experienced some high-profile cases of leaders who sinned and were removed from their positions. Some might think that rabbis are more inclined to forgive their colleagues. In my experience, that is true with some but the opposite is also true—some are less inclined to forgive because they feel their trust was violated and their reputation tarnished by their lapsed colleague. When one rabbi sins, all rabbis are tarnished, fairly or not. Setting personal biases aside, I prefer to engage the classical sources on the subject.

As should be obvious, leaders have been sinning since time immemorial; moral weakness is not a uniquely modern phenomenon. Halakhic literature is replete with discussions of how to deal with the aftermath. Sometimes people appreciate their flawed leaders for their positive attributes despite their weaknesses and sometimes they want the fallen leader to disappear. I see three main approaches among Medieval commentaries about whether a leader deposed for misdeeds may be reappointed. But before we get to that, let us discuss how this disgraced leader can regain his credibility.

II. Demonstrating Repentance I

Teshuvah, repentance, is always possible and even easy, if we just find the will. According to Ramban (13th century, Spain-

Israel; Deut. 30:11), the passage about the nearness of "this" commandment refers to *teshuvah* (Deut. 30:11): "For this commandment which I command you this day, it is not too hard for you, neither is it far off...." The Gemara (*Kiddushin* 49b) says that if a wicked man betroths a woman on condition that he is righteous, the marriage is valid because he may have had thoughts of repentance. However, a community needs verification. A claim of repentance that is convenient and financially or otherwise beneficial can hardly be trusted.

In Tannaitic times, there was an elite class of *Chaverim* that took extreme care with the rules of produce tithes and ritual purity. *Chaverim* were able to trust each other about these matters but were unable to trust regular people — *amei ha-aretz*. A *Chaver* who was caught cheating on these laws understandably lost his standing. How could he regain it?

The Gemara (*Bekhoros* 31a) records a debate among Sages whether a deviant *Chaver* could ever regain his status. The conclusion follows the view that a deviant *Chaver* can regain his status by reaccepting the laws in front of a court of three people. This process is called *kabbalas divrei chaverus*, formally accepting the rules of the *Chaverim*. It is sufficient for these purposes but still considered a lower level of demonstration because it only requires verbal commitment. A different Gemara passage discusses a higher level of demonstration.

III. Demonstrating Repentance II

Certain classes of people are rejected from testifying in court for various sins or improper conduct. For example, professional gamblers are not allowed to testify in court, either because their method of gambling involves a subtle form of theft or because gamblers are not involved in productive labor (*Sanhedrin* 24b).[26]

---

26. See *Search Engine*, vol. 1, pp. 343-344.

The Gemara (ibid., 25a) offers a formula for such people to regain their status in court and in society. They not only need to change but also demonstrate their commitment. A former gambler must never wager again, even when no money is involved, and must destroy his gambling paraphernalia.

Similarly, a *shochet* (slaughterer), appointed as a community functionary, who is caught fraudulently selling non-kosher meat as kosher must do more than merely recommit to the laws of kosher. He must demonstrate that he has changed his ways. He must move to another town where he is not known, live humbly and show a greater concern for law than for money, for example by returning a valuable lost object or losing a significant sum of money on an animal determined to be non-kosher.

The key here is demonstrating real change without an ulterior motive. Given what we know today about addiction and predatory behavior, I think we would maintain the high bar of personal transformation but measure it differently, depending on the transgressor. For some we may require therapy and for others we may assume an impossibility of proving change. Repentance is always possible but not always demonstrable.

IV. Reappointment

Because of the central position a *shochet* played in Jewish life and the constant temptation of profit by misapplying the *halakhah*, the literature on repentant slaughterers has grown long and complex. The *Pri Chadash* (17th century, Israel; *Yoreh De'ah* 119:28) surveys responsa, albeit with an analysis that has elicited heated debate.[27] Among those he cites are the Rosh (13th-14th century, Germany-Spain; Responsa 20:29), who writes that if a slaughterer lacks expertise, then he can study the laws and formally recommit to them, following the example of *kabbalas divrei chaverus*. However,

---

27. See *Pri To'ar*, ad loc., no. 20; *Birkei Yosef, Choshen Mishpat* 34.

if he already knew the laws and was either lazy or greedy, no amount of verbal commitment will suffice. The Rosh does not suggest nor reject the second, more extensive path of rehabilitation.

The *Pri Chadash* also quotes the Rashba (13th-14th century, Spain), who addresses this issue in three responsa (nos. 619, 632 & 782), offering different answers. In the first two responsa, the Rashba allows the *shochet* to return after *kabbalas divrei chaverus*. In the last, he restricts reappointment to a case where true change has been proven. The Rashba's reason for distinguishing between the cases is the subject of debate that need not detain us. In the worst case, he allows for sincere rehabilitation demonstrated to the satisfaction of the rabbis.

V. Accidental Murderers

Other views can be found when extrapolating from a communal leader who commits accidental murder. According to biblical law, an accidental murderer must flee to a sanctuary city and remain there until the *kohen gadol*, the high priest, dies, at which point the murderer may return home. In the Mishnah (*Makkos* 13a), two Sages dispute whether a communal leader can be reappointed on his return. According to R. Meir, he can; according to R. Yehudah, he cannot.

Rashi (11th century, France; Lev. 25:41) and Bartenura (15th-16th century, Italy-Israel; Mishnah, ad loc.) follow R. Meir and seem to allow appointment of an accidental murderer. However, Ritva (13th-14th century, Spain; *Makkos*, ad loc.) forbids such reappointment. He goes beyond the accidental murderer and discusses intentional sinners, as well. Ritva argues that only those who commit egregious sins, like murder, are restricted from returning to a leadership role. Lesser sins, including the surprising example of apostasy, do not preclude a return to a leadership position. The Ritva does not describe what kind of repentance is necessary.

In contrast, the *Magen Avraham* (17th century, Poland; *Orach Chaim* 153:49) quotes the *Mordekhai* (13th century, Germany; *Bava Basra*, ch. 3) who learns from this Mishnaic debate a general lesson. According to R. Yehudah, the commission of a sin precludes reappointment (see the *Machatzis Ha-Shekel*, ad loc.). Unlike the Ritva, the *Mordekhai* does not limit which sins preclude reappointment, implying that any sin that causes someone to lose his position of leadership prevents him from returning to that position.

We can speculate why the *Mordekhai* takes such a strong stand against reappointment. A leader's sins are a matter of public record. His return would lead to embarrassment and insult, for him and for his fellow communal leaders. Even if he has truly repented, he has turned himself into a spectacle and lost his ability to lead.

VI. Rambam

We have seen three views:

1. A repentant communal leader can be reappointed (Rashi; Bartenura; Rashba).
2. Depending on the severity of the sin, a repentant leader may be eligible for reappointment (Ritva).
3. A disgraced leader can never return to power (*Mordekhai*).[28]

In this spectrum of views, where does the Rambam (12th century, Egypt) fit? In *Mishneh Torah* (*Hilkhos Rotzei'ach* 7:14), Rambam rules that a leader who murdered accidentally may not be reappointed when returning from the sanctuary city after the *kohen gadol*'s death. The Rambam explains that since this terrible event (*takalah gedolah*) occurred by his hands, he can no longer

---

28. *Pri Megadim, Eshel Avraham* 153:49 quotes the *Eliyah Rabbah*, who rules leniently like Rashi. *Arukh La-Ner, Makkos* 13a, also concludes leniently. *Mishnah Berurah* 153:115 quotes all three views without indicating a preference.

rise to prominence. The implication seems to be that a lesser sin, which would not qualify as a "*takalah gedolah*," would not prevent a disgraced leader from returning to power. Perhaps the Rambam sides with the Ritva.

On the other hand, elsewhere (ibid., *Hilkhos Sanhedrin* 17:9) the Rambam writes that a *rosh yeshiva* who sins cannot return to his position. The *Kesef Mishneh* (ad loc.) explains that the reinstated *rosh yeshiva* would suffer public humiliation, perhaps damaging not only him but his position.[29] This would seem to imply that a public leader can never return to prominence.

I can think of several possibilities to distinguish between these two rulings. The most promising are:

1. Perhaps the Rambam believes that a reinstated leader would only suffer humiliation if he committed a terrible sin. If so, both rulings would allow for a repentant leader to resume his leadership for lesser sins. This might also help us define a lesser sin as one the public will not consider egregious.
2. Perhaps the Rambam only allows reinstatement for a sin that is both minor and accidental. The first ruling, with the distinction between types of sins, refers to an accidental sin. The second ruling, without the distinction, refers to an intentional sin.

However, more research needs to be done, and more proofs found, before we can reach even a tentative theory about the Rambam's overall view.

VII. Conclusion

Despite the differing views, even the most lenient one requires a demonstrated, sincere repentance. Any person has limited ability

---

29. The *Chasam Sofer, Responsa* 1:41 convincingly argues in favor of this explanation.

to see into another's heart. However, the Gemara (*Sanhedrin*, ibid.) assumes that despite this limitation, a court can determine that a person has repented. This does not mean that we ignore his past and act recklessly. But we can, at least according to some opinions, allow him to return to his former position. While according to others, even if we determine conclusively that he has changed his ways and regrets his past, reappointment is impossible because of the damage to the credibility of leadership.

I believe that there is a difference between appointing a repentant sinner for the first time and reappointing a disgraced leader. Regarding the latter, we saw above that the *Magen Avraham* follows the *Mordekhai*'s prohibitive view. However, regarding the appointment of a repentant cantor, the *Magen Avraham* (53:8) allows more room for leniency. I suggest that the distinction between these two cases is that the cantor is being appointed for the first time.[30] He has not disgraced the position and therefore can rise to it, once he overcomes his past. In the former case, the *shochet* violated the community's faith and trust, and has sacrificed his ability to serve them in that capacity.

---

30. Although the Ritva disagrees with this.

CHAPTER 2:
STUDIES IN LEADERSHIP

Whether in religious community or in government, today we all have a voice in leadership and thoughts on how to improve that leadership. Most of us wield only little influence. But even our small portions can generate real impact. Good citizenship requires careful thought about the issues and about expectations of our leaders. If we expect too much, we will face consistent disappointment and risk taking drastic measures to remedy a crisis created in our own minds. If we expect too little, we will experience instability as insufficiently qualified leaders stumble in their roles.

In this chapter, we examine role models for religious and political leaders. We explore religious theories of government and how individuals can function religiously in government positions of leadership.

Learning from Moshe

Our community discusses leadership frequently. Aside from Rav Jonathan Sacks' year of weekly leadership lessons on the Torah portion (5774, 2013-2014),[31] I have seen a few books in recent years devoted to the subject and a number of shorter discussions. I suspect that, mirroring general society, Jews feel a growing frustration with our current leaders and look to our tradition for inspiration on how to lead more effectively. This is all productive, indeed a very healthy and constructive response to a perceived problem, but perhaps it misses a bigger point.

I. Deconstructing Moshe

Rav Zvi Grumet (contemporary, Israel), in his *Moses and the Path to Leadership*,[32] argues that Moshe began as an imperfect leader but learned from his mistakes to become a great leader. In a book review,[33] Rav Francis Nataf (contemporary, Israel) expresses skepticism that Moshe ever became a great leader. Neither argument about Moshe's leadership flaws is religiously problematic, as Rav Nataf shows. Indeed, one could argue that Moshe's leadership flaws demonstrate the truth of the Torah,

---

31. Published as *Lessons in Leadership: A Weekly Reading of the Jewish Bible* (Jerusalem, 2015).
32. Jerusalem, 2014.
33. Rav Francis Nataf, "How Many Moshes Can There Be?," *Torah Musings*, March 18, 2014.

like the Ran argues about his speech impediment.[34] Only a deft charlatan could fool a nation into believing a non-existent revelation, not an uncharismatic, politically unsavvy man. This does not at all detract from his personal holiness. In my experience, the holiest people tend to be less skilled politically.

Yet, it still leaves me uncomfortable. So I was happy to see Rav Ari Kahn (contemporary, Israel) protest against this trend in the Preface to his book, *Echoes of Eden: Sefer B'midbar*.[35] He writes (p. xi):

> At times the book of B'midbar [Numbers] seems like a journey to nowhere; the Land of Israel, the exalted goal, remains out of reach and one may be tempted to call the entire enterprise a failure. Especially today, when true leadership seems rare, there are those who read the maladies of our own generation back into the past and project our own malaise onto the narrative of our ancestors' trek from Egypt to the Promised Land. This jaded view of history leads many to wonder what the results would have been had a different type of leader emerged to lead the people
>
> The resultant deconstruction of Moshe, popular in some circles, is anathema from the perspective of Torah and tradition. Moshe was our greatest leader; the challenges he faced were legion, the attacks he withstood from within the camp—at times from his own inner circle, and at times from enemies lurking in the distance—were sufficiently potent that a lesser man would have given up on at least a dozen different occasions…

---

34. *Derashos Ha-Ran*, no. 3.
35. New York, 2014.

I probably would not have worded it as stridently, but I appreciate the lack of comfort with the new approach. In the back of his book, Rav Grumet provides a timeline of leadership challenges Moshe faced and how he reacted to them. I found that particularly enlightening because it highlighted for me two key points:

1. Moshe was not the only one changing during the long stay in the desert. The people changed as well, both in terms of their own maturity and generationally, as those who left Egypt died and their children took their places. Perhaps Moshe reacted differently in the various challenges over time because the actual challenges, mainly the people, were different.
2. Just because an incident's outcome was bad (e.g., God causing a plague) does not mean that Moshe's leadership of the situation was less than ideal. Even the most skilled captain cannot navigate an impossible course.

II. Fire Pans and Violence

Let us consider a few examples. Rav Grumet points out that Moshe's suggestion that Korach et al bring fire pans with incense was a deadly test (Num. 16). Since Nadav and Avihu had died from doing that, this was a lethal challenge. However, it was much less violent than his rallying the Levi'im after the Golden Calf to kill the sinners. With Korach, Moshe had grown and instead of responding with violence, encouraged the sinners to bring violence on themselves. However, the result was further death and complaints, therefore a failure of leadership (Grumet, pp. 50-52).

In contrast, Dr. Erica Brown (contemporary, U.S.) sees great wisdom in Moshe's response to Korach. She notes that, on God's command, the fire pans were incorporated into the altar, a permanent holy memorial to the unholy rebellion. Rav Samson Raphael Hirsch (19th century, Germany) explains that the fire pans symbolize Moshe's successful leadership, his dedication to the true priesthood even in the face of great challenge. Dr. Brown writes (*Leadership in the Wilderness: Authority and Anarchy in the Book of Numbers*,[36] p. 147):

> Korach becomes, in these narratives, the quintessential bad follower.... Moses was able to choose trust over invulnerability, conflict over harmony, clarity over certainty, accountability over popularity, and results over status. He knew that his leadership would not be measured by how well he got along with others in this transitional stage of Jewish history, but by whether he was able to forge through contention to get close to the ancient finish line. And he was willing to sacrifice position and status, if necessary, to achieve his leadership goal.

Korach and his group were bad followers. Moshe remained authentic, committed to his leadership purpose. On God's command, this leadership success was permanently memorialized in the Temple. The difference in approaches between Dr. Brown and Rav Grumet lies in whether Moshe's unique reaction is due to his own changes or that in his challengers.

III. Prophesying Inside

Rav Grumet devotes Section Two to Moshe's separation from the people. He originally was one with them, then separated himself and finally learned to reconnect to them. He sees this as the message of the enigmatic passage about Eldad and Meidad (Num. 11:24-30). Those two men prophesied within the camp while Moshe and the elders left the camp to prophesy. Rav Grumet explains (p. 86) that "Eldad and Meidad, who prophesied in the

---

36. Jerusalem, 2013.

camp, are connected to the people! They serve as the next step in the bridge between Moses and the people, and represent the model of the prophet that Moses will need to emulate to become the kind of leader he would like to be."

Rav Mosheh Lichtenstein (contemporary, Israel), in his *Moses: Envoy of God, Envoy of His People*,[37] explains this passage in a different, very creative way. The people have changed. In the past, they lacked confidence and were scared. Now they were materialistically pursuing physical pleasure, as evidenced in the demand for meat in the immediately preceding passage. Eldad and Meidad felt that new leadership was needed, younger people more in touch with the nation, who prophesied within the camp. The elders needed to be replaced with young men like Eldad and Meidad.

Rav Lichtenstein continues, "Upon hearing the arguments put forward by Eldad and Meidad, Moshe acknowledged the justice of their criticism and took steps to recitfy the faults they had pointed out" (p. 115). He brought the elders back into the camp and appointed spies who were young, more in touch with the people. This change in direction led to disastrous consequences, with the tragedy of the spies' failure. However, Moshe's hands were forced: "In order to bring the people into the land, there was no choice but to select promising leaders from the younger generation, and this Moshe did. But Moshe did not realize that they were not ready for the challenge..." (p. 122).

Again, Rav Grumet sees the response to Eldad and Meidad as reflecting a change in Moshe. Rav Lichtenstein sees it as a change in the people.[38]

---

37. Hoboken, NJ, 2008, p. 105ff.
38. Although Rav Lichtenstein also sees a change in Moshe's leadership ability, but in the opposite direction. He writes (p. 170): "... Moshe's response to the incident of Mei Merivah is not an isolated reaction, but is part of a more comprehensive change in his attitude

IV. What is *Peshat*?

All this raises the question of whether we are discussing *peshat* or *derash*, the simple meaning or an elaborate interpretation. Because there is so much missing from the text, any attempt to fill in the blanks, to connect stories with an over-arching narrative, is *derash*. Even when based on *peshat* readings of all the passages, the connection of the dots is a construction of a theme that does not exist directly in the text. And there is nothing wrong with that

But with *derash* comes the interpreter's perspective. Rav Ya'akov Kamenetsky (20th century, Lithuania-U.S.; *Emes Le-Ya'akov Al Ha-Torah*, p. 186 n. 20) astutely observes that *derash* is valuable as a reflection of its practitioner's views, not of the text's message. There are so many mutually exclusive ways to read between the lines, to construct a meta-narrative beyond the text's direct words, that any commentator's view on the subject must reflect his own message.

When I first became enamored with what some call the "New School" of Torah commentary, one *rosh yeshiva* referred to it in private discussion as the "New Midrash." I found that surprising, since this is all based on a close, literal reading of the text. I now realize how correct he was. Meta-narratives look beyond the text, at themes and unwritten assumptions. However, the identification and interpretation of non-textual messages is an art, not a science. It reflects assumptions of the readers.

We see this in the study of Moshe's leadership. Was he a failed leader, an improving leader or the greatest leader in history? Your answer to that question determines how you read the text and not vice versa. If you see him as a great leader, then you blame any bad

---

toward the people that is taking place in the second half of Bamidbar. In the first half of the book, Moshe is disappointed and frustrated. In the second half, his reaction goes beyond disappointment; it is now interwoven with paralysis, resentment and anger." In other words, Moshe's leadership ability declines with the second generation.

outcomes on other causes. If you see him as a failed leader, you consider the bad outcomes his own failures. Both interpretations can be achieved plausibly, utilizing the finest *peshat* readings of the text.

In the end, the story of Moshe's leadership rests on the values and authority of the interpreter. Personally, I find Rav Kahn's approach most appealing, Dr. Brown's most enlightening, Rav Grumet's most exciting, and Rav Lichtenstein's most creative.

Growth into A Rabbi

I. Humanizing Leaders

The *New York Times* surprised many readers on February 20, 2016, when it published a human-interest story about a weekly tennis game among three rabbis and a judge that has been ongoing for about 45 years.[39] Judge Alvin Hellerstein and Rabbis Haskel Lookstein, Michael Shmidman, and Jonah Kupietzky—all in their 80s—play and joke around with each other on a Manhattan tennis court. This story is not just about comradeship among the surprisingly active elderly. It is about humanizing authority figures, breaking leaders down to a common experience.

In today's age of massive distrust of leadership, we revel in reminders that people in positions of authority are really the same as the rest of us. They put on their pants one leg at a time and hang out with friends just like everyone else. This story is newsworthy because it celebrates the humanity of leaders in an attempt to remove their authority. Implied in the narrative is that they are just like us so why do we have to care what they say?

There is no denying the ordinary aspects of leaders. They eat and sleep like the rest of us. They entertain doubts and worry about the future. However, good leaders have specific training and skills that enable them to serve the community. Even if we

---

39. This essay originally appeared in *The Jewish Link of New Jersey*, March 10, 2016.

all share certain aspects of life, we do not share every talent and experience. I'm pretty sure that Rav Moshe Feinstein (20th century, U.S.) could not do my job, because I have very specific training and experience that he lacked. He probably could not have written this essay because his English skills were limited. Likewise, I cannot fill his position because I lack both his genius and his vast immersion in Torah learning that are requirements for his role.

I am far from advocating the worship of *gedolim*, leading Torah scholars. Rav Moshe was a human being, with his own flaws and achievements. He had his own personality, with many unique traits that distinguished him from his colleagues, students and followers. He rose to a position of leadership because of his remarkable Torah expertise and his exceptional religious and interpersonal behavior. Accomplished Torah scholars would not have asked him questions if they had not respected his ability to answer, and they would not study his responsa today if they did not find important insights in them. He earned respect and even deference, despite being a person.

II. Balancing Respect

How do we balance the respect accorded to a Torah scholar with his obvious humanity? In the past, the human aspect—the normalcy—was taken for granted and generally ignored. Stories are told of Rav Yisrael Meir Kagan, the *Chafetz Chaim* (19th-20th centuries, Poland), which emphasize his greatness, not his ordinariness. This path risks forgetting the Torah scholar's humanity, affording him a superhuman stature, as has happened in some circles today. In other circles, the pendulum has swung in the other direction and people are emphasizing the human frailty of rabbis as a means of detracting from their scholarly accomplishments. Rabbi Dovid M. Cohen (contemporary, U.S.) offers a middle path.

Rav Cohen's book, *We're Almost There*,[40] tells stories from his own life about his personal and career challenges. After years of successful work as a lawyer but unsuccessful years of dating, he finally found his match and changed careers in a whirlwind story. All along, he, of course, had doubts and fears that he shares with readers. When his special needs child was born, new emotions arose but Rabbi and Mrs. Cohen learned to adjust and delight in their new child. This is a very personal story, not just biographical but psychological and emotional—the thoughts and feelings that accompany, and sometimes overwhelm, the author throughout his journey.

However, the personal story of this rabbi—until recently the rabbi of the Young Israel of the Upper West Side—adds, rather than detracts, from his rabbinic position because it includes more than his frailties. Rav Cohen also discusses his rabbinic training. He studied under the Torah giant Rav Dovid Lifshitz, apprenticed under two leading rabbis—Rav Benjamin Yudin and Rav Emanuel Gettinger, and developed close teacher-student relationships with two important educators—Rav Ari Waxman and Rav Moshe Weinberger. You become an expert by training under experts.

A rabbi learns his trade by studying and doing. Rav Cohen shares with us his fears and accomplishments—the first time he comforted a family mourning a tragic death and how that informed his future activities. "You can never be fully prepared for something like this, but the experience years ago alerted me to the potential issues and intricacies." In addition to his yeshiva studies, his experiences as a leader have trained him to occupy the position. Rav Cohen's personal interactions with experienced mentors prepared him to succeed as a leader. For example, he relates how Rav Gettinger "used a verse we were learning together to scold me and remind me about what topics are better left

---

40. White Plains, NY, 2015.

unaddressed in a public forum," affording Rav Cohen a lesson in both how to rebuke and how to preach.

In his controversial biography of his father, *Making of a Godol*,[41] Rav Nosson Kamenetsky (contemporary, Israel) tells how an elderly Rav Chaim Soloveitchik once visited Kovno for a snowy Shabbos. Some young students from the nearby Slabodka yeshiva walked through the raging blizzard to get a glimpse of the famous Torah giant. They entered the house where Rav Chaim was staying. Rav Chaim said to them, "You came to see so you see, *a poshuter mentch* (plain person)," in an effort to dispel the superhuman myth. Yes, he was just a *mensch*, but what a *mensch* he was. In Rav Dovid Cohen's book we learn that he, too, is just a *mensch*, but a *mensch* with insight and experience, someone trained to teach and lead the community.

---

41. Improved Edition, Jerusalem, 2004, p. 89.

The President's Rabbi

I first met Rabbi Menachem Genack, rabbinic administrator and chief executive officer of OU Kosher, on the momentous Inauguration Day of 2009.[42] During our conversation in his office, Rabbi Genack could not resist showing me his Lincoln memorabilia and pointing out that President Barak Obama would be sworn into office that day on the historic Lincoln Bible. Many remarkable ideas jump out at me from this treasured encounter, which was the beginning of my ongoing student-teacher relationship with the rabbi.

First, I was surprised to learn that a rabbi of world-renowned talmudic accomplishment, whose name carries weight in every yeshiva in the world, is an amateur historian of President Abraham Lincoln. Beginning years previously, I had studied Rabbi Genack's essays on talmudic law, even acquiring his short but brilliant 1969 book in memory of his father (since republished). I was expecting a rabbi whose sole focus is on the text, not one who waxes eloquently on the thoughts and behaviors of U.S. presidents.

Additionally, I learned about the importance of religious inspiration to many past presidents. Lincoln, who was very devout albeit in a non-traditional sense, summoned much of his great vision and leadership from biblical sources. His speeches are

---

42. This essay originally appeared in the OU Kosher magazine *Behind the Union Symbol*, Spring 2015.

replete with biblical references. They are also full of biblical cadence and spirit, radiating the charm and confidence of the ancient text. Lincoln was foremost, but hardly alone, among presidents who utilized Scripture for guidance.

I was also informed of an ongoing project, at that time over 15 years old, in which Rabbi Genack sent biblical insights to former President Bill Clinton. Among those letters was an essay containing musings on the historical significance of Lincoln's Bible, which Rabbi Genack discussed with me that day. At first glance, particularly to the uninitiated, this pairing of rabbi and politician seems unlikely. However, on thinking back to the Clinton years, it makes perfect sense. Those were heady times, when the Soviet Union had recently collapsed, when Middle East peace loomed temptingly close, when new technology was turbocharging the economy. We entered uncharted territory, faced a new world order, that posed difficult questions which politicians heatedly debated. More than ever, leadership required vision and wisdom. Where else do you turn for wisdom if not the foundation of Western civilization, the Bible?

The two unlikely friends, the Southern Baptist and the Orthodox rabbi, met at a fundraising event in 1992; Rabbi Genack introduced then Governor Clinton by quoting Proverbs (29:18): "Where there is no vision, the people perish." Clinton appreciated that biblical thought and incorporated it into his speech accepting the Democratic nomination for President. After that initial encounter, President Clinton invited Rabbi Genack to prayer meetings and official dinners. In advance of those events, Rabbi Genack prepared essays on biblical themes which he gave to the President. President Clinton enthusiastically read each essay, often replying in handwritten notes, one time even correcting a biblical reference.

Over the years, Rabbi Genack enlisted other scholars to write biblical essays for the President. This continual stream of religious insight serves as a reminder of the unique relationship in America between religion and government. While the Constitution wisely prevents government from endorsing religion, it allows for religious ideas to influence political views. The person holding the most stressful job in the world needs guidance and strength. In the U.S., presidents often find that inspiration in the Bible. This is a country where the President is sworn in on a Bible (of his choosing). The Declaration of Independence openly speaks about inalienable rights endowed by the Creator. Religion is a powerful force of American leadership and freedom.

The essays Rabbi Genack collected are published in *Letters to President Clinton: Biblical Lessons of Faith and Leadership* (New York, 2013).[43] Over 100 biblical essays by over 45 rabbis, scholars and leaders—including three Chief Rabbis, two university presidents and one U.S. Senator—offer Scriptural lessons of leadership and faith. This masterful collection of thoughts combines careful reading of the sacred text with profound understanding of the challenges faced by leaders in the complex world in which we live.

The letters Rabbi Genack personally wrote range across a variety of topics. In one essay, he emphasizes the biblical importance of personal privacy. He quotes the rabbis of the Midrash commentary who note the exceptional nature of Balaam's donkey's ability to speak. Why haven't other animals been granted this power? "If able to speak, animals would unmask our foibles, our pettiness, our inevitable failings." Residing in the background, they see too much and would reveal private information. This message is even more timely now than when written.

Faith, the need to look for strength and guidance from Above, the belief that circumstances will improve, represents a continual theme throughout the letters. While in office, President Clinton faced many daunting challenges. Rabbi Genack sent him lessons

---
43. I had a small advisory role in the book's publication.

in faith, biblical messages of sustenance. When God told Moses to challenge the powerful Pharaoh, He said, "Go to Pharaoh" in language that sounds like "Come to Pharaoh." The lesson, Rabbi Genack explains, is that "God is always standing next to us, giving us the strength to endure, and even the potential to be triumphant."

Aside from Rabbi Genack, the most frequent contributor of letters is Rabbi Lord Jonathan Sacks, the chief rabbi emeritus of the United Kingdom, who also wrote an impassioned preface to the book. Rabbi Sacks studied Bible privately with English Prime Ministers. In these essays, he offers the public a window into his lessons for world leaders. "A leader is one who shows the people where to look—down or up, short-term or long-term, at present dangers or at ultimate destinations. That is perhaps the leader's greatest power—to influence the mood of a nation." After pointing to the repeated biblical directive to tell our children about our past, Rabbi Sacks writes, "Moses taught that freedom is more than a moment of political triumph. It is a constant endeavor, throughout the ages, to teach those who come after us about the battles our ancestors fought, and why."

The sections of the book are arranged topically, including Leadership, Faith, Creation, Community, Dreams and Vision, Holidays, and, significantly, Sin and Repentance. Among the challenges President Clinton faced was the impeachment trial that emerged from a personal failing. In sympathetic but honest words, Rabbi Genack teaches the importance of repentance. Everyone sins; a great man learns from his mistakes and grows through repentance. Senator Joseph Lieberman, who publicly criticized the President's behavior at that time, wrote to the President a reflection on the significance that the biblical night always precedes day (as it says in Genesis, "and it was evening and it was morning... "). He profoundly explains, "To appreciate and properly evaluate the gifts of the day requires the experience of the emptiness of the night, because the night teaches us the importance of faith and courage.... After the night comes the day, with its promise of salvation and the hope for a new and better tomorrow."

This book is an important source of inspiration and guidance. The Bible serves as a guide to life for even—perhaps especially—those in the most trying situations. It reminds us to stop and reflect, to look beyond our own instincts, to seek insight from the ultimate source of wisdom. This book is also a historical record of the surprising spiritual influence of one prolific rabbinic scholar on the leader of the free world. After leaving office, President Clinton responded to a letter from Rabbi Genack as follows: "I think you know how much they've meant to me over the years, and I'm so glad you are continuing to send them."

The Talmud tells the story of Rabbi Judah's close friendship with Antoninus, the second-century Roman Emperor. They were friends and intellectuals, inspiring and challenging each other to grow. Perhaps future generations will look back at this book and declare Rabbi Genack and President Clinton as the modern incarnation of this ancient relationship, the political leader and his rabbi.

The Elected Official

I. Individual Punishment

The debate over the culpability of the biblical residents of Shechem reaches beyond the text to legal realms but should also extend to our philosophy of citizenship. Following Shechem-the-man's attack on Dinah, her brothers tricked and killed the male residents of the city. Ya'akov condemned the brothers, to which they firmly responded (Gen. 34).

Why were all the residents punished for a single man's sin? Rambam (12th century, Egypt; *Mishneh Torah, Hilkhos Melakhim* 9:14) uncharacteristically explains this biblical episode in his legal code. People in general are obligated by the Noachide code to establish courts to maintain justice. Since Shechem was unpunished for his crime, the city residents clearly were failing to enforce law and order, and therefore liable for violating the command to establish courts. According to the Rambam, administering justice is a personal obligation of each citizen.

II. Group Responsibility

Ramban (13th century, Spain-Israel; Gen. 34:13) strongly disagrees. In his view, the Noachide command is to interact with a legal system based on Torah's legislation. A society must regulate itself with the definition of torts and crimes given by the Torah. Rather, the brothers must have known that the town's citizens were generally wicked and deserving of punishment.

But how does the Ramban differ with the Rambam on the key obligation to establish courts? Certainly he would agree that part of legislating based on the Torah's definition includes establishing courts to administer justice. It seems that the Ramban believed this to be a communal obligation, devolving on society as a whole and not each individual. Therefore, each Shechemite could not be held liable for the lack of justice in the town. After all, one individual cannot enforce justice on his own. If so, he cannot be held responsible for its absence.

III. Political Theory

The nature of democracy may also revolve around this debate. Does an elected official serve as a representative of his constituents or as an individual selected by voters? Is he a bureaucratic functionary or an agent acting on behalf of his senders?

Jewish legal authorities dispute this topic. According to Rav Moshe Schick (19th century, Hungary; *Responsa Maharam Schick, Orach Chaim* 34), society is a partnership of citizens. Some partners are given senior positions out of organizational convenience—someone must do the dirty work of day-to-day governing. Elected officials do the work of all the citizens because not everyone can do it. But all are theoretically obligated to do so.

Rav Eliezer Waldenberg (20th century, Israel; *Hilkhos Medinah* 3:4:5) argues that elected officials act as trustees (*aputropsin*). They are the functionaries entrusted with public works. They are not doing the job that falls on everyone. Rather, they are performing an important role that the community needs filled.

According to the first theory, a government official is a representative acting on behalf of the citizens, a senior partner chosen for the role that each citizen might otherwise have to fill. The Rambam's view of personal obligation for justice finds its fulfillment in such a representative government. Each citizen plays a role in legislation—and enforcement—by appointing an agent to govern.

According to the second theory, the elected official is selected to serve on his own. He is chosen as a trustee. Ramban would presumably favor this view, whereby governance is a communal task and elected officials serve not as representatives but as communal functionaries appointed democratically.

IV. Communal Responsibility

Perhaps we can find echoes of this debate in explanations of the enigmatic *eglah arufah*. If a dead body is found outside of a city, the city's leaders must absolve themselves of sin over a ritual calf (Deut. 21:1-9). What is the meaning of this puzzling ritual.

Rambam (*Moreh Nevukhim* 3:40) explains this ceremony as a subterfuge to uncover the killer. With all the publicity over the killing, the public will enthusiastically search for clues and find the culprit. Ramban (Deut. 29:4) rejects this rationale because it renders the ritual inherently meaningless. Instead, he considers it a sacrifice of the community elders in penance for the killing.

According to the Rambam, the *eglah arufah* ceremony encourages each individual to find the killer, thereby atoning for the death. The communal activity serves to activate each member. However, according to the Ramban, only the central authority figures act in this ritual. Only they retain responsibility following this communal killing. Not each individual, but the community as a whole—represented by its leaders—must atone for the death.

The Ramban sees this *eglah arufah* ritual for the community as a single unit, while the Rambam sees it for the community as a group of individuals. Similarly, Ramban sees the obligation to establish courts as a requirement for the community as a whole while Rambam sees it as an obligation on the community of individuals.

How Should Jews Vote?

I gave a little groan when I first saw David Klinghoffer's book, *How Would God Vote? Why the Bible Commands You to Be a Conservative*.[44] However, once I opened the book I discovered that it is not at all what I thought it would be. I expected it to be a book that argues that the Bible commands such-and-such so we must support the Republican Party, which wants to enact that Torah legislation into American law. But the book is different.

Klinghoffer spends the first two chapters explaining that he does not believe that we should turn America into a theocracy. Rather, religious voters should look to the Bible as a place to find their own values, and that like all voters they should advocate laws that conform to their personal values. I agree with almost everything Klinghoffer writes in his first two chapters, although I take issue with his generalizations about liberals at the end of chapter two. One thing I found annoying about this book, and in much of conservative literature, is the generalizations about and the lambasting of Liberals. But I found that the book's good qualities outshone this aspect.

After the initial two chapters, Klinghoffer addresses some twenty major political issues and tries to extract the biblical (and talmudic) values on the subject. This is where he really surprises me. I was expecting to be lectured about how (conveniently) the Bible

---

44. New York, 2008.

advocates all of the stances taken by conservative Republicans. But that is not what Klinghoffer does. Instead, he works hard to try to follow the Bible's (and Talmud's) directions even when it takes him afoul of conservative Republicans.

For example, on school prayer Klinghoffer writes, "[M]y own reading of the Bible suggests that to the institution of such reforms at this moment, God Himself—if we picture Him first as a Supreme Court justice casting the deciding vote and then as a persuasive member of the local school board—would be indifferent" (p. 78). On abortion he writes (p. 66):

> We are left with abortion as a moral outrage whenever it is committed, but a punishable offense, subject to criminal penalties, only from the fortieth day on. This would not sit well, it seems, with either the extreme pro-life or the extreme pro-choice forces.

He goes where he sees the evidence pointing, and that sometimes takes him to a fairly moderate position, the book's subtitle notwithstanding. However, it must be mentioned that Klinghoffer is neither a biblical nor talmudic scholar. He knows his basic material fairly well but I disagree with many nuances and details in his presentation. For example, regarding the quote above about abortion before the fortieth day from conception, I hardly think that it is fair to call it a "moral outrage." Abortion as a substitute for contraception is a moral outrage. There exists a broad spectrum of reasons for an early abortion spanning from praiseworthy to understandable to contempible.

I found other readings of his to be enlightening. In extracting the ethos of immigration from the laws of a *ger toshav* (resident alien), Klinghoffer explains that "scriptural tradition expects that any immigrant, any *ger*, will meet demanding criteria—basically, moral criteria" (p. 186). In other words, we should require that immigrants follow a basic set of social rules (although he considers idolatry to be a moral issue, which I find questionable).

However, I also found some of his analyses wanting. In his chapter on poverty, he argues that help for the poor has to come from individuals and not a collective government: "I can find nowhere in Scripture where the state is commanded to extend generosity to the impoverished" (p. 89). Be that as it may, what about the hundreds if not thousands of years during which Jewish communities supported their local poor as collectives? Does not the Talmud speak about this, as well as centuries of rabbinic literature? They were all basing themselves on the same biblical values that Klinghoffer is trying to identify.

Overall, I disagree with many of Klinghoffer's conclusions and the resulting political views, but I found the book to be very thoughtful and thought provoking.

Religious Liberty

In a classic episode of *All In The Family*, a television repairman tells Archie Bunker that he cannot finish the job because sundown on Friday was approaching.[45] As a religious Jew, he had to observe the Sabbath. Archie offered to pay him extra to finish the job on Friday night, opining that turning down money is also against the Jewish religion.

Offensive stereotypes aside, neither Archie Bunker nor anyone else should have the right to tell someone how to observe his religion. Freedom of religion means freedom to practice my religion as I understand it. This country was built on the idealism and strong community spirit of religion. Yet, despite the great progress Jews and other minorities have made in the past decades, Orthodox Jews still face religious barriers.

Personally, I believe that Leviticus 19 forbids shaving beards with a razor but allows use of some electric shavers, which technically avoid this prohibition. Therefore, I feel religiously free to shave my beard and did so for many years. Other Orthodox Jews follow a stricter tradition, some never completely shaving off the beard and some never trimming it at all. Orthodox Jews who maintain their beards have recently suffered discrimination. In 2009, a medic in Pikesville, MD, sued for discrimination because he was forced to choose between his beard and his service as a

---

45. This essay first appeared in *Jewish World Review*, May 11, 2015.

medic. In the same year, a rabbi in Florida was rejected for service as an army chaplain because he refused to shave his beard.

While I believe my religion allows me to shave my beard, I do not want to be an Archie Bunker and tell others what their religion allows. Thanks to extensive legal intervention, both cases were resolved favorably. Orthodox Jews need laws protecting us so that we can observe our religion without government intervention.

Over the past few years, reports have emerged from around the world about governments attempting to ban circumcision and forbidding kosher slaughter. These laws would effectively exile most observant Jews from the country. Thankfully, most countries and regions that propose these laws do not pass them. But some do. Even in the U.S., similar laws find vocal advocates. Our religious liberty, our ability to practice the peaceful religion our ancestors have maintained for thousands of years, is currently under attack. We need to defend ourselves, both through vigorous legal action and by enacting new laws when necessary.

Imagine a kosher caterer that is sued for refusing to serve at a wedding on the Sabbath or a wedding hall owner who is sued for refusing to rent the premises for an interfaith wedding. Many people interpret Jewish tradition as allowing these activities. But the government should never serve in the Archie Bunker role, telling people what their religion allows and forbids. No Jew, no American, should be forced to violate his deeply held religious convictions.

All people, especially minorities, need their rights protected. Ideally, when conflicts emerge between the rights of different minorities, compromises can be found that respect everyone's needs. Alternative arrangements can often be found. However, we need laws to address those difficult cases that defy compromise. America is not Czarist Russia, where Jews were often forced by hostile government operatives to violate their religion. But this great country must strive for a higher standard. It must allow religion to flourish, because religious communities built this country into the great power that it is. Religious communities support the poor, provide healthy social frameworks for families, and encourage social activism.

Orthodox Jews and other religious minorities are vulnerable to discrimination. We need to vigorously defend our religious liberty or risk losing it. No American should be forced to choose between God and country.

Religious Politicians

Serving in political leadership requires occasionally leaving our comfortable community and joining with people who do not understand our beliefs and observances. Because the stakes are so high, *halakhah* recognizes the need for a balanced and realistic approach to maintaining loyalty to tradition while engaging in political activity at the highest levels.

In January 2017, the news reported that Jared and Ivanka Kushner received rabbinic permission to ride in a car back from President Trump's inaugural ball on Friday night.[46] Many people questioned this decision. We do not know the name of the rabbi who gave this permission nor the specific circumstances of the individuals, but we can discuss the possibilities. In general, I can understand the interpretation that allows this, but I would not have given this permission. Let's also keep in mind that Jared Kushner is not, and to my knowledge does not want to be, Chief Rabbi of America. He is just an Orthodox Jew trying to do his best. No one should be looking up to him as a religious exemplar, any more than they should Joseph Lieberman or Sandy Koufax.

I. The Questioners

The couple wanted to honor Ivanka's father on the greatest day of his life, as he was sworn into the most powerful office in the world.

---

46 "Report: Ivanka Trump Gets Pass To Travel on Shabbat for Inauguration," *Jerusalem Post*, Janury 19, 2017.

Sinca Ivanka is a convert, and a convert to Judaism is technically "reborn," the specific commandment of honoring her father no longer applies. However, she still has to show gratitude to the man who raised her and supported her. I don't know anyone who would advise a convert to do anything other than show respect for his parents. While honoring a parent or showing gratitude does not set aside any specific law, it does create a need that should be met if possible. Additionally, this was a state function and the Kushners were acting in political roles. If they could attend without violating Shabbos, on this one special occasion, there might be room to allow it. Normally people should spend Friday night in synagogue and at the Shabbos dinner table. However, for family sometimes you have to spend an unusual and perhaps uncomfortable Shabbos.

If your family or employer ask you to do something like this, tell them that you have to ask your rabbi (and ask him).

II. Questions

One question a rabbi would ask is the nature of the family dynamics. How would missing the event affect family relations? Would the President get insulted, or would the public perceive an insult, if the Kushners missed the event? I do not know the answers to these questions. An insult is not a free pass. You cannot violate Shabbos just because your father would be insulted if you observe Shabbos. However, it raises the question of whether there is a way to accommodate both Shabbos and the family need.

Additionally, why couldn't they just walk home? This would also resolve the main problem. Apparently, with hundreds of thousands of protesters in Washington, DC, security concerns prevented the Kushners from walking home even with security personnel surrounding them. There was a real danger to their lives that required them returning from the inaugural ball by car, if they attended. However, they could have avoided the danger by refraining from attending and returning home by car before Shabbos.

III. A Shabbos Bus?

In his book, *Shabbat, the Right Way: Resolving Halakhic Dilemmas*,[47] the late Rav J. Simcha Cohen discusses at length a dilemma facing his own community. As the rabbi of a retirement community, he led an aging membership that has trouble walking to shul. He analyzes whether he is allowed to hire a gentile bus driver to take elderly members to and from shul on Shabbos.

The community is surrounded by an *eruv* and all transportation will be done within the permissible perimeter (i.e., within both the *eruv* and the *techum*). Rav Cohen wrote an analysis and sent it to a number of prominent contemporary rabbis, receiving responses from Rav Moshe D. Tendler (contemporary, U.S.), Rav Norman Lamm (contemporary, U.S.) and Rav Yosef Carmel (contemporary, Israel), all reproduced in the book. Rav Cohen addresses the following issues.

IV. Gentile Labor

You are not allowed to ask a gentile to do work for you on Shabbos that you are not allowed to do yourself (*amirah le-nokhri*). However, this rule has many conditions and exceptions that allow for various extenuating circumstances. Rav Cohen works hard on this issue, harder than I think is necessary. He enters complex areas like having one gentile ask another gentile before Shabbos to do work for a Jew on Shabbos. Rav Yair Bachrach (17th century, Germany; *Chavos Yair*, no. 53) permits this arrangement, although others forbid. However, the consensus seems to only allow that in cases of great need and when the second gentile does not know

---

47. Jerusalem, 2009.

he is doing work for Jews (*Piskei Teshuvos* 307:13). Even in this unusual situation, the driver should not know that he is driving the Kushners because it is Shabbos. I'm not sure if that is feasible.

Some object that the ways to avoid this prohibition only apply to one-off situations, not when used every week. Rav Cohen dismisses this objection as incorrect. For example, the Rema (16th century, Poland; *Shulchan Arukh, Orach Chaim* 276:2) objects to those who asks gentiles to light candles for them on Shabbos but does not raise the objection that they did it every week. I find that to be a fairly weak response. However, this objection does not apply to the Kushners, because we are discussing a one-time permission for the inauguration.

V. Onlookers

Rav Cohen raises the issue that outsiders, unaware of the situation of this community's needs, will misunderstand the riding of a bus to and from shul under specific conditions. They will think that these people are violating a prohibition. Rav Cohen suggests placing signs on the bus explaining that these are special Shabbos buses, which should eliminate this problem. The announcement in the media that the Kushners received special permission also resolves this issue.

VI. Weight

Rav Cohen raises the question of whether sitting on a bus constitutes a violation of *halakhah*. If your weight causes the vehicle to do more work, then perhaps you are personally guilty of violating Shabbos. This is a serious concern that was debated in the context of Shabbos elevators, with great authorities on either side. Rav Cohen cites Rav Yosef Eliyahu Henkin and Rav Isser Yehuda Unterman as ruling leniently. In his response to Rav Cohen, Rav Moshe Tendler writes that those who permitted Shabbos elevators were unaware of the weight problem. This is surprising because his father-in-law, Rav Moshe Feinstein (*Iggeros Moshe*, vol. 1 no. 132), was among those who ruled leniently. Additionally, it is simply incorrect. Some explicitly permitted the weight issue, such as Rav Shlomo Zalman Auerbach regarding Shabbos elevators (*Shemiras Shabbos Ke-Hilkhasah*, ch. 23 n. 140).

VII. Weekday Activities

Rav Cohen proceeds to the nebulous prohibition of *uvda de-chol*, performing weekday activities on Shabbos. I'm not sure how or if he resolves it, other than stating that the Shabbos bus is for those who are elderly and weak or ill. I'm not sure it would be relevant to the Kushner issue, either. One could also add a concern of *shabbason*, that we must actively rest on Shabbos which precludes riding in a car. The *Chasam Sofer* invokes this concept to forbid riding on a train.

VIII. Responses

Rav Moshe Tendler responds that riding on a bus is tantamount to driving it, because one's weight adds to the work. He also argues that this innovation will destroy the sanctity of Shabbos and runs the risk of being extended to other situations that do not have the same urgency.

Rav Norman Lamm raises a historical precedent in India, that was only discontinued in the late 1950s or early 1960s. But he cautions that the risk of exiting the *techum* perimeter— a biblical violation — is too great to allow this innovation.

Rav Yosef Carmel quotes responsa by Rav Shaul Yisraeli (20th century, Israel) that permit somewhat similar situations and concludes that he would permit a Shabbos bus under a number of detailed conditions, including that it run at most every other week and that someone regularly monitor public impression about whether this is perceived as a farce or a sweeping abrogation of the law.

IX. Rav Soloveitchik

Rav Cohen misses Rav Joseph B. Soloveitchik's (20th century, U.S.) ruling on the matter. Rav Hershel Schachter (*Be-Ikvei Ha-Tzon*, pp. 34-35) quotes Rav Soloveitchik as rejecting a proposed Shabbos bus to bring people to shul because driving on Shabbos has become a symbol of anti-Orthodoxy. I suspect that the full force of this has passed with time but it still has sufficient relevance to prohibit. In the Kushner case, I believe it is still sufficient reason to forbid use of a car. Driving or even riding in a car is a public symbol of rejecting Orthodox Judaism, and cannot be permitted except when medically necessary.

X. Conclusion

Given the unusual circumstances, there is room for a rabbi to permit riding home in a car in this one case assuming no other Shabbos laws would be violated. At the inaugural ball, the Kushners would not be allowed to do anything contrary to Shabbos rules. This was probably an extremely uncomfortable situation but sometimes you have to do that for family.

Despite all the discussion, I think the *amirah le-nokhri* prohibition, *shabbason* commandment, weight issue and Rav Soloveitchik's concern would not allow me to permit this. I would tell the Kushners that despite all the other considerations, they should go home just before Shabbos. However, I know other rabbis who have said that they would rule leniently on this question.

In some communities in Israel, doctors and nurses routinely are driven home by gentiles when their shifts end on Shabbos. One of my children was once hit by a car early Friday afternoon.

The teenage child and my wife went to the hospital to get checked out (all was fine) and the child was released after Shabbos had started. We were told that my wife and child should have the gentile hospital staff call for a car service (with a gentile driver) to take them home because the walk was long and through a dangerous neighborhood. For one-time occurrences under unusual circumstances, there is room to be lenient. For ongoing practice, this would institutionalize possible violations of serious prohibitions that cannot be allowed.

Is A Politician Allowed To Retire From Public Office?

May an Orthodox Jew leave political office for the public or non-profit sectors? Does *halakhah* permit this? The community needs talented leaders in order to function. Is someone qualified, with a proven track record of success, morally and religiously allowed to keep his talents from benefiting the public? A 2017 article by Rav Avishai Ben David (contemporary, Israel) explores the parameters of a public official leaving office.[48]

I. Two Opinions

The Gemara (*Kiddushin* 32b) says that a king may not forgo his honor. Commentaries explain that showing honor to the king is a form of accepting his dominion, thereby fulfilling the commandment of "you shall surely appoint for yourself a king" (Deut. 17:15). *Shitah Mekubetzes* (16th century, Israel; *Kesubos* 17a sv. *ve-khasav ha-Ramban*) adds that if a king forgoes his honor, effectively he is abdicating his position, even if temporarily. Rav Pinchas Zabichi (contemporary, Israel; *Responsa Ateres Paz* 1:3:CM:1) deduces that only a king may not abdicate, since the mitzvah of appointment applies only to him. Any other public official, for which there is no mitzvah to appoint, may resign, given appropriate circumstances.

---
48. *Emunas Itekha*, no. 116, pp. 81-90.

Rav Amram Blum (19th century, Hungary; *Responsa Beis She'arim, Yoreh De'ah* 334) disagrees regarding Jewish communal positions. Since traditionally those positions are hereditary, a person does not choose those roles. The position-holder is chosen by powers greater than he and may not resign in opposition to those powers. Similarly, even someone who did not inherit the role was likewise chosen by great powers for his position. The Midrash (*Shemos Rabbah* 40:2) teaches that God showed Adam a book listing every generation and its leaders. Apparently, leaders were chosen for their roles at the time of Creation.

II. Historical Precedent

When Hillel came to Israel from Babylonia, the religious leaders were so embarrassed that they resigned from their position. The Gemara (*Pesachim* 61a) explains that in that year the day before Pesach, when the Paschal sacrifice must be brought, fell out on Shabbos. Bnei Beseira, the Israeli religious leaders, were not sure whether the *korban pesach* overrides Shabbos. Hillel, the immigrant scholar, proved to them that the Pesach sacrifice must be brought on Shabbos. In deference to his great scholarship, Bnei Beseira resigned so that Hillel could be appointed to the highest position of religious leadership.

Clearly, resignation is permitted. However, the Rivash (14th century, Algeria; Responsa 171) explains that Bnei Beseira only resigned because of their great humility. They are the exception that proves the rule. They truly believed that they were unworthy for the role. Anyone else for any other reason may not resign.

III. Modern Times

Rav Moshe Sofer (19th century, Hungary; *Responsa Chasam Sofer* 1:206) points out the incongruity between rabbinic contracts and careers. In his day, rabbis were given contracts for a few years but in practice the appointments were for life. He explains that the reason for the limited contracts was to allow the rabbi to resign at any point. If a rabbi accepted a lifetime position, he would be choosing a prison, placing himself into unlimited servitude. Similarly, Rav Ya'akov Ettlinger (19th century, Germany; *Responsa Binyan Tziyon* 124) rules that a rabbi may resign for personal reasons. He does not have to suffer for other people's benefit.

Rav Avraham Yitzchak Kook (19th-20th century, Israel; *Responsa Orach Mishpat, Choshen Mishpat* 21) argues that a rabbi may never resign from his position, because doing so could cause great spiritual damage to the community. Rav Ya'akov Epstein (contemporary, Israel; *Responsa Chevel Nachalaso* 6:26) tells the story that Rav Isser Zalman Meltzer (20th century, Russia-Israel) wanted to resign from the rabbinate of Slutzk. He asked Rav Chaim Soloveitchik (19th-20th century, Russia) and the Chofetz Chaim (19th-20th century, Poland), both of whom told him that he may not.

IV. Elected Officials

Rav Ben David suggests that elected officials are different from Jewish communal officials. They are elected for specifically delineated terms, after which their position is terminated unless they are reelected. (In some cases, there are even term limits forcing the elected official to retire from that position.)

Rav Ben David quotes a halakhic answer provided by Rav Ya'akov Ariel (contemporary, Israel) to a member of the governing body of a *moshav* community who wanted to resign. This *moshav* leader disagreed strongly over a timely issue with another member of the *moshav*. However, that person was next in line for his position. Rav Ariel responded that he may resign for two reasons. An elected official is supposed to do what he thinks is best for the community. If he thinks that his resignation is best, then he may do so. Additionally, voters understand that elected officials will sometimes resign. Otherwise, the community will have trouble finding people to take volunteer or low-paid positions.

According to the Rav Moshe Sofer and Rav Ya'akov Ettlinger, a rabbi or politician may resign if he wants to do so. Even according to Rav Kook who forbids, Rav Ya'akov Ariel (contemporary, Israel) argues that an elected official is different from a rabbi and may resign.

To add to this, I point out that rabbis frequently resign from one community to serve another community. Similarly, a politician should be able to resign from one position serving the public in order to take a different position serving the public, such as in a non-profit organization.

Finding Inspiration In Politics

We celebrate Purim every year to commemorate the celebration in ancient times, when joy conquered fear and good vanquished evil.[49] The story of Esther and Mordechai as told in the book of Esther takes place over many years. Too often, we skip the dates in the text and miss an important message hiding in plain sight in the final, short chapter of the book, a message that sheds light on both political leadership and personal inspiration.

I. Purim Timeline

The Gemara (*Megillah* 12a) says that Achashverosh ruled for fourteen years. In the third year, he made his enormous feast, to which Vashti refused to come (Esther 1:3). After this feast, Achashverosh began gathering young women to be his wife. Esther was taken to be Achashverosh's wife, after a year of preparation, in the seventh year of his reign (2:16). At the beginning of the twelfth year of Achashverosh's reign, Haman selected a day—eleven months later—to destroy the Jews (3:12). Within three months, Haman was dead and Mordechai was trying to undo the wicked plan (8:9). The fighting took place during the last month of Achashverosh's twelfth year as king (9:1). The next year, in Achashverosh's thirteenth year, the Jews established a celebration

---

49. This essay originally appeared in *The Jewish Link of New Jersey*, March 9, 2017.

on those days as Purim and Shushan Purim (9:22). This was probably the last Purim of Achashverosh's reign.

For at least four years, Achashverosh was taking young women to the capital so he could select a wife (or wives). This must have been a traumatic time for the nation, for parents whose daughters were taken away, most likely to be rejected and sent back to their disrupted youth. Esther could not have been the only Jewish girl snatched from her home.

After a queen was chosen, the other young women were sent home. Things returned to normal. While there was palace intrigue, this was largely invisible to the public. Even if they learned about it, they rightly saw it as politics as usual. For five years, life was good.

Then things got worse, very quickly. Seemingly out of nowhere, a genocidal decree was issued with the king's signature. After a miraculous reversal, the Jews had to fight for their lives. They not only won the fighting but rose to a position of favor. They even declared a holiday. It was all over and things could return to normal.

II. Normal Ending

Normalcy is the theme of the brief tenth chapter of Esther. In the first verse, we learn that Achashverosh raised taxes. What can be more normal than that? Instead of worrying about their lives, the Jews were concerned with taxes. The previous period of normalcy, after Achashverosh chose Esther, began with a reduction in taxes (2:18). The next period of normalcy also begins with a discussion of taxes. (Note that in the book of Esther, three things seem inevitable, contrary to the two in American tradition: death, taxes, and feasts.)

Verse 10:2 talks about Mordechai's and Achashverosh's legacies in running the empire. The third verse, the grand finale of the

Megillah, tells us that throughout his time in power, Mordechai was also a great leader of the Jews. Mordechai was "*gadol la-Yehudim*," which Targum translates as "a leader of the Jews." He was not just a successful politician but also an active leader of the Jewish community.

He was also "*ratzui le-rov echav*," a complicated phrase to translate. The Talmud (*Megillah* 16b) understands "*rov*" to mean majority, meaning that Mordechai was accepted by and popular with only a majority of Jews, but not all of them. Some of the Sages opposed Mordechai's decision to engage in politics rather than learn and teach Torah. Ibn Ezra explains simply that you can never please everyone, particularly given the natural jealousy of those in power. However, many modern commentators translate "*rov*" as very large number, which seems to be its consistent use throughout the Bible (e.g. Gen. 48:16).

Put differently, after the miraculous salvation, Mordechai faced ideological opponents and jealous critics despite enjoying widespread popularity. During the year-long threat, communal divisions took a back seat to survival. Crisis produced unity. When things returned to normal, ideological and political concerns returned.

III. Highs and Lows

On a personal level, we experience the same phenomenon. During a spiritual high, we embrace the moment and forget our mundane concerns. But when we return to normal life, our routine takes over and a multitude of concerns compete for attention. One of the great religious challenges of our time is apathy, or perhaps more accurately distractedness. Too many people don't feel the spiritual high of religion.

One solution is to create as many spiritual highs as possible, minimizing the downtime, all but eliminating the normalcy. For some people, this works. But one size does not fit all and many people lack the time or personal inclination to go *kumsitz* hopping. A constant high, like a constant crisis, is exhausting. No person can function at full capacity without rest.

Another solution is to find spirituality in the mundane, to bring God into the workplace and the living room. When we see ourselves fulfilling God's will in every large and small decision, we transform our days into religious worship. The beauty of the detailed halakhic life lies in the opportunity for constant God-awareness. Still another solution is to see God in the Torah, to rise spiritually in the pages of the Talmud. For some, Torah study is the highlight of their days, among the greatest joys in their lives. While people react differently based on their experiences and personalities, some will find value in all strategies.

From the time that Esther was taken, Mordechai sat in the palace courtyard. How did he do it? Was he living in crisis mode, looking for daily updates from Esther? Perhaps he felt that God wanted him to be politically aware, seeing spirituality in the mundane. Or maybe he spent most of his day learning and teaching Torah, taking a break to visit the palace.

We don't know. But we know that in the later period of normalcy, after the final crisis, he focused on two things that serve as the final words of the book of Esther. He was "*doresh tov le-ammo*" (10:3), he proactively helped his community, "*ve-dover shalom le-khol zaro*," he involved himself in Jewish education, either of his family (Ibn Ezra) or all children (modern commentators). Mordechai, the politician, found spiritual meaning in his community, his family and educating the next generation. We cannot all share the personality of Mordechai but we can learn from his example that there is beauty and inspiration to be found in community, family, and Torah education.

CHAPTER 3:
USING AUTHORITY

Authority is not a privilege but an obligation, even a burden. Rabbis serve both God and the community. They must answer questions based not on their opinions but on their best efforts to understand divine wisdom in all its manifestations. From time immemorial, people have complained that rabbis teach what benefits them personally. While individual rabbis of a lesser stature may have succumbed to their base human instincts, as a whole the rabbis have engaged seriously and honestly with their sacred charges. Rabbis today must continue on this noble path.

In this chapter, we explore some methodological aspects of rabbinic authority and specific responsibilities it entails.

A Rabbi's Obligation

A rabbi achieves his title through years of studying Torah. He implements that training when he teaches or rules on religious matters. However, unlike other subjects of study, Torah knowledge obligates. If a rabbi is asked a question to which he knows the answer, he must respond. It is his sacred duty.

I. Mitzvah to Respond

Rav Yitzchak of Corbeil (*Semak*; 13th century, France; no. 111) locates this obligation in a biblical verse. *Vayikra* (Lev. 10:8-11) teaches that priests may not drink wine because this will interfere with their obligation to distinguish between sacred and profane, between pure and impure. Drinking wine also interferes with the priests' obligation to teach Jewish law. *Semak* implicitly asks why the prohibition of getting drunk should only apply to priests. Rather, it must mean that every Torah scholar is obligated to teach and rule, and therefore may not get drunk.

In a lengthy responsum on a communal policy, Rav Chaim Palaggi (19th century, Turkey; *Chukos Ha-Chaim*, no. 93) points out an invalid clause in a communal agreement. The community leadership had forced local rabbis to sign that they would not teach people that the communal policy contradicts *halakhah*. Rav Palaggi argues that such an agreement, even if signed, is invalid because it contradicts a rabbi's obligation to respond to inquiries on Jewish law. Rav Palaggi locates the source of this obligation in a specific talmudic passage. The Talmud (*Kiddushin* 30a-b) explains the obligation to teach Torah (Deut. 6:7) as meaning that you must have a clear grasp on the law. If anyone asks you a question on *halakhah*, you must answer immediately without having to pause to think. This talmudic passage states that a Torah scholar is obligated to respond—immediately—to halakhic questions.

According to the *Semak*, there is a unique obligation for someone qualified to issue rulings on halakhic questions. It is a special mitzvah to inform and clarify halakhic obligations. A rabbi is tasked with enabling others to fulfill their religious obligations. According to Rav Palaggi, the obligation emerges from the mitzvah to teach Torah. Torah study is about learning and teaching, being part of the process of receiving and transmitting the Torah. Issuing halakhic rulings is a subset of this mitzvah to teach Torah.

The difference between these two views is whether a rabbi is obligated to answer a question on Torah without legal implications. If someone asks a rabbi the meaning of a verse or talmudic passage, or a theological question, must a rabbi who knows the answer respond or can he tell the questioner to ask someone else? According to Rav Palaggi, he must answer. According to *Semak*, he need not. Of course, in general he should answer. But if he has other pressing obligations, according to *Semak* answering this question need not take priority.

II. Mitzvah to Teach

Rav Akiva Eiger (18th-19th centuries, Poland; Responsa, introduction, cited by Rav Moshe Feinstein, below) explains that he fastidiously responded to inquiries because of the obligation found in a different talmudic passage. In warning those unqualified against issuing halakhic rulings, the Talmud (*Sotah* 22a) obligates those who are qualified to do so. The beginning of Prov. 7:26, "because she felled many corpses," describes someone unqualified who misleads people with incorrect halakhic guidance. The conclusion of the verse, "and many are its slain," refers to those who sought, but were denied, guidance of a qualified Torah scholar. Rav Eiger was a modest man but recognized his abilities and did not want to be guilty of leaving many slain by refusing them halakhic guidance. *Nimukei Yosef* (*Sanhedrin*, Rif 11a) preceded Rav Eiger in this approach.[50]

Rav Moshe Feinstein (20th century, U.S.; *Iggeros Moshe, Orach Chaim*, vol. 1, introduction) quotes Rav Akiva Eiger's view and adds another talmudic proof. The Talmud (*Berakhos* 4a) says that King David would spend time investigating the details of a woman's impurity in order to rule her permissible to her husband. Why was the king involved in this? Weren't there rabbis who could handle these matters while the king ran the country? Where were the members of the Sanhedrin? Rav Feinstein answers that if a woman asked King David a halakhic question, he was obligated to answer it even if there were others capable of responding.

Rav Eiger's prooftext seems to limit the obligation to ruling on halakhic matters, following the *Semak*. Rav Feinstein's prooftext is, in my opinion, inconclusive. Although the passage seems to only discuss offering halakhic guidance, the focus is on reuniting husband and wife. This means that King David was engaged in restoring peace in a home, *shalom bayis*, a very high religious priority.

III. Redirecting a Question

I think it is obvious that a rabbi is not obligated to be the victim of a persistent *nudnik*, someone who pesters him with unnecessary questions. A rabbi is allowed some peace and quiet. If someone legitimately asks a question, a rabbi is evidently required to

---

50. See also *Responsa Maharshdam, Choshen Mishpat* 1.

respond. However, I have seen and heard of famous rabbis tell questioners to ask a different rabbi. This has been in the context of someone asking a rabbi who follows an unusual stringency. If the rabbi would answer the question, he would have to be strict and cause the questioner extreme hardship. Instead, the rabbi tells the questioner to ask someone else, with a more mainstream view, and avoid the hardship of this stringency. I've only once had it done to me and I've heard of it being done to others. How is this allowed?

It could be that the rule is only speaking in general terms. A rabbi cannot entirely serve in academic functions but must also involve himself in the practical rabbinate. However, perhaps, on any given case there is no obligation for a rabbi to rule. This does not seem to me to be the simple meaning of this law, but I could be mistaken.

Rabbenu Chananel, in his commentary to *Avodah Zarah* (19b), explains that the obligation to issue a ruling only applies if there is no other, more qualified rabbi. Similarly, the Rambam (*Mishneh Torah, Hilkhos Sanhedrin* 20:8) writes that the rule only applies if the generation requires this rabbi to rule on *halakhah*.

While this seems to mean that a rabbi may entirely refrain from ruling on halakhic matters if there are capable experts already engaged in the activity, perhaps it also applies to specific cases. If on a given issue, this rabbi is unusually strict and will cause the questioner undue hardship, then there are others better than he *for this case*.

IV. Rabbis and *Kiddush*

A corollary of this rule is that a busy rabbi may not drink alcohol, even though most other Jews may freely partake within reason. The Torah (Lev. 10:8-11) forbids priests from ruling on religious matters after drinking wine. Rashi (ad loc., 11) points out that this prohibition applies to anyone who rules on religious matters. No rabbi may teach a practical law after drinking a small amount of wine (a *revi'is* — Eruvin 64a-b). Some rabbis are asked religious questions all the time. Are they allowed to drink wine, which would prevent them from answering questions?

A friend of mine, Rav Mordechai Tzion, has been sending interesting questions to a number of prominent Israeli rabbis for a few years. In 2016, he published a volume of their answers, titled *Shu"t Ha-Sho'el (Responsa of the Questioner)*. Question 38 is whether a rabbi should recite *kiddush* on grape juice, rather than wine, so he can rule on religious questions without concern for this prohibition.

V. Moderation

Rav Chaim Kanievsky (contemporary, Israel) responded that *kiddush* on wine is important, implying that it takes precedence over answering questions. Rav Avigdor Nebenzahl (contemporary, Israel) suggests fulfilling both on Shabbos by drinking less than a *revi'is*. In this way, you make *kiddush* on wine without removing yourself from responding to questions. He adds that on Yom Tov, when drinking wine fulfills the biblical mitzvah of enjoying the holiday, you should drink more wine and take a nap.

Many respondents relate the following three anecdotes:

1. Rav Shmuel Salant (19th-20th centuries, Israel), the former rabbi of Jerusalem, would rush through the Pesach *Seder* and sleep a little to remove the effects of the four cups of wine. He felt strongly that, at a time when everyone was drinking wine, he needed to make himself available to answer questions as soon as possible.
2. Rav Ovadiah Yosef (20th-21st centuries, Israel) gave a celebrated Saturday night lecture that was broadcast around the world.

Because of this lecture, he would recite *havdalah* at the end of Shabbos on grape juice rather than wine.
3. After reciting *kiddush* on wine, Rav Yosef Shalom Eliashiv (20th-21st centuries, Israel) would rest for half an hour before answering a question.

VI. What is Wine?

The implication seems to be that a rabbi may not rule after drinking wine and should find a way to minimize or avoid the situation. Rav Yirmiya Menachem Cohen of Paris points out that American grape juice is often made from concentrate. According to Rav Shlomo Zalman Auerbach, there is a question whether grape juice from concentrate can be used for *kiddush*. He adds that even European grape juice contains chemicals to prevent fermentation. Perhaps this also raises questions about whether the grape juice can be used for *kiddush*.

Rav Eliyahu Schlesinger (contemporary, Israel) distinguishes between talmudic wine and contemporary wine. Today, he argues, wine contains significantly less alcohol than in ancient times. Therefore, even someone who drinks a *revi'is* of wine may still issue religious rulings. In a somewhat similar vein, Rav Gamliel Rabinowitz suggests mixing one third wine with two thirds grape juice. In that way, you fulfill *kiddush* on wine without the prohibition against issuing rulings.

Rav Elchanan Prince (contemporary, Israel) concludes that a rabbi who is frequently asked questions should recite *kiddush* on grape juice. He adds that he personally only drinks wine on Purim, when he drinks a little and sleeps for an hour. Rav Shmuel Eliezer Stern (contemporary, Israel) similarly says that if a small amount of wine affects the rabbi's clarity, then he should use grape juice.

VII. Use Judgment

Rav Simcha Rabinowitz (contemporary, Israel) responded with two words: "*lefi ha-inyan,* depending on the circumstances." Presumably, he was hinting to what he wrote in his book, *Piskei Teshuvos* (99:1). Rav Yitzchak of Corbeil (*Semak* 133) writes that wine drunk as part of a meal is less intoxicating and therefore does not invoke the prohibition. Tosafos (*Ta'anis* 17a s.v. *ve-yodei'a*) distinguish likewise. *Magen Avraham* (99:1) quotes this view and adds that according to some opinions, wine drunk directly before a meal also has less of an intoxicating effect. *Pri Megadim* (ad loc.) concludes that if you drink with or before a meal there is no specific measure for the prohibition. Everyone is different. Therefore, you may pray or issue religious rulings as long as you feel sober. *Mishnah Berurah* (99:2) follows the *Pri Megadim*, as does Rav Rabinowitz. His son-in-law, Rav Aharon Aryeh Katz (contemporary, Israel), in the inaugural volume of *Pesakim U'Teshuvos* (242:9), concludes likewise.

Based on this *Magen Avraham*, it is hard to understand why anyone would disagree. Presumably, Rav Salant was concerned that after drinking four cups of wine at the Passover *Seder* he would not be thinking as clearly as necessary. Perhaps Rav Eliashiv was concerned likewise, especially in his later years, or maybe he ruled stringently against the *Magen Avraham*. Rav Ovadiah Yosef probably rejected this Ashkenazic leniency.

After all is said and done, maybe a rabbi can drink some wine for *kiddush*, but if he is going to advise people he has to drink in moderation. This is aside from the need to maintain the dignity of his position.

However we explain this exception, we see that a rabbi's expertise is also his burden. He must serve the public, answering their questions with practical guidance.

A Rabbi's Method

The Art of Halakhah:
Why Jewish law is more a
set of guidelines than of rules[51]

I. A Concise Code

In a fascinating article on law in Judaism,[52] Prof. Joshua Berman (contemporary, Israel) divides post-talmudic halakhic authorities into roughly two schools: those who follow a codified or statutory-law approach and those who adopt a common-law approach. As against this, I would contend that everyone—even the codifiers—approaches the task of halakhic decision-making through a unique mix of common and statutory law. If the results sometimes convey an impression of arbitrariness or inconsistency, the fault lies in a misunderstanding of the system by which those results have been reached.

On the issue of Berman's two jurisprudential schools, let me begin by citing a work that he would presumably include solidly within the statutory-law camp: Rav Shlomo Ganzfried's 1864 *Kitzur Shulchan Arukh* ("The Concise Code of Jewish Law"). In this short but wildly influential book, an adaptation and abridgement

---

51. This essay originally appeared in *Mosaic Magazine*, Dec. 8, 2013 https://mosaicmagazine.com/response/2013/12/the-art-of-halakhah/

52. "What Is This Thing Called Law? The Jewish Legal Tradition and Its Discontents" in *Mosaic Magazine*, December 1, 2013.

of the great 16th-century code by Rav Yosef Karo, Rav Ganzfried conclusively lays down the law on all common Jewish rituals.

But consider the sheer number of editions of this work that have since appeared in print. Not only are successive editions frequently accompanied by footnotes from dissenting authorities, but Rav Ganzfried's rulings themselves have often been revised, with the result that the burgeoning text itself includes disparate rulings. Among the leading participants in this ongoing enterprise have been at least two chief rabbis of Israel and other recognized luminaries of Jewish law.

II. Is It a Code?
All of these authors share the goal of codifying *halakhah*. But, you may well ask, doesn't it violate the very nature of a statutory code to revise—or even contradict—its black-letter provisions with one's own rulings? The answer is that these authorities, including Rav Ganzfried, are actually practicing not statutory but common law. For them, the legal code is a form, not an essence, a vehicle of publication rather than a mode of thought. Rav Ganzfried's code was a masterpiece, but his halakhic decisions reflect his own rulings and the nineteenth-century Hungarian community in which they were formulated. Later authorities, recognizing the usefulness of such a digest, then harnessed his language and organizing plan to the needs of their own time and their own views on Jewish law.
Another question: if so respected a work as Rav Ganzfried's code can be revised, on what grounds do Orthodox halakhic authorities treat the *Shulchan Arukh*, or for that matter the Talmud itself, as binding? In the case of the Talmud, its conclusions are religiously binding because they were irrevocably accepted by the Jewish people. The Talmud, then, serves as a source of statutory law. As for the *Shulchan Arukh*, it gained acceptance by representing the culmination of medieval Jewish common law: the summary of

an era. But it also reflected Sephardic practice alone, and for that reason was originally rejected by Ashkenazic Jews. Only when accompanied by Rav Moshe Isserles' glosses, adding Ashkenazic precedents and practices, did the *Shulchan Arukh* become influential for all. Which means that the resultant work is best understood not as a statutory code like the Talmud but as an extraordinarily influential compendium of common law.

III. The Halakhic Process

A significant factor in the makeup of Jewish law as common law, though one insufficiently treated by Berman, is the *method* by which halakhic authorities reach their decisions. In *The Making of a Halachic Decision*,[53] Rav Moshe Walter (contemporary, U.S.) tackles this issue by tracing the way that leading scholars across the generations, working backward from the conclusions of great authorities, have attempted to construct a methodology of the halakhic process. Their arduous work displays staggering genius, complete mastery of published materials, and an ability to assemble scattered pieces of a vast puzzle into a coherent map of legal reasoning. Unfortunately, the results are for the most part unimpressive. Exceptions accumulate quickly, making the whole process seem subjective and arbitrary.

In his effort to make order of this chaos, Rav Walter sets up a typology similar to Berman's. Some authorities—typified by Rav Eliyahu the Gaon of Vilna (18th century, Lithuania)—decide cases on a putatively common-law basis, which is to say strictly according to the evidence at hand, subject only to the authority of the Talmud. Others, operating from a putatively statutory viewpoint, assert the sanctity of codes like, preeminently, Rav Karo's *Shulchan Arukh*, building brick by brick on its foundation. In the middle lie people like Rav Chaim Soloveitchik of Brisk

---

53. Brooklyn, NY, 2013.

(19th-20th centuries, Russia), whom Rav Walter quotes as advising to rule in accordance with the evidence at hand but always reach the *Shulchan Arukh*'s conclusion.

To Rav Walter, and presumably to Prof. Berman, this division among the authorities demonstrates a fundamental difference in kind; I see it as a difference in degree.

In brief, the halakhic process is more a set of guidelines than of rules, and decision-making itself is a religious act—one that mobilizes all of a jurist's God-given skills, talents, and personality. It is art, not arithmetic. A halakhic authority is afforded a good deal of leeway to follow the texts; his method is fluid, bounded by precedent but not enslaved to it, and mindful of the force of proof and counterproof. He decides not on the basis of whim but compelled by his deliberations, and he is as religiously bound by his conclusion as are his inquirers.

For these reasons, it is false to assert, as some have done, that "where there is a rabbinic will, there is a halakhic way." Halakhic authorities do not choose their conclusions; they follow them.

IV. Common Law in Practice

Throughout the centuries since its initial publication in 1565, the *Shulchan Arukh* has served as the standard of discussion; because it is such an important precedent, jurists face a high burden of proof before disagreeing with it. But if it were a real statutory code, authorities would not be allowed to disagree with it at all; no Jewish work since the Babylonian Talmud has attained such a status.

We can see in contemporary developments precisely this mixed nature of Jewish jurisprudence at work. Berman discusses two contrasting examples of difficult issues facing jurists in Israel today. In the first case—whether to relax halakhic standards of conversion to Judaism for recent immigrants from the former

Soveit Union—jurists advocating leniency have had some relative success. In the second—whether to allow the ordination of women as rabbis—the lenient side has gotten no traction. Berman explains the discrepancy by reference to the agendas being pursued in each case: a comfortably Religious Zionist agenda in the conversion case versus an uncomfortably feminist agenda in the case of ordaining women.

There is a simpler explanation. Statutory law is egalitarian in that it places greater emphasis on the argument than on the person advancing it. By contrast, common law requires a person—a judge or judges—with standing. The Religious Zionist rabbis who are behind the conversion leniencies have long careers as accomplished halakhic authorities. They have published responsa covering a broad cross-section of law and serve also as community leaders, accepted by their peers and the public. In addition, they have acquired international reputations, so that even those (like me) who may not support them on this particular issue respect their expertise. They are serious halakhists making bold, controversial, but legitimate decisions.

No equivalent figures are to be found among the feminists—the "Open Orthodox" or "neo-Conservatives" (large "C"), as they have been called. Their ranks include brilliant academics and educators, accomplished speakers and clergymen, but no established halakhic authorities who have published rulings on a broad array of halakhic topics. In a common-law system, the greatest responsibility lies with the judge. The neo-Conservatives have no judges—no halakhic authorities—and are therefore outsiders to the system. So far, for a variety of reasons, they have failed to convince any authority to embrace their cause. Lacking a qualified judge, they are powerless to enact real change.

The final paradox is this: by virtue of the fact that *halakhah* is a mixed system in which precedent plays such a strong role, conservatives (small "c") will always have the stronger argument. Progress and innovation are important to the vitality of the halakhic community, but proposed changes have to be measured by expert jurists who command respect from their colleagues and the broader community. Deviation requires justification, and justification requires authoritative judges.

A Rabbi's Approach

There are two ways of looking at Judaism, the Jewish community, and the world.[54] These views are not mutually exclusive but require definition and separation. If we keep the difference alive in our minds, we better understand ourselves and our world. I sense that we urgently need to remind ourselves of this distinction.

I. Is vs. Should Be

A sociologist sees things as they are. He keenly observes practices and attitudes, noting cross-cultural similarities and key differences that distinguish phenomena. The sociologist records rather than judges, examines rather than expounds.

A rabbi sees things as they should be. He teaches right from wrong, correcting improper practices and attitudes. He must be sensitive and wise to accomplish his goals, to inspire rather than offend. But his goals are markedly different from those of a sociologist. A rabbi prescribes proper behavior; a sociologist describes existing behavior.

Some sociologists are also rabbis but they are sufficiently expert to bracket off their different roles. Obviously, every individual's various activities inform each other and a rabbi-sociologist uses all of his capacities to his advantage. However,

---

54. This essay originally appeared in *The Jewish Link of NJ*, February 19, 2015.

a professional knows when to describe and when to prescribe. Our community is suffering from a blurring of these boundaries. What is, how people behave, is being confused with what should be. For too many people, surveys of attitudes and behaviors are becoming the new *Shulchan Arukh*. Sociology is important but plays only a small role in defining proper behavior. Our goal should be religious growth, strengthening our practices and attitudes. I am not calling for stringencies (*chumros*) but for recognition that we all fall short of perfection and must strive for improvement. Mistaking sociology for rabbinics prevents that growth because it transforms current practice, including occasional flaws, into the ideal. We say "yes" to *minhag* (custom), but "no" to complacency and indifference.

II. Learning From Grammar
I recently compared two works of English grammar and style, and surprisingly found this same distinction in a very different context. The *Chicago Manual of Style*[55] is the dominant American guidebook for writing style. Before discussing proper usage, the book takes pains to explain that it makes no claim to authority of what is right, only what is most stylistically acceptable. The background seems to be linguists who insist that language is merely a convention and grammar is only what people agree is correct. Therefore, whatever English speakers decide to accept is correct by definition. There is no right or wrong, just common practice.

Gwynne's Grammar,[56] a recent best-seller, presents an ardent contrary attitude. With great intellectual force, N.M. Gwynne contends that the rules of English grammar developed for good reasons. Language is not merely convention but a carefully evolved

---

55. Sixteenth edition, Chicago, IL, 2010.
56. New York, NY, 2014.

amalgam of logic, felicity, and clarity. Changes occur, for sure, but on the margins and only within the pre-existing rules. Changes that do not conform to the logic of the English language must be opposed.

If I may once again recreate our simple dichotomy, linguists tell us what is and grammarians tell us what should be. Gwynne is a grammarian, one who is very dogmatic and unforgiving. The editors of the *Chicago Manual of Style*, however, presumably under enormous pressure, attempted to act as both linguists and grammarians. They wished to prescribe without judging. In this misguided attempt, they confused categories to avoid judgment at the very time they should be judging.

III. Maintaining Standards

You do not have to be a grammar enthusiast to appreciate the cultural trend Gwynne is fighting. Relativism, the denial of right and wrong, deprives all religious rules of authority. Whatever people decide is religiously appropriate becomes acceptable no matter how outrageous the deviation may be. A biblical historian may say that Judaism accepts idolatry because many Jews in the biblical era committed this ultimate transgression. According to news reports, many Conservative rabbis are currently agonizing over their prohibition on officiating at interfaith marriages. Since Jews are intermarrying, why should rabbis stand firm in opposition? When the highest standard is common practice, there is no standard whatsoever. Leaders are supposed to lead, not merely provide a stamp of approval.

I have remained intentionally vague about what common practices in the Orthodox community are easily overlooked and justified. Listing them would cause offense and divert attention from the methodological point. In general, I am arguing that just because members of the Orthodox community engage in new or old practices, or entertain new or old beliefs, that does not automatically legitimate those beliefs and practices. We must constantly reexamine our actions, conduct a *cheshbon ha-nefesh*, and ask ourselves what room remains for religious improvement.

The biblical book of Ruth begins: "And it was in the time when judges judged." Commentators throughout the ages have pondered the redundancy of "when judges judged." Perhaps our generation has found the answer. When sociology dominates rabbinics, when we elevate current practice to the ideal, the judges fail to judge. Rather than encouraging improvement, they justify religious failures with complex, often strained talmudic arguments. Woe to the generation whose judges fail to distinguish between rules and common practice, between ideal and current reality, between what should be and what is.

Religious Law and Change

I. Justifying Behavior

Over three decades ago, Dr. Haym Soloveitchik proposed that communal self-image plays a crucial role in the development of religious law. His revision of that thesis raises questions not only about Medieval Jewish history but also about contemporary Orthodox Jewish society and the much-discussed and perhaps mislabeled "turn to the right."

One essay in Dr. Soloveitchik's *Collected Essays volume 1* (London, 2013) that caught my eye is an important revision of an earlier essay. In 1982, Dr. Soloveitchik published an article titled "Religious Law and Change: The Medieval Ashkenazic Example," included as chapter 9 in this volume. In this article, Dr. Soloveitchik contrasts the attitudes of Ashkenazic and Sephardic rabbis to religious practices that deviate from authoritative texts. The Ashkenazic Tosafists struggled to justify contemporary practice, while Sephardic rabbis stuck to the texts and condemned deviant practices. He explained this by pointing to the differences in communal self-image (p. 246):

> [W]hat we unquestionably have before us is the way in which a community's self-image can change the course of its legal thought. The Franco-German community was permeated by a profound sense of its own religiosity, of

the rightness of its traditions, and could not imagine any sharp difference between its practices and the law that its members studied and observed with such devotion. The Provencal Jewish community and the Spanish communities, on the other hand, wrestling as they were with, or with what they perceived to be, widespread religious laxity, had no such self-image, and it never occurred to the scholars of these communities, many of whom were in every sense the intellectual heirs of the French Tosafists, to seek to align their people's practices with the written word.

In other words, Ashkenazic rabbis saw a pious laity and could not imagine that its members would be sinning, intentionally or not. Therefore, they sought religious justification for common practices. Sephardic rabbis saw a community that was slipping in its devotion and therefore expended no energy to justify behavior. Dr. Soloveitchik expands on this split, adding further nuance, caveats, and examples. In his later "Rupture and Reconstruction,"[57] he seeks to explain why this is no longer the case. Why has the Ashkenazic community rejected this veneration of practice and moved toward a purely textual religion? Even those on the right, with a strong religious self-image, fail to follow this pattern. His article attempts to explain this change of attitude. (It is also interesting that some rabbis today of communities with weak religious self-images attempt to justify common practice, which also seems to be against the historic paradigm.)

II. Different Types of Behavior
However, chapter ten of this volume is a translation of a chapter from Dr. Soloveitchik's 2008 book *Ha-Yayin Bi-Yemei Ha-*

---

57. *Tradition* 28:4 (Summer 1994).

Beinayim, titled here, "'Religious Law and Change' Revisited." In this second look, Dr. Soloveitchik significantly revises his original thesis. It is not true, he agrees, that the Tosafists justified all religious practices. In fact, Rabbenu Tam declared non-kosher all the meat eaten by recent generations (Tosafos, *Chullin* 47a, s.v. *hainu*) and invalidated all the Torah scrolls in Germany (Tosafos, *Megillah* 19a, s.v. *al*). A strong communal self-image did not prevent rabbis from declaring past practices wrong. Rather, Dr. Soloveitchik proposes, only practices for which Jews specifically sacrificed greatly were justified (p. 263): "The difference lay in the cost of the observance." When Jews observed their religious practices despite great external pressure, the rabbis strove to validate textually those practices. On other issues, sometimes the Tosafists justified communal practice (e.g., early night prayers[58] and clapping on Shabbos[59]) and sometimes they criticized contemporary behavior (as above).

This claim is certainly weaker than the earlier one. Communal self-image does not explain everything. Even a community with a strong self-image, which sees itself as possessing pious ancestry and devoted laity, will sometimes find its practices faulty when subjected to textual scrutiny. If so, perhaps the changes Dr. Soloveitchik describes in his "Rupture and Reconstruction" are not part of a new phenomenon but representative of a long historical trend. While there are multiple ingredients that go into his thesis in that article, the revision of this particular argument may take that argument in a slightly different direction. I anxiously await Dr. Soloveitchik's revised thoughts in the forthcoming volume on this subject.

The idea that rabbis must justify the questionable practices of the religious community is so limited that it can hardly be cited

---

58. Tosafos, *Berakhos* 2a, s.v. *me'eimasai*.
59. Tosafos, *Beitzah* 30a, s.v. *tenan*.

in contemporary legal discussion. *Mussar*, constructive rebuke, has a long Jewish history. It is not the only possible response to communal failings but it cannot and should not be ruled out in exchange for redefining halakhic standards.

Religious Law and Historical Context

Critics of the traditional practice of Jewish law point out the important role of historical context in its development. They argue that when we recognize the social and economic considerations that went into halakhic decisions, we will reach different decisions today.

I. Independent *Halakhah*

I have responded to this claim in the past that while I believe that the influence of context is often wildly overstated, thereby minimizing the important religious act of honest Torah study, I accept that sometimes context matters. However, that impact has to be incidental, not intentional. Torah study and halakhic decision-making are part of a living Torah tradition. The leading scholars who reach those decisions use their full talents and experiences to best understand and implement the Torah. In order to be part of the chain of Torah, they must be true to themselves, including their personal contexts.

A self-conscious *halakhah*, a Jewish law that actively attempts to incorporate sociological and historical studies, is inauthentic. Rather than being part of the tradition, it ends up on a different plane, looking down at the process from the outside.

Additionally, it becomes irrelevant. A *halakhah* that is subject to cultural study becomes secondary to contemporary mores. If *halakhah* is seen as a representation of contemporary culture, and that culture is consciously imposed on *halakhah*, then *halakhah* becomes the handmaiden of secular culture. You merely need to look at the weather vanes of zeitgeist to know what *halakhah* demands. At that point, who needs *halakhah*? You can lead a purely secular life and achieve the same results, with the same values.

II. Expertise

In the Fall 2015 issue of the journal *Shofar*, Prof. Tzvi Novick of Notre Dame reviews Prof. Roberta Kwall's *The Myth of the Cultural Jew: Culture and Law in Jewish Tradition*.[60] One of the book's main arguments is that *halakhah* should incorporate a cultural analysis, yielding a more inclusive result (for example, on issues of gender and homosexuality).

In addition to criticisms of the book in general, Prof. Novick points out a practical difficulty with including such a cultural analysis within halakhic decision-making. He writes (p. 135):

> One of the difficulties in making the historical role of culture in halakhic decision making a basis for self-conscious incorporation of cultural considerations is that it demands that contemporary halakhic decision makers be historians, at least to a certain extent. Even if this demand is theoretically coherent and attractive, it poses a real challenge in practice. Learning to be a jurist is hard enough; can we really also ask our jurists to be historians? The at best mixed results of Supreme Court Justices' attempts to read the Constitution in its original context should counsel caution.

---

60. New York, 2015.

If we expect halakhic authorities to be experts of academic Jewish Studies, we will inevitably end up with scholars who are less than expert in both fields. Even if they train in both fields successfully, and reach the top of both fields, they will have difficulty keeping current with the literature as their careers progress. A century ago, Rav David Tzvi Hoffmann (19th-20th centuries, Germany) was able to do it. The field of Jewish Studies has since grown exponentially, making the task much more difficult.

A *halakhah* that includes the insights of academic Jewish Studies is not only inauthentic, it is subpar on either halakhic or academic criteria, if not both.

Contemporary Changes

If you want to know why Rabbi Shlomo Riskin (contemporary, Israel) was nearly forced into retirement at the age of 75 by the Israeli Chief Rabbinate,[61] you have to read his book, *The Living Tree: Studies in Modern Orthodoxy*.[62] I don't claim any insight into the complex politics of Israel's governmental organizations, of which the Chief Rabbinate is one. I don't know enough to understand the power struggle that occurred. However, in terms of ideology, I see why the Chief Rabbinate Council would express concern over Rabbi Riskin. His book is more radical than many might expect. This is not the same Rabbi Riskin you may remember from the 60's and 70's.

The most surprising thing about the book is what is missing from it. On multiple occasions, Rabbi Riskin wrote programmatic essays about what Modern Orthodoxy needs to do to succeed. These were essays full of passion, exhorting both faith in God and Torah as well as devoted observance of the commandments. While the book consists almost entirely of previously published articles, these programmatic essays were replaced with a new introduction titled "What is Modern Orthodoxy?" This introduction is a call for radical change in halakhic decision-making. For example (p. xiv):

---

61. "Chief Rabbinate to weigh ending Rabbi Riskin's tenure in Efrat" in *Times of Israel*, May 25, 2015.
62. Jerusalem, 2014.

The Modern Orthodox decisor must orchestrate the interplay between both of these directives, taking into account the guiding principles used by the sages of the Talmud in their religio-legal discussions, the meta-halakhic principles such as, "for the sake of the perfection of the world," "in order to respect the integrity of the human being created in the divine image," "for the sake of freeing a wife chained to an impossible marriage the sages found leniency," "in order to provide spiritual satisfaction for women," and "you must love the stranger and the proselyte."

If you are familiar with rabbinic literature of the past century, you will immediately recognize that these are legitimate principles that can and have been (ab)used to overturn wide swaths of Jewish law. The essays in the book provide many examples of Rabbi Riskin's applications of these principles. There are two things going on here. First, Rabbi Riskin is promoting his own fairly radical agenda, as would be expected. Second, he is setting the stage for future rabbis to make even more changes to Jewish practice according to their own understanding of what is needed, regardless of what traditional texts allow.

Another troubling trend I find in this book seems to be the result of an editorial oversight. Most of the essays were written over the course of decades, as Rabbi Riskin's experiences and outlook changed. While the essays were edited for consistency and maybe updated a little, the conclusions were largely left intact. Here we see a troubling difference in how Rabbi Riskin reaches conclusions. Regarding changing the daily blessing "Who has not made me a woman," Rabbi Riskin writes: "I would not permit even so minor a change without the approval and approbation of several leading halakhic authorities" (p. 159). While Rabbi Riskin advocates annulling marriages, he does not plan on doing so unilaterally. Rather, "this should be effectuated by a special *beit din* for agunot in Jerusalem with impeccable halakhic credentials who would render judgments, and rule on urgent issues of *mesuravot get* throughout the world" (p. 188). In his call for theological interfaith dialogue with Christians, Rabbi Riskin repeatedly invokes Rav Soloveitchik, albeit in what I believe is a twisting of his words but at least as an appeal to an eminent authority.

However, in his essay on women halakhic scholars and judges, Rabbi Riskin does not submit his proposal to leading authorities. The most he does is quote a responsum of Rav Eliyahu Bakshi-Doron, who is alive and well and could be consulted.[63] Instead, Rabbi Riskin started a program for ordaining women on his own.[64]

When it comes to women dancing with a Torah scroll on Simchas Torah—which I acknowledge lacks the gravity of some other issues under discussion—Rabbi Riskin likewise does not mention consulting with other scholars.[65] When discussing establishing a Hesder yeshiva for women—a matter of great communal importance—Rabbi Riskin also omits discussion with great authorities.

What I see is a rabbi whose agenda has become increasingly radical. Realizing that he was engaging in activities for which he would not gain approval of his elders, he stopped asking. Instead,

---

63. In fact, the RCA consulted with Rav Eliyahu Bakshi-Doron, who denounced the ordination of women. See https://www.torahmusings.com/wp-content/uploads/2015/11/Rav-Bakshi-Doron-on-Women-Rabbis.pdf

64. Rabbi Riskin writes that his program's first two graduates published a book of responsa that "has received much praise, and—at least to my knowledge—no negative reviews" (p. 132). I published a negative review by Rav Yosef Gavriel Bechhofer to which one of the authors responded. See *Torah Musings*, November 10, 2014; December 4, 2014.

65. See *Search Engine*, vol. 1, pp. 157-160.

he moved forward on his own authority. A young R. Shlomo Riskin regularly consulted with Rav Soloveitchik, Rav Moshe Feinstein, and the Lubavitcher Rebbe. When they passed away, he was no longer restrained.

In America, Rabbi Riskin was a defender of Orthodoxy against the Conservative movement and a defender of Judaism against Christian missionaries. That is not the Rabbi Riskin you will find in this book. Maybe in Israel he found himself in a different situation which has given him a new perspective. He now has Christian supporters in his role as a defender of modernity against Charedi Judaism. Maybe he simply underwent a personal evolution

However, this is all speculation. Regardless of why, Rabbi Riskin has taken some communally radical actions and created surprisingly unorthodox institutions entirely on his own initiative. Some people love him for it. We should not be surprised that others believe he has gone too far on too many issues. Whether that is cause for him to be forced into retirement I leave to his employers and constituents.

Proposed Changes

Who Creates Jewish Customs?

I have a vague recollection from my early years in Solomon Schechter of being taught by a guest teacher how to write a midrash. I do not know precisely what the teacher intended but my perception was that midrash is man-made so any person can make one. If the rabbis of the talmudic era could weave complex legends surrounding the biblical narrative, so can we.

There is a basic logical fallacy in this thinking—it ignores the expertise of the midrashic writer. The greatest rabbis of ancient generations, steeped in piety and learning, explored the depths of Jewish texts and thought through midrash. I was both literally and figuratively a child in comparison, and will remain the latter throughout my life. Just because a great rabbi could write a midrash does not mean that I can. Socrates was a philosopher. Socrates was a man. Not all men are philosophers.

This came to my mind as I read the learned, passionate book, *A Jewish Ceremony for Newborn Girls: The Torah's Covenant Affirmed*,[66] by my old friend, Sharon Siegel. The book represents the ideal to which feminist Jewish writings should aspire. Siegel researched her topic expertly. She pored through texts and manuscripts, conducted interviews and picked the minds of the greatest scholars. Her history of Jewish naming practices for girls, while somewhat Germany-centric, is the authoritative work on the subject.

---

66. Waltham, MA, 2014.

Women and Covenant

Additionally, Siegel's main thesis is sound. She argues that girls are just as much a part of God's covenant as boys. I find the view against which she argues odd, and believe she successfully knocks it down from multiple approaches. The only source I think Siegel overlooks is the comment of Tosafos (*Berakhos* 20b, s,v. *nashim*), quoted by the *Magen Avraham* (186:1), that women are not part of the *bris*, the covenant. But they clearly mean circumcision, *bris milah*, and not the general covenant. If women are not part of the covenant, why would they have to observe any commandments—including keeping kosher and observing Shabbos—at all?

But this conclusion takes Siegel on a strange and unnecessary path. If girls are part of the covenant, she wonders, why do they lack a *bris* celebration? Most people would answer that girls are not circumcised in the Jewish tradition but Siegel would frustratedly respond that *bris* means "covenant," not "circumcision."

Siegel exhaustively and authoritatively explores Jewish ceremonies for newborn girls throughout the ages and concludes that today's celebrations are inadequate. Therefore, she proposes a *bris bas* ceremony for girls, held on the eighth day after birth but obviously omitting circumcision. She then proceeds to explore possible texts and rituals that are appropriate for such a ceremony, including an optional blessing similar to that recited at a circumcision. With a keen eye for traditional symbols and an understanding of Jewish liturgy, Siegel constructs an original ceremony for a girl's *bris*.

The Full Cup

Judaism abhors a vacuum. Important life-cycle events will not lack a Jewish ritual for long because how else do we mark important moments if not religiously? Siegel's mistake is that she tries to fill an already full cup. Orthodox synagogues regularly feature celebrations of the birth of girls. Everyone, with the exception of uniquely troubled people, values the birth of a daughter. It is one of the miracles of life, a universal joy that embraces parents, family, and community. Of course there is already an Orthodox formula for that celebration! While local rituals vary, most communities with which I am familiar celebrate with a naming in synagogue and generally a *kiddush*, as well, although often on different days.[67]

Siegel argues that this is insufficient. Her two main points are that: (1) the current ceremony is not meaningful to parents, and (2) friends and family do not insist on attending the naming and/or *kiddush*. Therefore, she proposes a mandatory ceremony for girls on their eighth day in this world, replete with meaningful prayers and symbols.

I sympathize with my old friend's instincts but believe her direction is wrong. If our current ceremony is insufficient, an argument with which I will disagree shortly, we should not look to the future but to the past. As Siegel expertly demonstrates, current naming practices descend from the Medieval Ashkenazic welcoming of the mother and daughter into the community four weeks after the baby is born. If we are looking for a meaningful ceremony that is consistent with Jewish tradition, why not reinstate our own past customs?

Who is an Expert?
The creation of a new ceremony is religiously dangerous. Neither Siegel nor I are Socrates, so to speak. How can we dare to compose prayers and rituals, pretending that we can access the deepest meanings of Jewish symbols and texts? This is especially true when the new practice is redundant. We already have the tools in

---

67. Orthodox legend has it that parents who fail to make a kiddush for a newborn girl risk her marriage chances through divine calculation. This is an oft-repeated *bubbeh-ma'aseh* that is still telling on many levels.

Ashkenazic tradition; we only need to take them out of the toolbox. We move forward by embracing our past. "*Chadeish yameinu ke-kedem*, renew our days as of old" (Lam. 5:21).

Siegel devotes an exhaustive chapter to cataloging the various ceremonies for newborn girls that people have created since the 1970's. This chapter highlights my concerns. Some of the people listed are Orthodox Jews, albeit perhaps overly bold. Most are not Orthodox, nor are they consistently observant nor completely believing Jews. Yet the customs they create are taken as serious precedents, options to consider in making our own customs. Elsewhere, I have argued at length that *halakhah* forbids tailoring customs after the actions of non-traditional Jews.[68] I find it hard to take seriously the notion that those who do not believe in the Torah as traditionally understood should be deciding or creating Jewish practices. Put differently, you cannot change the system unless you are part of it. Non-believing and/or non-practicing Jews are outside the system.

How to Create a Custom

Lacking expertise ourselves, we can at most look to precedent for inspiration. In our case, we have two excellent options. The first and most obvious is the Medieval and Early Modern Ashkenazic celebrations of newborn girls, which Siegel documents so well. Reviving them would be meaningful to parents, Siegel's first concern. However, we may not need to change anything. The current practice of making a *kiddush*, essentially a meal with a *devar Torah*, is how we celebrate Rosh Chodesh and Chanukah. Patterning the celebration of a newborn girl on other, familiar celebrations is a wonderful and meaningful way to mark the joyous occasion.

---

68. "The Adoption of Heterodox Practices," *Torah Musings*, December 8, 2011.

As to Siegel's concern that family and friends are less zealous to attend a girl's ceremony than a boy's, this is a sociological problem, not religious. No amount of tinkering with customs can force old habits to die quickly. The way to deal with lack of courtesy is through gentle rebuke.

Siegel's book can be divided into four main parts: (1) describing historical customs, (2) arguing that women are part of the covenant, (3) describing recent practices, and (4) advocating for a new ceremony. I found the first three to be expertly done and of lasting scholarly value. The fourth, what is clearly closest to Siegel's heart, is where I have to take issue. A new ceremony is unnecessary, overly presumptuous and decidedly non-traditional. Our customs tie us to our personal and communal history, the memories of our youths and recent generations that have passed. In the transient society in which we find ourselves today, with weakened communities and loose affiliations, we need to strengthen, not weaken, that bond to the past.

Communal Impact of Strict Standards

I. Two Reasons for Punishment

Beruriah famously inferred from the Bible that God does not want sinners to suffer punishment but rather to repent (*Berakhos* 10a). Does this desire for repentance mean that religious authorities should tread lightly with a sinner to prevent his going further off the path? On the other hand, if authorities fail to punish wrongdoers, others will be emboldened to follow in their path.

Put differently, one purpose of punishment is rehabilitation, bringing the perpetrator back toward good citizenship. Another is to serve as a deterrent, scaring away other would-be criminals. When the goal of rehabilitation clashes with that of deterrence, which should Jewish authorities prefer?

In the modern Jewish community, post-Enlightenment and post-Emancipation, religious authority means something very different than it did when the Jewish community was autonomous and largely self-governing. For the current study, we will only examine pre-Modern texts, with the latest being a responsum by Rav Ya'akov Emden, who lived at the time that the Enlightenment began to flourish. Later literature overflows with the dilemma of dealing with sinners, the struggle of tradition in a non-traditional era. Rabbis of this time are full of angst over this dilemma but their reality is so different from that of prior eras that their discussions deserve separate treatment.

II. Rebbe's "Prophecy"

Three talmudic passages are particularly relevant. The Gemara (*Kiddushin* 72a) records R. Yehudah Ha-Nasi's surprising last words. He listed four places in Babylonia and denounced their residents. One city, he said, was full of *mamzerim*, illegitimate children. Another of Amonites. In a third city, wife-swapping occurred. And in a fourth, they caught fish on Shabbos. R. Achi Bar Yoshiah was so upset that he excommunicated the people of this fourth city, who in turn proceeded to leave Judaism entirely.

Rav Yisrael Isserlein (15th century, Austria; *Terumas Ha-Deshen* 2:138) quotes Rav Alexander Suslin (14th century, Germany; *Sefer Ha-Agudah*) who uses this Gemara as proof that religious authorities should punish wrong-doers even if it will push them further away from Judaism. The Talmud seems to approve of the action despite the unfortunate, albeit predictable repercussions. A century later, far from Rav Isserlein's home Vienna, Rav David Ibn Zimra (16th century, Egypt; *Responsa Radbaz* 1:187) infers the same conclusion from this passage.

Rav Binyamin Ze'ev (16th century, Greece; *Responsa Binyamin Ze'ev*, no. 287) reads the passage similarly. He was dealing with a man who consistently insulted rabbis and denigrated conversos who had escaped Christian lands and returned to Judaism. This latter group had suffered religious persecution and now had to suffer this man's insults. The offender deserved excommunication until he apologized and repented of his ways. However, apparently there was a concern that he would leave Judaism over the punishment. Based on the above Gemara, Rav Binyamin Ze'ev ruled that the punishment should be applied.

Significantly, Rav Moshe Isserles (the Rema; 16th century, Poland; *Shulchan Arukh, Yoreh De'ah* 334:1) rules according to the *Terumas Ha-Deshen* (and the Radbaz and Rav Binyamin Ze'ev). However, Rav Yair Chaim Bacharach (17th century, Germany;

Chavos Yair 141), while agreeing with this ruling, questioned the interpretation of this passage.

The *Chavos Yair* was asked whether the community should fine and denounce a man who drank gentile wine if, in response, he likely would eat non-kosher food and leave Judaism entirely. The local rabbi decided not to punish the man so as not to push him further away. When the *Chavos Yair* was asked, he strongly disagreed because leniency on this man might encourage other sinners by removing their fear of communal consequences. A court is even empowered to execute someone for a minor violation in order to prevent widespread lawlessness (*Sanhedrin* 46a). Certainly, the religious leadership may punish someone appropriately to similarly prevent lawlessness.

However, the *Chavos Yair* did not see the text about R. Yehudah Ha-Nasi as conclusive. In his opinion, the Gemara was only telling the story and not rendering judgment on the outcome.[69]

III. The Idol Servant

The Gemara (*Kiddushin* 20a-b) discusses the case of a man who sells himself as a slave to an idol, meaning to work on its behalf by chopping wood or cleaning the area around it. Perhaps such a person who would sell himself to an idol should be abandoned. After all, he has clearly separated himself from Judaism. Maybe we should "throw a rock after the fallen." No, the Gemara concludes, we must still redeem him from his servitude.

Rav David Ha-Levi Segal (17th century, Poland; *Taz*, *Yoreh De'ah* 334:1) cites this passage as a counterproof to the Rema's above ruling. Since we are willing to save someone from apostasy,

---

69. Rav Ya'akov Emden (*She'eilas Ya'avetz* 1:79) was puzzled by the *Chavos Yair*'s change of opinion at the very end of the responsum when discussing this text. However, I think it is clear that he was merely discarding this proof without changing his opinion.

certainly we will refrain from causing someone to leave the fold. It is better to be passive than to cause someone to abandon Judaism.

However, Rav Shabsi Cohen (*Nekudos Ha-Kesef*, ad loc.), a younger contemporary and frequent sparring partner, disputes the relevance of this text. An individual must redeem his relative, even a servant to an idol. But that is about individuals. Why should we be surprised that we must care for our family, even if they are wayward? However, a court must fulfill its duty to punish wrongdoers, come what may. Otherwise society will crumble.

The *Taz* further quotes a ruling by Rav Yehudah Mintz (15th century, Italy; *Responsa Mahari Mintz*, no. 5) about a divorced woman who married while still nursing, which is rabbinically forbidden. If the court attempted to force the couple to divorce, there was a distinct possibility that they would leave Judaism to avoid the verdict. Mahari Mintz ruled that the couple may stay together. The *Taz* sees here a proof for his approach that it is better to allow a violation rather than risk losing Jews to religion.

However, as Rav Shimshon Morpurgo (18th century, Italy; *Shemesh Tzedakah*, *Yoreh De'ah*, no. 48) points out, the Mahari Mintz only reaches that conclusion because he found other reasons for leniency. He argues that a minority opinion among earlier authorities would allow this marriage. Additionally, he believes that, as a single woman, this nursing mother would act promiscuously. He felt that the minority opinion combined with his concern for the woman's possible improper activity and that this couple might leave Judaism were sufficient for leniency.

Rav Morpurgo's case was even more vexing. Should the court censure a licentious woman who threatens to convert to Christianity along with her four young children? Even if you follow those who are unconcerned for the sinner's possible apostasy, what about the innocent children? Rav Morpurgo quotes the Rema's ruling (*Yoreh De'ah* 334:6) that a religious court may prevent the circumcision of an excommunicated man's children or even expel them from school as proof that we punish deviant parents even if it affects their children. While this approach is surprising, it recognizes that any action against parents causes the children to suffer. Should we refrain from executing murderous parents so the children will not be abandoned?

IV. Let Him Suffer the Consequences

The Mishnah (*Ma'aser Sheini* 5:1) states that you should mark your forbidden food to prevent others from eating it by mistake. R. Shimon ben Gamliel says that this does not apply to food that others can only steal. The Gemara (*Bava Kamma* 69a) explains that R. Shimon ben Gamliel holds the surprising view of "*haliteihu le-rasha ve-yamus*, let the wicked stuff themselves and die." In other words, if they want to sin then they have to suffer the consequences, as serious as they may be.

Rav Yair Chaim Bacharach (ibid.) applies this to the case of someone who may leave Judaism over punishment for his sin. He sinned and must suffer the punishment. If that causes more problems for him, it is his fault. The literature on this passage has grown significantly in recent years but that takes us past our chosen timeframe and must wait for separate discussion.

V. Community Priority

In an astonishing passage, Rav Yitzchak Arama (15th century, Spain; *Akedas Yitzchak, Vayera* no. 20) discusses the general communal ambivalence to the use of Jewish prostitutes and the existence in a few places of communally supported brothels. The religious leadership in those places had decided that it was better for people to commit this sin than more severe sins with married or gentile women.

Rav Arama rails against this practice. He distinguishes between the sin of an individual and of the community. If an individual sins then he will be punished, either by human or divine hands. But if the community in general and the religious authorities in particular allow the sin, or even support it, then it becomes the sin of the entire community, a massive undertaking of sinfulness. Better an individual commit a terrible sin than the entire community commit together a smaller one. Therefore, the religious authorities cannot look the other way but must condemn and attempt to prevent such sin.

There is a concept in Jewish law of preferred ignorance. If someone is going to ignore warnings and commit a sin, better not to inform him that the act is forbidden. In this way, at least he is sinning accidentally rather than intentionally (e.g., *Shabbos* 148b). However, this rule has limitations. For example, it only applies to rabbinic violations and not biblical (ibid.). Rav Shimon ben Tzemach Duran (15th century, Algeria; *Responsa Rashbatz* 2:47), rules that we set this concern aside for the sake of the community. We inform a community that an act is forbidden to prevent the general populace from sinning, even if an individual will thereby become an intentional sinner. Similarly, Rav Bacharach (ibid.) writes: "we worry about the interests of the community even if it is against the interests of the individual."

VI. Other Considerations

The Radbaz (ibid.) adds other considerations. First, Jews are responsible for one another—*kol Yisrael areivim zeh ba-zeh* (*Sanhedrin* 27b). However, the application of this principle could easily be reversed on the Radbaz. If we are responsible for other people's sins, certainly we should avoid causing them to commit even worse sins. The Radbaz quotes the verse (Lev. 20:4): "And if the people of the land hide their eyes from that man...." On this

Using Authority

verse, the Sages (quoted by Rashi) say that if the court ignores one sin they will eventually ignore many sins. In other words, by failing to properly rebuke a sinner you are enabling him and others to sin more.

Additionally, if we decide not to punish sinners then society will break down. Without law enforcement, there will be no order. Theft, violence, adultery and the like will proliferate. In other words, society as a whole needs the deterrence, which prevents us from reducing the criminal's sentence. Similarly, Rav Ya'akov Emden (ibid.), in discussing someone who stole from a man, committed adultery with the victim's wife, defamed him and caused his death (presumably through aggravation), rules that the perpetrator may not be accepted into the community without returning the stolen money to the deceased's family and asking their forgiveness—even if this requirement causes the transgressor to leave Judaism. Rav Emden argues that if we fail to enforce the law then not only will justice be perverted but the deterrence will be diminished and violations will spread further. Additionally, we cannot maintain the strength of deterrence if we enforce the law selectively. If we force other people to repay what they stole then the authorities must also force this man.

The Radbaz also suggests that someone like that will often leave religion regardless of what the religious authorities do. Others point out that some people who threaten to leave the community do not really intend to. It is generally difficult to gauge whether these possibilities are serious concerns.

VII. Conclusion

The Radbaz reaches a wise and important conclusion. He points out that this is a sensitive matter that must be carefully considered by the generation's highest leadership. Every person is different and every transgression is different. If we truly believe that mercy will rehabilitate the sinner, then we should help him return to good standing. Ultimately, the judge must decide based on his best judgment.

Contemporary Jewry faces very different communal challenges than pre-modern Jewry. Of course, that does not mean we ignore the ample precedents. However, these rulings must be carefully applied, taking into account the changed circumstances. Unsurprisingly, there is a large body of literature of religious authorities of the past two centuries doing just that. I leave surveying that literature as a subject for a future time.

Threatening Halakhah

Community members deeply unhappy with a specific rule sometimes charge that this rule is pushing them out of the community. As a description, this may be accurate. As a call for change, it is scandalous. We can see this with a comparable parenting claim. As we saw above, pre-Modern scholars engaged with this dilemma. Modern rabbis confronted a different reality, more complex socially. Here we look at one informative example from a broad literature.

I. Threats and Life

Parents are often disappointed if their children choose a different religious path than planned. While reactions will differ based on the people and circumstances, some responses are morally intolerable. *Halakhah* must grapple with these improper reactions, responding as appropriate.

Rav David Tzvi Hoffmann (19th-20th centuries, Germany; *Melamed Le-Ho'il*, no. 61) responded to such a question from a student attending a professional school. Like most general schools of the day, its classes met on Shabbos. This student attended those classes but refrained from writing on the holy day. However, his parents, concerned about his professional future, felt strongly that he needed to write. His mother was so upset that she threatened to commit suicide unless he wrote in class on Shabbos.

Normally, a threat to life (*piku'ach nefesh*) overrides Shabbos. You may write to save someone's life, such as a vital medical prescription, even if the threat is self-inflicted. Certainly, you may call the police or a psychologist to prevent someone from committing suicide. May the son write in school on Shabbos in order to save his mother's life? I cannot imagine having to answer this question.

Rav Hoffmann responds with horror. Even if entirely serious, such a case does not constitute *piku'ach nefesh* if one person intends to remove another from religious behavior. It is potentially violent anti-religious coercion to which we may not submit. If we were to concede, any anti-religious activist would threaten to commit suicide unless Jews refrained from observance. The entire Torah would be subject to dismissal because of one crazy person's suicidal threat.

II. Responding with Confidence
Rav Hoffmann quotes Rav Yehudah Assad (19th century, Hungary; *Yehudah Ya'aleh, Even Ha-Ezer* 140) regarding a *kohen* who wishes to marry a woman freed from levirate marriage (*chalutzah*), which is forbidden. Even if the couple threatens to leave religion unless the union is allowed, we do not set aside a prohibition, even one of rabbinic origin such as a *kohen* marrying a *chalutzah*.

The significance of the ruling regarding a *kohen* becomes particularly relevant when we consider that in the original case above, the son could write with his left hand (i.e. halakhically differently), which is only prohibited on a rabbinic level. However, Rav Hoffman does not permit this either.

We cannot allow the laws of the Torah to be used against each other, forcing someone into non-observance through religious duress. While the parenting instinct that led to this threat is abhorrent, the entire concept also must be rejected halakhically. Similarly, the community cannot be held hostage by those threatening to leave if *halakhah* fails to change to their satisfaction. Despite all the real emotions we sense in others and feel in ourselves, we must reject this approach.

Losing the Next Generation

I. The Millennial Challenge

I sometimes hear concerns about the future of Orthodox Judaism if it fails to adapt to the times.[70] People say that the generation of Millennials, those born roughly between 1982 and 2000, will not accept traditional teachings on gender roles, homosexuality, the authorship of the Torah, or whatever pet issue is bothering the speaker. Therefore, it is claimed, we must find a way to change Orthodox Judaism or risk losing the next generation. Not only do I reject this argument, but I see it as pointing in the other direction.

First, as a parent of Millennials, I do not see these attitudes among my children and their friends. Maybe my sample size is too small or too right-leaning, but I hear this from other parents in different communities. Let us not allow the media to control our perceptions. Even if the claim is true, I deny that we risk losing the entire generation. We may lose some, even many, to the right or the left, as Orthodoxy has consistently experienced for over 200 years. The recent period of high communal retention rates may have been a historical anomaly. If true, this would be a tragedy, particularly for the parents who have to navigate contemporary complex and difficult situations. But it would not be the end of Orthodoxy, merely a difficult period we will have to endure. However, there are more important reasons to reject this argument.

---

70. This essay appeared in *The Jewish Link of NJ*, January 5, 2015.

In a column in the January 2015 issue of *First Things* magazine, the editor, R.R. Reno, writes about the recently translated memoirs of the Nazi-era Catholic thinker, Dietrich von Hildebrand. Throughout the 1930's, Hildebrand tried to raise the alarm within Catholic leadership about the dangers of Nazism and the need to oppose the evil regime. Time and again, he was frustrated. He faced many arguments, such as that Fascism is better than Communism and that its victory was inevitable. Additionally, he was told that the youth wanted the fascist nationalism. Indeed, there was ample and enthusiastic membership in Nazi youth groups. If the Catholic Church opposed the Nazis, Hildebrand was warned, it would lose the young generation.

II. Dangerous Trends
Hildebrand rejected that line of thinking, and he was obviously right—this is why Reno raises this historical episode. While we cannot compare contemporary challenges to Nazism and we dare not equate our religious or political rivals to such odious villains, we can learn a lesson from the arguments and ideas of the time. Polls do not tell the full story because public opinion is fickle. What is popular today may be despised in a year. Intellectual fads rise and fall faster than gas prices. Imagine the embarrassment and regret of someone who abandons a cherished belief because he finds it morally unsustainable, only to find a decade later that the intellectual climate has changed and the belief has regained acceptability. Sometimes, losing the youth today means being in the right place when they return later.

More importantly, we cannot set aside our principles for the sake of embracing the public mood. Yes, emphases can be adjusted and methods of engagement modernized to meet the needs of the day. But we must stand resolutely and proudly on our principles, even—perhaps particularly—when they are unpopular. We should be proud, not embarrassed, of the Torah. Popularity can justify anything, even pure evil. If the youth truly want to go in that direction, we must try to lead in the other direction. The Torah has always been a corrective to societal views, a countercultural push of divine values. We are morally obligated to stand firm in our Torah principles in the face of opposition.

In the decades before and after Hildebrand's battle with the Nazis, Jews in America were rejecting Torah observance in large numbers. The young generation had little interest in strict adherence to the commandments. Some communal leaders chose to compromise, whether by allowing driving on Shabbos or otherwise changing laws and beliefs. However, the leading Orthodox rabbis, who were the custodians of a tradition dating back thousands of years, refused to compromise. Torah is not subject to a popular vote. Even if the youth demand something else, Jewish leaders have no right to fundamentally alter the tradition because it is not theirs to change. Judaism is not for sale to the bidder with the most adherents.

III. Thinking Long Term

Even if we could change Judaism in substantial ways, doing so would be unwise. We may very well find that the youth respect people who are consistent and principled, if not immediately then later as they mature. Today's youth will be tomorrow's middle-aged. If we change the religion every 20 years to fit the mood of the youth, to ensure we do not lose the next generation, we will lose prior generations.

Rabbi Norman Lamm (contemporary, U.S.), writing in 1972 about the need for strong but gentle leadership, described the early Reform response to emancipation in a way that I think applies well to the pressures we face today:[71]

---

71. *Derashot Ledorot: Numbers*, New York, 2014, p. 128.

What was the rationale for this radical surgery performed [by Reform] on the Jewish tradition? Simply, that this is what people demanded, as reflected in the popular saying, 'Give youth what it wants!' What they forgot was that, first, youth does not always know what it wants (that is the special privilege of youth); second, youth changes its wants every few years; and third, the word of God is permanent and the plaints of whining youth are temporary. Halakha must always remain superior to fashion.

We all must be concerned about losing young people from our tradition. It is difficult to live a restrictive lifestyle in the middle of a prosperous, permissive and intellectually exciting society. Therefore, it is our responsibility to teach our children and students that the Torah is a beautiful inheritance that is true and just. Intellectual fads come and go, but God's word will never change.

The Israeli Chief Rabbinate: Why?

The Israeli Chief Rabbinate was established by Imperial Britain and developed under the fledgling socialist Israeli government. Given that origin, its overly bureaucratic and allegedly corrupt nature should be unsurprising. Under one particularly unpopular Chief Rabbi, the Israeli government removed much of the ability of the Rabbinate's senior officials to manage the bureaucracy. The current result of that history is an organization drowning in internal and external politics, with the Chief Rabbi sometimes forced to use the media to shame his employees into compliance. In short, the Israeli Chief Rabbinate is a mess. Before we decide whether the institution deserves a quick death, let us examine its purpose.

In honor of the 70th anniversary of the Israeli Chief Rabbinate in 1992, then-Ashkenazic Chief Rabbi Avraham Shapira (Chief Rabbi from 1983-1993) spoke at a special session of the Knesset in honor of the occasion.[72] Rav Shapira offers a concise description of the role of the Chief Rabbinate. Among its functions are:

1. Working toward national unity
2. Responsibility for the spiritual status of rabbis, religious judges and other religious functionaries

---

72. The text of his speech appears in *Ha-Rabbanut Ha-Rashit Le-Yisrael: Shivim Shanah Le-Yisudah* (Jerusalem, 2002), vol. 1, pp. 56-59.

3. Determining who is a rabbi, thereby preventing those unqualified from entering the rabbinate
4. Kosher supervision
5. The religious propriety of marriages and divorces
6. Operating religious courts (for civil matters)
7. Determining the Torah view on any issue the government needs
8. Establishing the country's religious atmosphere through local religious councils

Rav Shapira adds (based on *Sotah* 49a) that nowadays we not only lack Torah scholars of the quality of past years, but even our ignorami are on a lower level. Some rabbis lack the scholarship but fool people into believing they are scholars.

Rabbis carry the Torah. Their job is to rule and decide according to the tradition they received from prior generations. They do not own the law and therefore cannot change it—the law owns them. They are compelled by their conclusions, and not vice versa.

The source of many difficult communal problems is spiritual, particularly the lack of faith. The country suffers from a spiritual darkness, widespread ignorance that risks becoming a culture of anti-Judaism. It is more important now than in past generations to study the fundamentals of Jewish faith in God, Torah, the Jewish people and the land of Israel in order to prevent assimilation into Western culture.

Rav Yisrael Meir Lau published an article highlighting activities of the Chief Rabbinical Council during his term as Chief Rabbi (1993-2003).[73] He notes the following issues:

---

73. Ibid., pp. 3-9.

1. Israel and Jerusalem: dealing with the halakhic issues surrounding Disengagement and the sanctity of the Temple Mount, and establishing guidelines for holy places across the country,
2. Personal Status and Marriage Registry: determining the status of gentiles of Jewish descent and intermarried couples who moved to Israel from the FSU and elsewhere, the Beta Israel and Falashmura, and children adopted from South America,
3. Kashrus: deciding on kosher issues in cities across the country and sometimes dealing with kashrus supervisors against whom complaints were filed, responding to challenging secular court rulings, and working with legislators to strengthen the kashrus laws,
4. Shabbos: opposing the opening of shopping malls and entertainment places on Shabbos
5. Independence of the Rabbinate: working with the prime minister to establish the independence of the Chief Rabbinate,
6. Reform and Conservative: objecting clearly to the spiritual danger of these heretical movements and preventing representatives of those movements from joining local religious councils,
7. Local Religious Councils: supporting the cooperation of local religious councils with local rabbis and working to ensure that only those who accept the authority of the Chief Rabbinate serve on local religious councils,
8. Torah Law and Secular Law: addressing issues that were litigated in the court, such as halakhic conversions, opening kosher certified restaurants on Shabbos and approving imported meat,
9. Burial: establishing guidelines for the burial of gentiles,
10. Rabbis and Rebbetzins: appointing rabbis, supporting them while requiring that they fulfill their duties including moving

to the communities they serve,

11. Medicine and *Halakhah*: decided in favor of premarital genetic testing, testifying before the Knesset on medical issues and addressing an assortment of medical halakhic issues,
12. Certifications: established committees for testing and certifying city rabbis and complaint boards for rabbinic lawyers, enacted rules for the certification of rabbis and marriage registrants,
13. Other Issues: called for improvements in Jewish education across the country and greater care in avoiding car accidents, worked to prevent spousal abuse, and supported the families of fallen soldiers.

In my opinion, the functions and activities mentioned by Rav Shapira and Rav Lau can be divided into three categories. Note that my comments assume a well-functioning Chief Rabbinate. Much—but not all—of the opposition to the Chief Rabbinate would disappear if it operated efficiently and effectively:

I. Activities that require an authorized official rabbinate — these include:

- Determining who is a rabbi and certifying various rabbinic functionaries—a centralized authority is best placed to maintain quality control. Rabbinic organizations have their own methods of quality control but without a Chief Rabbinate, anyone can set up shop and call themselves a rabbi.
- Deciding on personal status and marriage registry issues—without a central authority to make decisions on borderline cases over which scholars disagree, such people will be subject to a life of uncertainty as some communities will accept them and some reject them.
- Determining burial policies—cemetery owners will do

whatever they want unless they are forced to listen to a rabbi, and only government regulation can force them. I don't see how market forces can realistically do that except in unusual circumstances.
- Supervising rabbis and religious functionaries—without a centralized licensing body, unscrupulous rabbis will do whatever they can get away with.
- Operating religious courts—because of the stakes in terms of money and power, unsupervised religious courts easily devolve into a general state of chaos, with many unscrupulous figures taking advantage of them. There needs to be an authority with the power to overrule and punish improper judges.

II. Activities that operate better with an authorized official rabbinate:

- Working toward national unity—an official Chief Rabbi, as a government figure, has many unique opportunities to reach out to the public, other government figures and religious leaders.
- Advising the government on religious issues—anyone and any individual can advise courts and politicians, but a Chief Rabbi is uniquely positioned to serve as an advisor at the highest levels of government.
- Lobbying for laws supporting Shabbos observance—same as above.
- Deciding on issues regarding Israel and Jerusalem—individual or groups of rabbis can issue rulings that will be effective with their followers. However, these are national issues that are best handled by a national authority.
- Enhancing the country's religious atmosphere by serving as an effective spokesman of religion and influencing curricula—a Chief Rabbi has greater access to the public, and therefore

Using Authority

greater influence, than any individual rabbi, even greater than the leaders of rabbinic organizations.
- Supporting local religious councils—religion is often best run locally but centralized support greatly helps local officials do their job more effectively.
- Kosher supervision—a single, central supervision greatly benefits consumers. In the U.S., confusion reigns when a consumer encounters an unfamiliar supervision.
- Limiting non-Orthodox advancement—some people will think this is a reason to abolish the Chief Rabbinate. Those who believe that non-Orthodox movements bring spiritual damage to Israel will agree that an authorized Chief Rabbinate is best poised to prevent non-Orthodox movements from encroaching on kosher supervision, marriage registration and other activities that threaten to confuse the public.

III. Activities that any rabbinic group can do equally well if not better:

- Ruling on issues of medicine and *halakhah*—I don't see why this cannot be left to individuals.
- Calling for improvements in education and greater care in avoiding car accidents—these activities are hardly limited to a Chief Rabbi. Any organization can work on these issues.
- Working to prevent spousal abuse and supporting the families of fallen soldiers—this seems like issues that can be handled by other organizations and not a Chief Rabbinate.

Of course, all this assumes that a Chief Rabbinate has the tools, talent and authority to be effective in its mission. On many of the issues above, the Israeli Chief Rabbinate currently is ineffective. I wonder whether the answer to many people's concerns is fixing the Chief Rabbinate rather than ending it. This is no small task and will probably require massive legislation and institutionalized checks on power.

I make no claims to expertise in Israeli politics or the corruption that too many people allege, fairly or not. My only point is that an effective Chief Rabbinate carries many benefits over the current "Wild West" situation that exists in the U.S. and elsewhere. This deserves inclusion in our ultimate evaluations of the situation.

Determination of Jewish Status

The disputes over the past few years regarding whose validations of personal status of immigrants the Israel Chief Rabbinate accepts raises a crucial question: Why should anyone need their Jewish status validated? Why don't we accept someone's word that he is Jewish? The Jewish media incorrectly reports this issue; the complex answer to our question will explain what they have gotten wrong. The key is splitting this issue into two related subjects.

I. Religious Identity
The Gemara (*Yevamos* 46b) states that someone who comes to a community and says he is a convert is not accepted as a Jew unless he brings proof of his status. What if someone comes and says that he is Jewish? Rabbenu Tam (quoted in Tosafos, ibid., 47a, s.v. *be-muchzak*) states that we believe him because most people who say they are Jewish are in fact Jews. Therefore, Rabbenu Tam continues, the Gemara is discussing someone who has established himself as a gentile. In order to change that presumption he must bring proof. But someone who comes in out of the blue and says that he is a convert is believed because (*migo*) he could have said that he is Jewish and would have been believed.

However, Rambam (*Mishneh Torah, Hlikhos Issurei Bi'ah* 13:10) says that this only applies in Israel where most people are Jewish. By implication, he seems to say that in the Diaspora we cannot accept someone who says he is Jewish so the *migo* deduction no longer applies. Therefore, we cannot automatically accept a convert's claim without testimony. The Ritva (*Yevamos* 47a, s.v. *bein*) says that, absent a presumption to the contrary, we believe someone who claims to be Jewish or to be a convert because the truth will eventually come out (*milsa de-avida le-igluyei*). I assume he means that in a world in which most men are uncircumcised, a gentile pretending to be a Jew will eventually be discovered, either at the mikvah or when he gets married. (It is not clear why, according to the Ritva, we accept a woman's unsupported claim that she is Jewish.)

The upshot is that, according to Rabbenu Tam, someone in the Diaspora who says he is Jewish should be believed without any testimony. According to Rambam he should not. It is not clear what Ritva would say in this world in which Jewish identity is so confused that sometimes people who are halakhically gentile are raised as Jews.

The *Shulchan Arukh* (*Yoreh De'ah* 268:10) follows the Rambam. However, the *Shakh* (ad loc., 21) quotes the *Bach* who says that common practice follows Rabbenu Tam. The *Shakh* also suggests that perhaps the Rambam really agrees and was only strict for a convert's marriage.

However, there might still be an underlying assumption that we accept these claims when the person acts like a Jew. If not, perhaps he undermines his claims with his actions. For example, if he does not observe the commandments does he create a presumption that he is not Jewish? Two former chief rabbis of Israel disagreed about this. Rav Mordechai Eliyahu (Sephardic Chief Rabbi, 1983-1993; *Responsa Ma'amar Mordechai*, vol. 2, *Orach Chaim* no. 32) points out that Rashi (*Yevamos* 46a, s.v. *yakhol*) writes that if we accept someone's claim that he is a convert then we do not require him to undergo pseudo-circumcision (*hatafas dam bris*) and immersion in a mikvah. Why, Rav Eliyahu asks, doesn't Rashi include acceptance of the commandments in his list of what we demand of someone (re-)converting? He explains that, according to Rashi, the entire discussion of the Gemara revolves around someone who observes the commandments. If not, we certainly do not accept his claims. (Although he allows that Jews from the former Soviet Union are different.)

Rav Avraham Shapira (Ashkenazic Chief Rabbi, 1983-1993; "*Yichus Olah Chadashah Le-Tzorekh Nisu'eha*" in *Techumin*, no. 15, pp. 265-267) states that all this only applies where all Jews are observant. In such a time and place, someone who is not observant is not believed. However, this is only a matter of acting like other Jews. When it is common for Jews to be non-observant, lack of observance does not undermine a person's credibility about Jewish identity.

II. Personal Status

An additional concern is personal status. When we believe someone that he is Jewish, do we also accept that he may marry into the Jewish community? For example, he could be a *mamzer*, who may not marry a regular Jew, or a *kohen*, who may not marry a convert or divorcee. The Gemara (*Kiddushin* 76b) states that all families have a presumption of acceptability (*kol mishpachos kesheiros*). Ostensibly, that means that anyone claiming regular status is accepted as such.

However, the *Tur* (*Even Ha-Ezer* 2) quotes Rav Meir Halevi Abulafia (Ramah; Spain, 12th-13th centuries) who holds that this rule only applies to families that are known to us. When someone comes from a distant, unknown family, he must prove his personal status. Even though we accept him as Jewish, we cannot let him marry another Jew until he proves he is not a *mamzer*. The *Beis Shmuel* (*Even Ha-Ezer* 2:3) follows this Ramah. However, the

Shakh (cited above) rules leniently, that everyone is presumed permissible to marry. Later authorities split on this issue. The *Ba'er Heitev* (ad loc., 4) quotes the Maharit and *Beis Hillel* who follow the *Beis Shmuel*, while the *Pischei Teshuvah* (ad loc., 2) quotes the *Sha'ar Ha-Melekh* who follows the *Shakh*. Rav Shlomo Kluger (*Ha-Alef Lekha Shlomo*, EH 15) says the common practice is to be lenient, while the *Arukh Ha-Shulchan* (ad loc., 13) rules strictly regarding individuals (he holds that the presumption of "kosher" status only applies to families and not to individuals). The *Otzar Ha-Poskim* (ad loc., 4) contains a long summary of the different rulings on the subject. Significantly, the *Otzar Ha-Poskim* quotes the *Beis Hillel* as saying that there was an enactment of Lithuanian rabbis requiring proof of lineage before officiating at a wedding.

There is a further question whether this presumption of validity applies to personal status for marrying a *kohen*. The *Tur* (*Even Ha-Ezer* 2) quotes Rabbenu Tam as saying that presumption of "kosher" status does not apply to a *kohen*. The *Bach* understands this as meaning that an unknown *kohen* who presents himself without proof of his status cannot serve in the Temple in a priestly function. However, the *Beis Yosef* understands Rabbenu Tam as referring to marital status. A *kohen* may not marry an unknown woman on the basis of merely her unsupported word that he is permitted to marry her. Later authorities disagree about this in practice. The *Arukh Ha-Shulchan* (ad loc., 12-13) believes we must be strict about a *kohen* while Rav Shlomo Kluger (ibid.) and Rav Avraham Shapira (ibid.) rule leniently.

III. Who Can Say?

Returning to the controversy regarding the Israeli Chief Rabbinate, we find that someone who claims to be Jewish and is observant should be believed. If he is not observant,[74] then

---

74. I use "he" as neutral, to refer to both men and women.

according to Rav Avraham Shapira he should still be believed, but according to Rav Mordechai Eliyahu he must prove his Jewishness. When someone who is believed about his Jewish status comes to marry, according to the *Shakh* he may marry any regular Jew, and according to the *Beis Shmuel* he must prove his status before marrying. According to the *Arukh Ha-Shulchan*, he (or rather she) must also prove his status before marrying someone with a *kohen* status, although others disagree.

In other words, there is a debate about whether we accept someone's word about his Jewish and personal status. Apparently, the Israeli Chief Rabbinate is strict and requires testimony even about Jewish status. However, when it comes to a woman's status as eligible to marry a *kohen*, many would argue that proof is halakhically required.

Therefore, the acceptability of a rabbi to the Chief Rabbinate is not just about his testimony regarding who is Jewish. It is also, perhaps primarily, about his testimony regarding who is a *kohen*, *mamzer*, divorcee, *chalal*, etc. This is not the place to discuss the expertise or track records of individual rabbis on these issues. However, the evaluation of one's qualifications must clearly involve more than whether he can adequately determine if someone is Jewish. Testifying about marital status not only requires more expertise but sometimes involves difficult halakhic interpretations. The Israeli Chief Rabbinate's rejection of someone's testimony could mean that they reject him personally. But it could mean also (or instead) that they don't trust his interpretations and applications of Jewish law on marital status, particularly regarding a *kohen*.

The Decline and Fall of Local Rabbinic Authority[75]

The issue of rabbinic authority[76] in the Orthodox Jewish community is not a matter of how wide a rabbi's authority spreads—whether his opinion is decisive on issues of esthetics, politics, etc., or just ritual.[77] Today's debate is whether rabbis have any authority at all. A rabbi who has shown himself to be wise will be consulted on issues ranging from religious to personal. His advice will be taken seriously because of his insight—but is it binding? When the issue is not halakhic, it is assumed in our community that his advice is nothing more than helpful suggestions. The question before us deals with halakhic issues. In the following three sections, I argue that there is a need for a personal halakhic decisor, that this guide

---

75. This essay was original published in Shmuel Hain ed., *The Next Generation of Modern Orthodoxy* (Jersey City, NJ, 2012). I thank Rabbis David Berger, Arie Folger, Dovid Gottlieb, Adam Mintz, Simon Posner, Gidon Rothstein, Moshe Schapiro, David Shatz and Dov Zakheim, and Prof. Jerome Chanes for their thoughtful comments. Of course, they bear no responsibility for the final content of this essay.
76. I am intentionally avoiding the term "*da'as Torah*" because it is so politically loaded and religiously ambiguous.
77. On this, see Rav Moshe Z. Sokol ed., *Rabbinic Authority and Personal Autonomy* (Northvale, NJ, 1992); Prof. Suzanne Last Stone ed., *Rabbinic and Lay Communal Authority* (New York, NY, 2003).

should be your synagogue rabbi, and that today people often do not turn to their synagogue rabbi for halakhic guidance due to a variety of reasons. I then offer practical suggestions for changing this situation by establishing a partnership among rabbis, communal leaders, and *roshei yeshiva*.[78]

I. The Need for Authority

Asking A Question

The idea of asking a personal inquiry on halakhic matters seems to be rooted in an explicit biblical passage: "If there arise a matter too hard for you in judgment, between blood and blood, between plea and plea, and between stroke and stroke, even matters of controversy within your gates; then you shall arise, and go up to the place which the Lord your God shall choose. And you shall come to the priests the Levites, and to the judge that shall be in those days; and you shall inquire; and they shall declare to you the sentence of judgment. And you shall do according to the tenor of the sentence, which they shall declare to you from that place which the Lord shall choose; and you shall observe to do according to all that they shall teach you" (Deut. 17:8-10).

The context of this passage[79] and the initial words "*ki yippalei*"[80] led the Sages to see this passage as obligating religious judges to take their unresolved questions to a higher authority.[81] Despite the

---

78. On reading this essay, you may notice the frequent appearance of the word "I," as in "I believe" and "I view." I wrote in this way with the intention of making everything provisional, one person's opinion that is subject to revision based on the input of those wiser and more knowledgeable.
79. Cf. Malbim and *Torah Temimah* ad loc.
80. Cf. *Sanhedrin* 86b.
81. *Mishneh Torah, Hilkhos Mamrim* 1:4. R. Dr. David Shatz pointed out that even Moshe had to ask a "*she'eilah*" — see Num. 27:5 and Rashi ad loc.

sensible *kal va-chomer* deduction, I have not found any midrash or commentary that derives from this verse an obligation on a layman to present his halakhic difficulties to a religious authority. The reason for this, I believe, is that this need is so fundamental and obvious that it requires no compulsion. Of course, anyone interested in following the word of God who is unsure of the proper route will ask an expert for clarification of the law. We will otherwise be paralyzed by uncertainty or forced into stringency.

One of the many duties of the pulpit rabbi is to serve as this needed halakhic expert. That is, however, an understatement of his role. Rulings on Jewish law are not merely clarification or the offering of an opinion. *Pesak*, a personalized halakhic decision (*pesikah* in Modern Hebrew), is binding. This can be seen most clearly in the rule of *chakham she-asar ein chakham acher rashai le-hattiro* (when one authority prohibits, another may not permit).[82] The standard approach to this issue is that the classical authorities debate why this is the case—whether the inquirer accepts on himself to follow the authority's ruling in an implicit prohibitive vow or the respect due the first rabbi prevents annulling his ruling.[83] I believe that there is also a third approach among commentators, perhaps the majority, which asserts that a rabbi's ruling creates a metaphysical status; it establishes an halakhic reality for this object[84] that had heretofore been undefined.[85] When there is

---

82. *Chullin* 44b; *Niddah* 20b; *Berakhos* 63b; *Avodah Zarah* 7a.
83. The former is proposed by *Nimmukei Yosef* (*Avodah Zarah* 7a) and the latter is adopted by Rashi (*Niddah* 20b, s.v. *me-ikara* and Ran (*Chiddushim* to *Avodah Zarah* 7a, s.v. *ha-nishal*). See R. Yehudah Henkin, *Responsa Bnei Banim* (Jerusalem, 1998) vol. 3 no. 8 for a long list and discussion of sources.
84. This rule only applies to the specific case brought before a rabbi and not other cases. Rema in *Shulchan Arukh, Yoreh De'ah* 242:31.
85. The phrasing used is "*shavya chatikha de-issura*" and not "*shavya a-nafsheih chatikha de-issura.*" *Revid Ha-Zahav* (*Parashas Shoftim*, s.v. *asher yorukha*) has it as "*shavya chakham chatikha de-issura.*" Cf.

halakhic uncertainty, a rabbi is needed to render a decision and determine the law, not just teach it.

Similarly, while a *minhag* (custom) is binding because it has the status of a vow, the *Pri Chadash* asserts that this only applies to an extra-halakhic practice, one that is beyond biblical and rabbinic obligations. Following a specific ruling on a purely halakhic matter is not a *minhag* but the nature of *halakhah*.[86] In other words, when a rabbi rules for a questioner on an halakhic matter, his ruling shapes the questioner's Torah obligation, creating a new halakhic reality for him.[87] Such is the power of the halakhic decisor.

The Art of Halakhah

I have heard talk about the proposed creation of an halakhic database with an artificial intelligence interface that will provide halakhic guidance. This is impossible for two reasons: (1) the vast complexities involved in creating a comprehensive database render the enterprise impractical, (2) it represents a misunderstanding of the nature of halakhic guidance. Initiates in many professions recognize that while their field projects an image of mathematical precision, it is in reality highly subjective and personal. The complex formulas and models seem purely objective but, in reality, they operate with a great deal of subjectivity.

R. Shaul Yisraeli, *Amud Ha-Yemini* (Tel Aviv, 2000) 1:6:4, p. 53; R. Menashe Klein, *Mishneh Halakhos* vol. 16 (Brooklyn, 2003), no. 59 p. 173; *Encyclopedia Talmudis*, entry for "hora'ah" section 6, vol. 8 col. 507.

86. *Shulchan Arukh, Yoreh De'ah* 214; *Pri Chadash, Orach Chaim* 596:7. Cf. *Chayei Adam* 127:10. Regarding family customs, see *Pischei Teshuvah, Yoreh De'ah* 214:4; R. Hershel Schachter, "Hashbei'a Hishbi'a" in *Beis Yitzchak* 39 (New York, NY, 2007), pp. 513-520.

87. It is noteworthy that the *Pri Chadash* states that such a ruling may only be overturned by a uniquely outstanding scholar, of which there is only one or two in a generation. Cf. *Chayei Adam*, ibid.

Similarly, *le-havdil*, halakhic decision-making is an art and not a science.[88] Authorities throughout the ages have adopted multiple approaches to innumerable issues and contemporary decisors have different methods of reaching a *pesak*. Some rabbis choose, whenever possible, the side of a debate they find most convincing based on an examination of the primary sources. Others take into account the multiple existing views among later authorities and reach decisions based on rules such as allowing for leniency in rabbinic matters and requiring stringency in biblical matters. The majority of rabbis, it seems to me, stake positions somewhere along the spectrum between those two poles.

There is also an element of *chiddush*, innovation. Sometimes a rabbi will have an original approach to a subject which he will incorporate into his ruling. Others will rely only on precedent. But even precedent allows wide room for disagreement because how you weigh prior authorities, whom you consider to be of prime importance and whom lesser, will impact your conclusion.

Besides these methodological issues, a factual analysis is also required. You need to tease out of the questioner all of the necessary details to gain a full understanding of the question. This is no small feat, and people differ on how they do this and therefore what constitutes the full question to which the rabbi will then respond. No computer can do this.

Specialists

There was a time in history when the canons of knowledge were sufficiently limited that individuals could master all of them. Scholars such as Da Vinci and Galileo were capable of fully comprehending the breadth and depth of multiple disciplines,

---

88. Cf. R. J. David Bleich, "*Lomdut* and *Pesak*: Theoretical Analysis and Halakhic Decision-Making" in R. Yosef Blau ed., *Lomdut: The Conceptual Approach to Learning* (New York, NY, 2006), p. 87ff.

making important contributions that advanced different fields. This phenomenon of the Rennaissance Man is aptly a thing of the past. The current specialization of knowledge is a result of the extended study of hundreds of thousands of scholars in thousands of fields over hundreds of years. It is, in itself, a full-time job to keep abreast of developments in any given subject. The unique genius of the Renaissance Man that once allowed a savant to master all knowledge is now sufficient to master, at most, two or three fields.

Le-havdil, Jewish studies developed at a slight lag. The era of the Renaissance Yid was the late eighteenth and early nineteenth centuries, when a Maharatz Chajes could master all rabbinic literature and simultaneously keep abreast of the developments in all of the various areas within the academic study of Judaism.[89] With the advent of inexpensive printing, widespread advanced yeshiva studies, and the maturation of academic Jewish studies, this mastery is no longer possible. The proverbial "*Ish Ha-Eshkolos*" is a relic of the past.[90]

Halakhah, the application of Jewish law to the nuanced realities of daily life, is no less a specialty. We cannot realistically expect every Jew to be a master of practical *halakhah,* and would be misguided to advise amateurs to reach their own conclusions

---

89. On his accomplishments, see Meir Hershkowitz, *Rabbi Tzvi Hirsch Chajes* (Jerusalem, 1972); Bruria Hutner David, "The Dual Role of Rabbi Zvi Hirsch Chajes: Traditionalist and Maskil" (unpublished doctoral dissertation, Columbia University, 1971); Jacob Schachter ed., *The Students' Guide Through The Talmud* (Brooklyn, NY, 2005), pp. xi-xiv.

90. Although exaggerated honorifics are still a thing of the present, and this writer is equally guilty of it. See my review of the *Machzor Mesorat HaRav* in *Jewish Action* 68:2 (Winter 5768/2008), pp. 85-88. See also *Bnei Banim* (Jerusalem, 2005) vol. 4 no. 26 where R. Yehudah Henkin chastises his correspondent—this writer—for addressing him in overly laudatory terms, and more generally in vol. 2 (Jerusalem, 1992) no. 35.

when experts are readily available. Yet this type of anti-intellectualism, of "common sense" rule over studied decision, is a frequent occurrence. Many people think that after examining the relevant texts—often for the first time—they have gained sufficient insight into the subject to critique established authorities and offer their own opinions.[91]

Non-Specialists

There is a bit of a contradiction, or at least an inconsistency on first glance, in Rav Avraham Besdin's book *Reflections of the Rav*.[92] In chapter 6, Rav Besdin quotes Rav Joseph B. Soloveitchik (20th century, U.S.) as defending the religious intuition of the average Jew. Jewish values and traditions are so ingrained in the Jewish psyche that they infiltrate the subconscious thought of the community. Yet in chapter 13, Rav Besdin quotes Rav Soloveitchik as insisting that authentic Judaism must come from its authoritative representatives because the masses are misguided in their "common sense" approach. Are the masses subconsciously enlightened or not? Can their religious instincts be trusted or not?

I think the resolution to this question can be found in the repetition in *Avos* chapter 1 of the dictum: "Make for yourself a teacher" (*Avos* 1:4, 16). According to Rashi, this is an example of two *Tanna'im* teaching the same idea. The Rambam, however, sees two different concepts being advocated. The first is an instruction to find a mentor who will teach you Torah. The second is a command to find a rabbinic authority who will rule for you on halakhic matters. The former is about a teacher of Torah theory and the latter about an adjudicator of Torah practice.[93]

---

91. Cf. *Sanhedrin* 99b-100a regarding those who say "Of what use to us are rabbis?"
92. Hoboken, NJ, 1993. A close reader of the book will find the following answer implicit in the words.
93. Rashi and Rambam, *Avos* 1:16.

When it comes to Torah knowledge, it exists in abundance in the Jewish psyche. Torah attitudes inform the views and practices of traditional Jews. Jewish law, however, must be decided by an expert in its application who knows all of its sources and understands how different circumstances affect it. Torah study and teaching are universal activites but Torah ruling is only for experts. This is aptly described in a biography of Nehama Leibowitz (20th century, Israel), who, despite her expertise as a Bible scholar, made no claim to halakhic authority and regularly consulted with and deferred to noted rabbis:

> Nehama abided by the halakhic rulings of her day, refraining from voting, in compliance with R. Kook's prohibition of women from doing so. She took her halakhic questions to rabbis she admired—to her local rabbi, R. Yohanan Fried, or R. Shlomo Zalman Auerbach and R. Shlomo Min Hahar. She also asked halakhic questions of R. Isaac Herzog.... In the final decades of her life she regularly phoned the late R. Yosef Kapah with her questions. He recalled that she knew Halakhah very well, and frequently already knew the answer. Nehama was turning to him, not for information, but because it was important to her to rely on a recognized authority in her religious practice. Thus she was careful to ask about seemingly minor issues such as making tea on Shabbat, even calling again to double-check.[94]

It is worth noting that even advanced Talmud scholars may not be experts in practical *halakhah*. Stories abound about *roshei yeshiva* who have refused to rule on practical matters, leaving them for pulpit rabbis. These stories, though, speak mainly of the past. *Roshei yeshiva* today generally feel free to rule on practical

---

94. *Nehama Leibowitz: Teacher and Scholar* (Jerusalem, 2009), p. 336.

matters, only sometimes due to experience and expertise. This can lead to numerous problems, including overly technical answers that ignore important human factors and the application of stringencies that are appropriate only for the *beis midrash* and not for the community in general. In particular, there is always a disconnect between the experiences of a rabbi who has spent his whole life in a yeshiva environment with a layman who spends the majority of his waking hours in a secular businessplace. Without ever having been there, it is extremely difficult for a rabbi to understand the environment and its challenges. A *rosh yeshiva* is often at a disadvantage to a pulpit rabbi in this regard, because the latter has greater secondary exposure through the time spent talking to his congregants. That disconnect sometimes leads falsely confident *roshei yeshiva* to issue rulings on situations they do not fully understand. This is, of course, a broad generalization that has many exceptions.

Nevertheless, it is commonplace for yeshiva graduates to take their halakhic questions to their *rosh yeshiva* or another of their teachers rather than their synagogue rabbi. Indeed, I too have been guilty of this at times. Not only does this sometimes lead to an improper answer, and also impedes the development of a rabbi-congregant relationship, it undermines the authority of the local rabbi, to which we now turn our attention.

II. The Loss of Authority

The Outsiders

Until now, we have discussed the need to ask your halakhic questions to a qualified authority. Let us now focus on the proper address for these questions and why it has declined in popularity. Today's heightened level of communication is a mixed blessing.[95]

---

95. I discussed another aspect of this in "Are Blogs Good for the Jews?" in *The Jewish Press*, Oct. 7, 2009.

Using Authority

It is now commonplace for laymen to know on any given subject the views of multiple local and international rabbis. The proximity of very different communities in large Jewish enclaves and the omni-present book, article, and website summarizing multiple views allow for an open marketplace of ideas. This is a godsend in terms of creating large amounts of stimulating Torah content that attracts the attention of those who might otherwise lack a sustained interested in studying Torah. In theory, this also keeps rabbis informed.[96] But it also allows laymen to choose the opinion that suits their temperaments and needs. The stringency addicts are fed by Haredi newspapers and the leniency seekers are satiated by renegade blogs. Many see no reason to ask their local rabbi.

Historically, the rabbi of a town was called its *mara de-asra*, "master of the place." This title is reminiscent of the Gemara (*Mo'ed Katan* 6a), which states that all matters of the town are the rabbi's responsibility. Today, in the U.S., most rabbis serve congregations and not towns. However, it seems to me that their religious authority still applies to their community, i.e., those families who voluntarily join a rabbi's synagogue.[97] Even though families

---

96. In reality, it tends to keep the layman better informed than the rabbi, which is a different problem.
97. We see an halakhic concept of intra-city sub-communities regarding customs. See Responsa of *Mahari Ben Lev* vol. 3 no. 14; Responsa of R. Eliyahu Mizrachi no. 13; *Responsa Maharshdam, Yoreh De'ah* no. 40; *Pri Chadash, Orach Chaim* 596:19. Given the phenomenon of "shtiebel hopping," I would define someone's synagogue as the one he attends on Shabbos morning (when and if he attends). Rav Dr. David Shatz, however, pointed out that some people even alternate where they pray on Shabbos morning. I leave defining the affiliation of such people to others, fairly certain that they cannot be defined as having more than one community any more than one who maintains residences in two cities, traveling back and forth between his two homes on an equal basis.

choose their synagogues based on a number of criteria,[98] the very act of settling within a rabbi's domain is, I suggest, a submission to his halakhic authority. I see no difference between choosing a contemporary synagogue for the quality of its *kiddush* and moving into a pre-Modern town for business reasons. The latter certainly obligated a Jew to follow the city rabbi's halakhic decisions and so, I contend, does the former.[99]

The Rema (16th century, Poland; *Shulchan Arukh, Yoreh De'ah* 245:22) writes that a rabbi is not allowed to rule on ritual matters within the domain of another rabbi. The Vilna Gaon (18th century, Lithuania; ad loc., no. 36) points to talmudic examples of rabbis refusing to rule inside another rabbi's town (e.g., *Chullin* 53b). In contemporary application, a rabbi is the sole halakhic authority for members of his synagogue and no other rabbi has the right to rule on halakhic matters for them. When an outside rabbi of any stature rules on a local matter, he infringes on the local rabbi's jurisdiction, an infraction so serious that it is punishable with excommunication.[100] This stringency, I suggest, is well deserved because divergent rulings on many issues can and do lead to disuniform practice and often communal *machlokes*.[101]

---

98. Rav Dr. Gidon Rothstein suggested this point and added that most synagogue members have no real say in the hiring of a new rabbi.
99. Cf. R. Shaul Yisraeli, *Ammud Ha-Yemini* (above note 88), 1:6:10; R. Shlomo Aviner, *She'eilas Shlomo* (Jerusalem, 2006, 2nd edition), vol. 1 no. 204 par. 8; vol. 2 nos. 223, 226, 227, 254; vol. 3 nos. 259-261; vol. 4 pp. 272-276.
100. Cf. *Shabbos* 19b, *Eruvin* 94a, *Pesachim* 30a, *Chullin* 53b; *Tashbetz* 3:210; *Sheyarei Knesses Ha-Gedolah, Hagahos Beis Yosef, Yoreh De'ah* 242:17; R. Samson Raphael Hirsch, *Collected Writings* (New York, 1984), vol. 6 pp. 271-277.
101. Rav Dr. David Shatz raised the issue of *machlokes* (loosely defined as "friction") in this case. R. Shlomo Aviner (above note 99) states that the custom is to accept local rabbis as authorities on all public matters but not on private matters, for which people may consult any rabbi.

That is one of the reasons that my standard answer to people who e-mail me halakhic questions is that they should ask their rabbi. I find it difficult to understand the halakhic legitimacy of "Ask the Rabbi" features in newspapers and on websites, or, additionally, the "*Kol Korei*"/broadside-type of halakhic pronouncements, unless they are attempts to fill the holes left by rabbis (and society)—answer the questions that will never be asked to a rabbi—rather than create local disconnects.

In 2005, in response to a pamphlet that advocated a recently built *eruv* in Flatbush (in addition to the prior *eruv* that had existed for over twenty years), a mailing was sent widely within the Flatbush community condemning any *eruv* in Flatbush. The denunciations were strictly by prominent local *roshei yeshiva* and synagogue rabbis, with a separate section containing letters from Israeli rabbis.[102] While it is significant that the statement was from local rabbis, it is unclear what right they have to impose their position on members of other local synagogues/communities who do not normally turn to them for guidance. I was particularly struck by the response of one blogger, who created a mock mailing that read simply: "The Flatbush Eruv: Ask Your Rabbi."[103] This was a sharp critique of what can be viewed as an infringement on the prerogatives of many pulpit rabbis by the issuer of the Flatbush mailing.

---

102. See *Torah Musings*, June 15, 2005 at https://www.torahmusings.com/2005/06/flatbush-eruv-2/. The local rabbis pictured on the cover are Rav Shmuel Berenbaum, Rav Feivel Cohen, Rav Hillel David, Rav David Feinstein (from Manhattan), and Rav Aharon Schechter. The Israeli rabbis are Rav Yosef Shalom Eliashiv, Rav Chaim Kanievsky, Rav Aharon Leib Shteinman, Rav Shmuel Wosner, and the Gerrer Rebbe.

103. As of this writing, I cannot locate this blog post and am relying on my memory.

Distance

There are other reasons that some people do not address their halakhic questions to their local rabbi. Whether due to embarrassment over lack of knowledge, shyness about discussing private details with an outsider, intimidation by someone so different, or personality clashes, some people are simply uncomfortable asking their rabbi questions. Some may ask rabbis who taught them in school, others may venture to websites where they can ask questions anonymously, while still others may choose not to ask and to instead act as they see fit.

There is also a general distrust of authority. A desire for independence is part of human nature, but for at least the past few decades, a profound skepticism of authority figures has dominated Western culture. Rabbis are certainly not exempt from being targets of this attitude. This is further aggravated when great rabbis are perceived, rightly or not, as ruling on matters they do not fully understand or being manipulated to rule based on incomplete or incorrect information. This leads to a dismissal of all rabbinic authority. This is certainly aggravated by the all-too-frequent news story about rabbis involved in financial and sexual scandals. The reality is that when one rabbi sins, all rabbis look bad.

Some people ignore great rabbis while others bypass their local rabbi and go directly to a leading authority—whether a *rosh yeshiva* or the rabbi of a different community. An important reason for this attitude is the vast gap in expertise that often separates rabbis. Many competent rabbis lack the training, knowledge, and experience of their colleagues, particularly after years of communal service that have limited their available time for personal study. Laypeople want the most expert halakhic opinions, just like they want the most expert medical and financial opinions.[104]

---

104. Rav Dr. Gidon Rothstein and Rav Dovid Gottlieb emphasized this point.

Sometimes a rabbi undercuts his own authority by accepting a position in a synagogue with a significantly different worldview than his own, whether to the right or the left, and then tries to "convert" his congregants. This common phenomenon creates an alienation that is unnecessary and counterproductive. A rabbi needs to work with his congregants and generate goodwill so they will have confidence in his views.[105] Part of this is to allow hashkafic pluralism, to recognize that his congregants have different backgrounds, worldviews, and temperaments, and to either answer questions appropriately or to direct questioners to someone who can.[106] For example, if someone Modern Orthodox were to ask his Charedi rabbi about college choices, the rabbi must either answer taking into account the questioner's worldview that values secular education or direct the questioner to a different rabbi who is able to advise within this framework. This takes a high level of sensitivity and humility that is difficult to achieve.

Lowering the Barrier

An additional diminution of rabbinic authority can be found in the recent debate regarding the ordination of women.[107] Proponents advance two main strategies to avoid the prohibition of *serarah* that entails when women attain positions of communal

---

105. Rav Dr. Gidon Rothstein pointed this out.
106. Cf. R. J. David Bleich, "*Lomdut* and *Pesak*: Theoretical Analysis and Halakhic Decision-Making" in R. Yosef Blau ed., *Lomdut: The Conceptual Approach to Learning* (New York, NY, 2006), p. 109 n. 5. While *Shulchan Arukh* (*Yoreh De'ah* 242:14; *Choshen Mishpat* 10:3) seems to obligate a rabbi to answer a practical halakhic question presented to him if he can, I suspect that this is only a general requirement and does not obligate a rabbi to answer every question posed to him.
107. I refer to arguments I have seen in informal discussion and not to specific published articles. I thank Rav Arie Folger for suggesting this general point.

authority. One is to adopt the minority view that the prohibition of *serarah* does not apply to women. The difficulty with this is that it leaves ample room for those who oppose the ordination of women to adopt the majority view that accepts *serarah* limitations on women.[108] Therefore, another approach is strategically more advantageous—namely, arguing that a rabbi has no authority over the community. While a coherent argument to this effect can be constructed, the embracing of the decline of the local rabbinate is, I believe, to the detriment of the entire community.

A friend described the following incident: At a synagogue event, a man went to wash his hands before eating bread. Not finding the regular washing cup, he took a different vessel to use but was unsure of its halakhic suitability. He asked a local educator who was standing nearby, and this rabbi told him that according to one opinion it is good and according to another it is not. My friend, another local educator, witnessed the paralysis this response caused and stepped in, telling the man that the vessel is acceptable and he should proceed. My friend told me this to describe how some teachers of *halakhah* fail to instruct people what to do. My reaction, though, was that my friend had no right to issue a ruling for this man, given the other available options.[109] Who is he to decide on an halakhic matter of legitimate dispute among major *poskim*? The dilemma he witnessed should be solved by a rabbi with local authority, with the mandate to render a decision that is conclusive for members of his community.[110] If the rabbi has no

---

108. Cf. R. J. David Bleich, *Contemporary Halakhic Problems*, vol. 2 (Hoboken, NJ, 1983) pp. 254-267.

109. I would have either asked the rabbi or said, "I think this is allowed. Let's check with the rabbi when we have the opportunity."

110. On the rare occasions when I am forced to answer a halakhic question in my synagogue, when the rabbi is unavailable and an answer is needed immediately, I try to determine how the rabbi would answer and then, afterwards, tell the rabbi the entire story to give him the opportunity to disagree for future occurrences, to know

authority, his rulings, teachings, and exhortations become nothing but friendly advice, another voice among the many that crowd our lives in this hyper-connected day.

There is also a widespread lack of appreciation of the importance of meta-halakhic, values-based aspects of *halakhah* that require expertise in application. One can speculate as to whether the origins of this attitude is a growing textualism and/or a desire for scientific precision. Regardless, axiological principles that have guided halakhic authorities for centuries are regularly dismissed by laypeople in their desire to self-*pasken*.[111]

Independent Minyanim

A few examples of the diminished respect for rabbinic authority are in order. One phenomenon that was covered extensively in the media a few years ago is the "Independent *Minyan*." This "new" concept of a group convening for prayer without a formal synagogue structure is hailed by some as the future of Judaism.[112] The novelty of this phenomenon is debatable. It is actually the third wave or generation of the "*Chavurah* Movement," following

---

that I did not try to infringe on his domain, and to be aware of the halakhic questions raised by his congregants, i.e., to know what is going on in various people's lives.

111. See *inter alia* R. Mayer Twersky, "Halakhic Values and Halakhic Decisions: Rav Soloveitchik's *Pesaq* Regarding Women's Prayer Groups" in *Tradition* 32:3 (Spring 1998), a critique of this in R. Reuven Singer, "*Halakhic* Values: *Pesaq* or Persuasion" in *The Edah Journal* 3:1 (*Tevet* 5763), and my response to that critique in "Values, Halakhah and Pesaq: Continued Discussion Of 'Halakhic Values: Pesaq or Persuasion'" in *The Edah Journal* 3:2 (Elul 5763), reprinted in my *Posts Along the Way* (Brooklyn, NY, 2009), vol. 1 pp. 176-183.

112. See, for example, "'New Jews' stake claim to faith, culture" (CNN. com, Oct. 28, 2009) at http://www.cnn.com/2009/LIVING/10/28/new.and.emergent.jews/index.html and "Minyanim Grow Up, Turn Inward" (*The Jewish Week*, Nov. 25, 2008) at http://www.thejewishweek.com/viewArticle/c36_a14128/News/New_York.html.

its innovation in the 1960's with the original three *chavurot* in Boston, New York, and Washington; and a second wave in the 1970's beginning in New York and Los Angeles. This second generation was a "counter-move" to the earlier *chavurot* in that it represented a measure of return to more traditional synagogal forms while maintaining egalitarianism and innovation. This third generation is more formalized and is represented by "congregations of renewal" rather than informal prayer gatherings, among other differences.[113]

Allow me to offer a few thoughts based on my childhood experience attending a *chavurah* in the early 1980's.[114] This *chavurah* was a gathering of families every Shabbos morning for egalitarian prayer in the basement of a Reform Temple. The participants were local families of varying levels of observance and Jewish education. A core group of knowledgeable, observant people—including one JTS ordainee—led the group, said *divrei Torah* in lieu of sermons, and taught synagogue skills to those interested in learning. The friendships made in this group remain strong over thirty years later. After a few years of regular attendance, my family drifted back to our synagogue but continues to remain within that group of friends.

After polling many of the regulars at my elementary school reunion, I see a few factors that attracted people to this *chavurah*: (1) The informality of structure and attire made it a welcoming environment, (2) The lively, participatory services, (3) The democratic nature—while in reality almost all decisions were made by the core group, everyone's input was encouraged and taken seriously, (4) The completely egalitarian services was, at that time, fairly radical and not widely available in Conservative

---

113. Prof. Jerome Chanes proposed these distinctions which require further elaboration in a more appropriate venue.

114. This *chavurah* was featured in Abba Eban's film Heritage, although I was not there for the filming.

synagogues, (5) Perhaps most important, it provided a fun, Jewish experience for the children, who had wide leeway to run around and play.

After interviewing a few people involved in the "congregations of renewal," the independent *minyanim* at the border of Orthodoxy,[115] I found significant similarities and differences.[116] The atmosphere is welcoming and informal, and the services are lively. The attendees have a wide variety of backgrounds and levels of observance. Decisions are fairly democratic, although some form of halakhic authority is regularly consulted and often given veto power. Perhaps the biggest difference is demographic—the attendees of independent *minyanim* are young, abundantly single and/or without children, and living in a city. While on the one hand, this prevents family needs—such as preparation for a synagogue bar mitzvah—to interfere with attendance and allows for continuous replenishment of the ranks as long as young people continue to move into those neighborhoods, it also leads to a constant exodus as members move on to another stage of life.

In general, it seems to me that the *chavurah* movement had more potential staying power than independent *minyanim* yet largely failed to become a permanent fixture, despite the influence they exerted on the broader Jewish community. I expect independent *minyanim* to be an equally transient phenomenon, whose influence has yet to be fully seen. As high schools and colleges know well, the constantly changing student body make trends short-lived, as new students arrive with different needs and interests than those who preceded them. The same can be said about the predominantly transient members of independent *minyanim*.

---

115. Which side of the border depends on whom you ask.
116. Rav Adam Mintz correctly pointed out that there is a wide variety of independent *minyanim*. I attempt here to discuss characteristics that are typical of most such *minyanim*, aware that experiences will vary.

One important commonality is that of ritual experimentation. The *chavurot* were free of rabbinic oversight and were therefore able to democratically choose full egalitarianism. The independent *minyanim* have a little more fealty to the halakhic process but are still the places where egalitarian experimentation is taking place, each *minyan* based on the boundaries its members decide. If a religious guide chooses to stop this democratic process, he or she runs the risk of members starting a new independent *minyan* where they have more freedom from unwanted authority (and such has happened).

Like everything, the *chavurah* and independent *minyan* phenomena have both positive and negative aspects. The positive aspects speak volumes about the state of American Jewry and its needs, information that synagogues ignore at their own peril. Some of the negative aspects include the democratization of halakhic decision-making, the bypassing of local and communal authorities, and the general atmosphere of halakhic experimentation.[117]

Bans

Another example that I witnessed up close is that of book-banning. I first learned of the impending ban on three of Rav Natan Slifkin's books on the day it was issued—Sep. 21, 2004, a few days before Yom Kippur. Despite my expectation that the controversy would quickly die down, a few months later the bans were further publicized in the newspaper *Yated Ne'eman*. The ban led Rav Slifkin's publisher and distributor to drop his books, after which he asked me to distribute his controversial works through Yashar Books, a company I had recently started. My inclination

---

117. One occasional attendee at the *chavurah* to which my family belonged was the wife of a prominent Conservative halakhist. I have reason to believe that her husband refused to attend on principle, because he felt that the *chavurah* undermined rabbinic authority and communal structures.

was to accept but I first consulted with a number of synagogue rabbis, asking whether they wanted the books available for their communities. They responded positively and I took on the distribution of the controversial books. I later obtained approval and encouragement from many other rabbis and *roshei yeshiva*.

This episode highlights another area in which the authority of synagogue rabbis is undermined. When leading Torah scholars issue wide-reaching rulings that are highly publicized, synagogue rabbis feel their hands are forced. If these local authorities disagree or think that their communities reflect different circumstances that necessitate alternate conclusions, they will need to take the uncomfortable position of publicly disagreeing with giants of Torah. Not every rabbi has the courage and the political capital to do so. In effect, many rabbis have had the halakhic authority over local matters snatched away from them by the assistants and publicists of leading Torah scholars.[118]

All of these many factors we have discussed contribute to the situation we have today where even sincere people striving to fulfill the will of God choose not to abide by the halakhic decisions of their rabbis.

III. Regaining Authority

Deference

Many of these problems are, one way or another, caused by rabbis, and their resolution will also be through their efforts. The solution will not be synagogue rabbis preaching about their own prerogatives to determine local *halakhah*. Only the most forgiving audience will fail to note how self-serving that approach sounds. The answer, I believe, rests in a partnership among rabbis and communal leaders, each emphasizing the authority of a local rabbi

---

118. Blaming assistants is an intentionally generous assumption.

and the local rabbis recognizing the need to consult with more expert authorities on complex cases.

Roshei yeshiva need to send their students to local rabbis as appropriate. Of course, I am not suggesting that the yeshiva is not a place for teaching practical *halakhah* by answering questions. However, there are questions and there are questions. When a student wants to know whether his torn *tzitzis* have been invalidated, that is certainly an appropriate question for a *rosh yeshiva*. But when he wants to know whether he should attend his cousin's intermarriage, it is entirely appropriate for a *rosh yeshiva* to send a student to his local rabbi (and maybe even call the rabbi directly as well). The *rosh yeshiva* can also send a married *kollel* student to his local rabbi for household questions, such as those relating to *kashrus* and *taharas ha-mishpachah*.

In lectures, also, *roshei yeshiva* and communal leaders can speak about the importance of respecting the domain of the local rabbi. People often never consider that they should submit to the halakhic authority of their *mara de-asra*. They need to be reminded—by someone other than their rabbi—of this obligation.

Stories about great scholars deferring to proper authorities need to be emphasized. It is told that a Vilna layman once inadvertently asked both the city rabbi and the Vilna Gaon about the *kashrus* of a chicken. The former permitted it and the latter forbade. In order to emphasize his authority as the city's official halakhic authority, the city rabbi insisted that the Vilna Gaon join him in tasting this cooked chicken—to which the Ga'on assented (the story continues that a piece of forbidden fat fell onto the chicken as a divine commutation of the Gaon's sentence).[119]

Roshei yeshiva who are expert halakhists certainly have a role in local *halakhah* but as consultants for local rabbis. Pulpit

---

119. Betzalel Landau, *Ha-Ga'on He-Chassid Mi-Vilna* (Jerusalem, 1978), pp. 253-254; Betzalel Landau (Jonathan Rosenblum tr.), *The Vilna Gaon* (Brooklyn, NY, 1994), pp. 179-180.

rabbis should serve as the gatekeeper to prominent authorities. When people ask their rabbi a question, they know that he will take a difficult case to a world-class expert. This allows for the development of rabbi-congregant relationships and maintains the local rabbi as the sole source of halakhic rulings, even for those pulpit rabbis who are not themselves renowned experts.[120] This also enables maintaining the rabbi-congregant relationship while still allowing for the conscientious objector, the congregant who belongs to a different ideological community than his rabbi and feels a need to obtain guidance in certain issues from those who share his ideology.[121] The pulpit rabbi should serve as the gatekeeper for such questions or, at the very least, be informed about the discussion. A rabbi unaware of, and uninvolved with, his congregants' hashkafic and halakhic dilemmas is significantly impeded in his communal work.

Guard Your Tongue
But the burden of restoring local authority should not be placed solely on the shoulders of *roshei yeshiva*. We all need to be careful in our speaking patterns to preserve the dignity and prerogatives of the synagogue rabbi. One of the many humorous aspects of the Jewish community is the frequent call for care in speech. While preaching greater *shemiras ha-lashon* is certainly praiseworthy, the way some rabbis can lecture about its importance while still insulting other people, sometimes in the very same speech, seems straight out of a stand-up comedy routine.

One of the standard messages relayed to an adult struggling with the consuming needs of an elderly parent is that his children are watching. They will emulate his treatment of his parents.

---

120. Rav Adam Mintz contributed to this formulation.
121. Cf. Rav Aharon Lichtenstein, *Leaves of Faith* volume 2 (Hoboken, NJ, 2004), p. 289ff.

Aside from the impetuses of gratitude and fulfilling a biblical commandment, an adult should treat his own parents well if he wants his children to treat him well. Of course, there are no guarantees in life. I suspect, though, that this powerful idea is true more often than not.[122]

Similarly, a rabbi who wants respect from his followers needs to show respect to other rabbis. When a rabbi displays public respect for the domain of another rabbi, he will be respected himself. When all rabbis respect each other's prerogative to serve as a *mara de-asra*, congregants will observe and learn. We need to free ourselves from the sadly common habit of delegitimizing the rulings of other rabbis and instead learn the language of "*eilu va-eilu*."

The Incompetent Rabbi

When all is said and done, however, a synagogue rabbi needs to know his own limits. Not everyone who manages to pass a *semikhah* examination is truly fit to rule on Jewish law. A rabbi can have many wonderful skills that make him an asset to his community but still be unqualified for all but the simplest halakhic questions. The Mishnah (*Avos* 4:7) has harsh words about such a person who despite his shortcoming still rules on halakhic matters, calling him a "wicked, arrogant fool."[123] He needs the self-awareness to recognize the issue and consult with those more qualified in this aspect of the rabbinate. All of the advocacy for the prerogatives of the synagogue rabbi will be dismissed if the problem of the overstepping rabbi is not resolved. While Rav

---

122. In a sense, it is based on the rabbinic dictum "Who is repected? One who respects others" (*Avos* 4:1) and the theological concept of "measure for measure." Cf. *Shabbos* 105b, *Nedarim* 32a, *Sanhedrin* 90a.

123. Quoted in *Shulchan Arukh, Yoreh De'ah* 242:13, *Choshen Mishpat* 10:3.

Menashe Klein writes that he was told by Rav Moshe Feinstein that he is obligated to disagree with the older authority whom he thought was wrong,[124] at the time Rav Klein already had the Talmud and codes at his fingertips. This certainly does not apply to someone of dramatically lesser learning. Even if the precise definition of someone entitled to an opinion is unclear, that does not mean that we can entirely disregard the vague definition. If local rabbis do not *pasken* responsibly, they cannot expect the cooperation of *roshei yeshiva* and other rabbis.

Regarding such rabbis who do not defer to greater authorities when appropriate, I found a noteworthy paradigm of balancing the prerogatives of a *mara de-asra* with potential incompetence in Rav Eliezer Melamed's (contemporary, Israel) *Revivim: Kovetz Ma'amarim Be-Inyanei Am, Eretz, Tzava*.[125] Asked whether an Israeli soldier is bound by the halakhic decisions of an army rabbi or should instead consult with his *rosh yeshiva* or hometown rabbi, Rav Melamed answered as follows: There are many excellent army rabbis but some are unqualified and/or too deferential to military superiors. Therefore, a soldier should follow the ruling of the army rabbi, who is the *mara de-asra*, unless his decision does not "make sense," in which case the soldier should ask an outside rabbi.

Rav Achiah Amitai (contemporary, Israel) wrote a letter disagreeing, pointing out that the determination whether a ruling "makes sense" is so subjective that it effectively dismisses the authority of the army rabbinate for anyone who prefers to look elsewhere for guidance. Additionally, outside rabbis frequently do not understand the immediate circumstances and often are

---

124. R. Menashe Klein, *Mishneh Halakhos* vol. 8 (Brooklyn, NY, 2000), no. 137 p. 202; idem., *Om Ani Chomah* (Brooklyn, NY, 2000), p. 332. Cf. idem., *Mishneh Halakhos* vol. 16 (Brooklyn, NY, 2003), no. 63 p. 187.

125. Har Berakhah, Israel, 2007, pp. 250-254, taken from his columns in the newspaper *Be-Sheva* in late 2004.

educators without training in practical *halakhah*. This approach will also lead to religious disunity within units consisting of soldiers from different towns or *yeshivos*. And officers will ignore army rabbis when they see that even religious soldiers do not follow their instructions.

Rav Melamed's response was, essentially, that despite all these problems, this is the way it has to be. I believe that his approach can be reformulated as follows: When a soldier receives a ruling that does not "make sense" to him, he should ask an outside rabbi whether this ruling falls under the category of a mistaken and reversible decision as defined in *Shulchan Arukh* (*Yoreh De'ah* 242:31) and commentaries (admittedly a complex discussion). If it does, then the outside rabbi, who must make every effort to determine and fully understand the exact circumstances, can give a ruling to the contrary. Otherwise, the soldier must follow the army rabbi's ruling even if his outside rabbi reaches a different conclusion. As long as the army rabbi's ruling is not so mistaken as to be reversible, it is binding because he is the *mara de-asra*.

This same approach can be applied to synagogue members. An outside rabbi who is consulted and is concerned about the competence of his questioner's local rabbi, should only provide alternate rulings if the first rabbi's decision is reversible. Otherwise, he should advise people to follow their local rabbi's decision even if he disagrees with it.

Global Halakhah

When it comes to issues that affect broad segments of the community—beyond a single synagogue, neighborhood or town—broader halakhic shoulders are required. This is both because such issues are more complex and require balancing numerous halakhic and public policy concerns at once, and also because the decisor must be capable of commanding the respect and deference of rabbis throughout the multiple communities. In short, he must be recognized as an outstanding halakhic expert with a deep understanding of general and local socio-religious dynamics.

Beyond the problem of the overstepping rabbi, which we already discussed, a dilemma arises when the few rabbis who have achieved sufficient prominence disagree on a particular subject, as is inevitable. The halakhic system allows for such pluralism. Some people, however, mistake pluralism for chaos. They believe that allowing for multiple opinions means allowing for all opinions, that unless there is a single authority there is no authority. Local rabbis need to have their own outstanding authority, who shares the local communities' values, with whom they consult on global matters. Even then, laypeople often find it difficult to accept one position when there is widespread debate, particularly when they fail to understand the reasoning behind a specific view.

Show Your Work

The solution, albeit only partial, to this problem is greater transparency. There is a need for halakhic authorities or their disciples to proactively justify and defend their rulings in publicly accessible forums, perhaps by writing and publicizing lengthy responsa. The processes by which information is gathered and a decision is reached needs to be disclosed. While criticism will be fierce and immediate, there are ample mechanisms available for responding to those critiques and, when appropriate, revising decisions based on valid criticisms.

A few years ago, someone posted a popular essay on an halakhic topic by Rav Shlomo Aviner (contemporary, Israel) to an e-mail list on which I participated. I proceeded to critique his approach in detail, and the person who posted the original essay brought my critique to Rav Aviner who then responded to each point. While I was not entirely convinced by his response, I gained respect for his position and intellectual openness. A few years later, I responded to a surprising position of Rav Aviner's that a colleague of his e-mailed with a request for sources. I was pleasantly surprised by an e-mail with a list of responsa that supported his position. I believe that this is a new model that has great merit. In theory, the local rabbi should be charged with the task of defending his and/or his authority's ruling. However, local rabbis often lack the expertise and information to do so.

Additionally, the wording of proclamations and responsa needs to be crafted in a way that is strong and confident but still allows for other competent authorities to disagree. This will not only tone down the rhetoric in communal discourse but also preserve the dignity and prerogative of the local *mara de-asra*.[126]

We have discussed how the local rabbi's authority is currently being challenged from many different sides. In multiple ways, the local rabbi's authority has diminished, to the detriment of responsible halakhic decision-making. It behooves us to consider the consequences of this continuing decline and to actively protect this embattled, age-old institution. Through a partnership of rabbis and communal leaders, we can, in some measure, increase awareness of the need for local *halakhah*.

---

126. While newspapers that print stories magnifying disputes do much to aggravate the problem, it would be unrealistic to expect them to cooperate with preserving the dignity of the local rabbinate when so much of their revenue depends on controversy. Our "relief and deliverance" will have to come from "another place."

CHAPTER 4: FOLLOWERSHIP

In past eras, rabbis held formal positions of authority that gave them power over the lives of community members. Today, people enjoy the freedom to choose whether to accept a rabbi's authority. While they may face communal pressure or their own sense of religious obligation, they retain the legal right to disobey rabbinic guidance. Leadership now, more than ever, requires followership. The responsibility for the contiuity of Jewish tradition rests on every community member. This great responsibility comes with a moral obligation to serve faithfully, empowering leaders to fulfill their roles without ceding too much autonomy.

This chapter explores different manifestations of the conflict between individual initiative and communal authority. Whether the synagogue, the rabbi or the rabbinate, these institutions of communal authority challenge the inherent human desire for freedom. Perhaps the defining religious challenge of the Modern era lies in balancing individual freedom with commitment to communal authority.

The Need For A Rabbi

I. Jewish Autonomy

My wife's grandfather, a *chasid* who was trapped behind the Iron Curtain for decades before moving to Brooklyn, used to enjoy being asked who his *rebbe* was.[127] After all, every good *chasid* needs a *rebbe*. He would say that God is his *rebbe*, not any man. He answered to God and only God. That was a nice personal statement but, in reality, he took all his halakhic questions to his synagogue rabbi and followed that rabbi's decisions to the letter. He found his own way to deal with a dilemma that all modern Jews face: How much religious independence do we retain and how much do we cede to rabbis?

Judaism greatly values autonomy. It expects people to be independent thinkers who evaluate ideas and make their own decisions. God does not want robots. He gave people minds with which to think, to judge right from wrong, to distinguish truth from falsehood. If we simply place our fates in the hands of rabbis, how are we different from members of a cult who suffer abuse because they leave the thinking to their leader? If we give up some of our freedom to rabbis, are we sure they will use that power responsibly?

Rabbis are human, sometimes painfully so. They have strengths and flaws, just like the rest of us. We would be neglecting

---

127. This essay originally appeared in *The Jewish Link of NJ*, January 30, 2015.

our duties as beings created in God's image if we surrendered our freedom to rabbis. But that does not mean that we can disregard what rabbis have to say.

II. Expertise

All right-thinking people value true expertise. Doctors know more about medicine than laymen; lawyers can guide you through the legal system better than others, and so on. This does not mean that all opinions of all doctors are equal. Some are greater experts than others and most are specialists with unique insight only in their area of specialization. Even experts disagree and sometimes, maybe not often, all of the experts turn out to be wrong. But someone with no medical or legal training has limited insight into those fields. Even if he turns out to be right, it means he guessed correctly and got lucky. When a complex issue arises, the layman's opinion is generally too uninformed to be worthy of consideration.

Torah has experts, as well. God gave the Torah to the Jewish people as an inheritance for all, but that does not mean that everyone is equally knowledgeable. Some rabbis specialize in specific topics and others are well-rounded generalists. When complex Torah issues arise, the voices of the greatest experts are most important. I am not discussing deference to rabbis on matters of personal preference or politics but on Torah issues, where they are clearly more qualified than most. If we are truly interested in God's revealed word of Torah in the broadest sense, we must turn to Torah experts on religious questions. Failing to do so would be neglecting our duty to seriously search for the truth of the Torah.

Keep in mind that even rabbis defer to their teachers and others greater than they. This is not an issue of rabbis demanding obedience but inhabiting the same awkward place between freedom and submission. Even teachers need a teacher.

III. Limits on Authority

Some people say that they will only accept a rabbi's opinion on pure Torah issues, not on matters of judgment, worldviews, or social policy. But this minimalist view of Torah ignores all that our texts and traditions have to tell us about life in this world and the next. Torah is much more than *halakhah*, Jewish law. And even *halakhah* is more than just "do this and don't do that." It has nuance and depth, sensitivities and broad implications. It is a guide for life.

Rav Joseph B. Soloveitchik (20th century, U.S.) argued very strongly about the need for rabbinic expertise with words that resonate to this day. As summarized by Rav Avraham Besdin in *Reflections of the Rav*:

> When people talk about a meaningful Halakhah, of unfreezing the Halakhah or an empirical Halakhah, they are basically proposing Korah's approach. Lacking a knowledge of halakhic methodology, which can only be achieved through extensive study, they instead apply common-sense reasoning which is replete with platitudes and cliches.... This *da'at* [common-sense] approach is not tolerated in science, and it should not receive serious credence in Halakhah. Such judgments are pseudo-statements, lacking sophistication about depth relationships and meanings.[128]

Do-it-yourself Judaism, Rav Soloveitchik seems to be telling us, is doing it wrong. This analogy about experts holds true when thinking about rabbis who abuse their roles in any of a variety of ways. Like a doctor, a rabbi who oversteps his bounds should be dismissed. But in doing so, we do not reject the entire medical

---

128. Revised edition, Hoboken, NJ, 1993, p. 147.

field nor the entire rabbinate. We discard the individual, not the system. If an expert fails, we pick up the pieces of our lives and look, with the great care of hard-learned experience, for another expert.

IV. Sacred Experts

However, the analogy strikes me as incomplete for two reasons. First, it diminishes the role of a rabbi to that of a knowledge expert. But a rabbi is also a role model, an example of someone enriched by the holiness of Torah. A rabbi who succeeds is much more than a doctor and one who fails is much worse.

Additionally, we are talking about the most intimate religious aspects of life. A rabbi is your guide to the sacred. He teaches you not just how to act but how to bring the divine into your life. He is directly involved with your personal relationship with God. That requires much more than book smarts.

There is much more to discuss about this subject but given space considerations, I want to go straight to how we can—indeed, we must—place limitations on our rabbis. As responsible adults, we need to maintain a balance between the autonomy we cede to rabbis and that which we retain for ourselves. We have two key powers that remain in our hands. The first is the power of our feet, the ability to choose. If we don't like our community and its leadership, we can move to another yeshiva, another synagogue, another city and even another country. Life always has complications but certainly in theory, if not always in practice, we can free ourselves from any rabbi or other leader we do not like. Even a leading, globally recognized rabbi does not control every synagogue in the world.

The other power is that of review. A rabbi is subject to scrutiny, to outside evaluation. If we ever suspect him of acting improperly, if his answers ever seem out of line with the Torah or his behavior seems to deviate from our expectations, we must obtain a second opinion from another rabbi, another expert we believe is qualified to render judgment. No individual has free reign over our lives; only God can tell us what to do. If a rabbi is not legitimately transmitting God's message, as determined by other experts, he can and should be dismissed.

Perhaps most importantly, a successful balance of freedom and submission requires a shift in perception. We have to focus on the process, not the individual. Asking a rabbi is a method of determining what God expects of us. Since a rabbi is not a prophet and can only deduce answers from texts and traditions, he is a conduit, a decipherer, a connector. This process of inquiry is indirect and often imprecise, but the best we have in this world lacking direct revelation. We have to keep our eye on the target, which is God's word as traditionally understood within Judaism. The rabbi is there to use his best abilities, which are better trained than ours, to tell us God's expectations. The rabbi is only a human being, with his own personality, strengths and weaknesses. But so are we, so we should be able to look past the individual's quirks at the Torah he teaches and the guidance he provides.

When I was first married, I attended the synagogue of a world-famous halakhic authority. Often when I asked him a question and he gave me an answer, I would challenge him from various texts. He did not appreciate that. He was the rabbi, the expert, and I, the 20-something seeking his guidance; his decision was final.

At the next synagogue I attended, after moving, the rabbi was equally skilled albeit less famous. He enjoyed the arguments and rebutted my prooftexts with explanations and counterproofs. Personally, I "clicked" more with the second rabbi. Even when I thought he was wrong, when he had failed to convince me that my arguments were insufficient, I followed his rulings. I may have learned a few texts in my life but you cannot compare someone who learned a text 101 times to someone who learned it 100 times (*Chagigah* 9b), and certainly not fewer. Because I respected him so much, I could defer to his judgment on religious matters.

We all need a rabbi, someone whose judgment and expertise we trust. For some of us who are more argumentative, that means a rabbi we can challenge. For others, it is a figure who speaks from authority. As the Mishnah (*Avos* 1:4,16) says, "Make for yourself a rabbi." We make the rabbi by choosing wisely and maintaining a healthy relationship. We accept authority willingly but insist it be wielded responsibly.

Communal Cynicism

I. Miriam's Offense

Miriam's sin and punishment serve as not only a cautionary moral tale about interpersonal care but also the unintended theological consequences of cynicism. Both aspects—behavior and attitude, cognizance of which according to one authority are formalized in a mitzvah observance—are important to take with us as we travel on the Internet.

In Numbers (12:1-16), we learn that Miriam (primarily) and Aharon speak against Moshe, apparently about his marital relationship. They add, "Has God indeed spoken only with Moshe? Has he not also spoken with us?" (12:2). As punishment, Miriam was stricken with the *tzara'as* disease (12:10). The Torah later (Deut. 24:9) declares that we must remember Miriam's punishment, which Ramban (13th century, Spain-Israel; ad loc.; *Sefer Ha-Mitzvos*, supplemental positive commandment 7) lists as a daily obligation. Even *Megillas Esther* (*Sefer Ha-Mitzvos*, ad loc.), whose goal is to defend the Rambam (12th century, Egypt), concedes this point to the Ramban.

Lashon hara, slander, destroys people's lives. It undermines their authority, the reputation they spend years building. Careless words, quick judgments, uninformed conclusions cause real damage. The argument that something is true or that you are willing to be corrected is no defense. Too many on (and off) the Internet fail to remember Miriam's punishment.

II. Valuing Moshe

However, the selection for daily remembrance of *lashon hara* among all the commandments demands explanation. Is it really worse than other interpersonal violations, such as revenge, theft, and shaming? Rav Chaim Soloveitchik (19th-20th centuries, Russia)[129] explained that there is another reason for remembering Miriam's punishment. It reminds us about the qualitative difference of Moshe's prophecy.

Miriam acknowledged that Moshe was a greater prophet than all the rest. However, she failed to recognize that his prophecy was of a different nature. "My servant Moshe is different... with him I speak mouth to mouth, plainly, and not in riddles" (Num. 12:7). Rav Joseph B. Soloveitchik explains:[130]

> Miriam's sin was her failure to acknowledge this difference. The inclusion of the passage referring to her in the *shesh zekhirot* [six daily remembrances] was to emphasize the uniqueness of Moses' prophecy, since acceptance of the authority of his teachings is the foundation of Judaism.

III. Undermining Authority

Rav Menachem Genack (*Birkas Yitzchak Al Ha-Torah*, p. 278) quotes Rav Shmuel Kamenetsky as finding a similar idea in the Rambam's own words. Rambam (*Mishneh Torah, Hilkhos Tzara'as* 16:10) writes:

---

129. Rav Menachem Genack (*Birkas Yitzchak Al Ha-Torah*, p. 278) quotes Rav Joseph B. Soloveitchik as saying this in the name of his grandfather. *Reflections of the Rav* (pp. 123-125) does not mention Rav Chaim.
130. Rav Avraham Besdin, *Reflections of the Rav* (Hoboken, NJ, 1993), pp. 124-125; I thank Rav Elly Storch for bringing this passage to my attention. See also Rav Soloveitchik, *Vision and Leadership* (Hoboken, NJ, 2012), pp. 177-179.

On this, the Torah warns, "Take heed in the plague of *tzara'as*... Remember what the Lord your God did to Miriam, on the way [as you came out of Egypt]" (Deut. 24:8-9). It tells you to consider what happened to Miriam the prophetess. She spoke against her brother, whom she was older than, whom she raised on her knees and for whom she endangered herself to save him from the river. She did not denigrate him but made a mistake by comparing him to the other prophets.

Rambam describes Miriam's sin, her *lashon hara* for which she was so severely punished, as a statement diminishing his prophecy, ultimately undermining the sanctity of the Torah. She intended to criticize an individual but, by doing so, criticized authority and prophecy.

Our attitudes toward others have a compounding effect. Our thoughts take unexpected turns and sometimes rebound in surprising directions. Cynicism about authority figures and leaders, when taken to an extreme, undermines even divine authority. The reverse is also true. Indiscriminate acceptance leads to tolerance of even the most absurd and abhorrent distortions of right and wrong, while indiscriminate rejection descends into moral and theological anarchy. Miriam's lesson is that we need to be cognizant of the unexpected impact of our moral choices and attitudes on our thought processes.

Challenging Your Rabbi

I. Respect

A person can challenge his rabbi in many different ways, some of which undermine his authority socially. There is also a legal venue for a challenge, which we will explore here. If a student believes that his rabbi has committed a financial wrong against him, can the student call him to a religious court? Perhaps the respect due to a Torah teacher prevents this legal action. Rav Avraham Shmuel Binyamin Sofer (19th century, Hungary; *Responsa Kesav Sofer, Yoreh De'ah* 107-109) argues that a student is allowed to follow such a course of action. But he adds two surprising and important points that go beyond technical law.

The case involves a man who wished to sue his father-in-law, who was also his teacher, for money he believed was owed to him. Apparently, Rav Sofer's correspondent found this lawsuit disrespectful and sought the famous rabbi's prohibition. However, Rav Sofer did not comply with the request and instead attempted to deduce a lenient answer from a similar case.

II. Losing to Your Father

The Talmud (*Kiddushin* 32a) debates whether a son must spend his own money to honor his parents or the parents should pay for the financial expenditures. The Rambam (12th century, Egypt; *Mishneh Torah, Hilkhos Mamrim* 6:3) rules that the parents must pay. For example, if the son buys groceries for his parents, he is not required to pay for the food with his own money if his parents can afford it (if they have no money, then he must pay).

However, the Rambam later (ibid. 7) seems to contradict that ruling. He says that a son is obligated to honor his parents even if they throw his wallet into the sea. Apparently the son must pay for his parents' honor. Rav Yosef Karo (16th century, Israel; *Beis Yosef, Yoreh De'ah* 240) differentiates between honoring and dishonoring a parent. A son need not pay to honor his parent; the parent must pay. However, the son may not actively show disrespect to his parent, even if it costs him money. If the only way to stop a father from throwing his son's wallet away is by grabbing it from the father or even tackling him, the son must suffer the financial loss instead.

Rav Sofer adds, based on the language of the Rambam and the *Tur*, that a son must suffer a financial loss rather than insult his parents even if they have money of their own. Unlike honor, for which the son must pay only if the parents lack money, when it comes to dishonor, the son must pay regardless of the parents' financial situation.

III. Protecting Your Assets

This is according to the Rambam. However, Rav Yitzchak of Dampierre (Ri; 12th century, France; quoted in Tosafos, *Kiddushin* 32a sv. *Rav Yehuda*) disagrees. The Ri rules that a son need not lose money in order to honor his parents. *Shulchan Arukh* (*Yoreh De'ah* 240:8) rules like the Rambam, while the Rema (ad loc.) follows the Ri.

According to the Ri, a son may sue his father in religious court in order to avoid losing money. Indeed, the Rosh (quoted by the *Tur*, ad loc.) says this explicitly, and the Rema (ibid.) follows this Rosh. However, one could argue that according to the Rambam a son may never sue his father in a religious court because doing so is arguably insulting and dishonoring the father. Therefore, it would be a dispute between the Rambam and the Ri whether a son can sue his father, and presumably whether a student can sue his rabbi.

IV. Lawsuits and Respect

However, Rav Sofer points out that elsewhere (ibid., 5:15) the Rambam describes the common procedure when a son obligates his father to take an oath, what the son may and may not obligate the father to swear. The case is clearly in a religious court, which implies that a son may sue his father. Rav Sofer considers this conclusive proof that even the Rambam allows a son to sue his father.[131]

As to the disgrace of going to court at one's son's hands, Rav Sofer suggests that either the Rambam does not consider this sufficient dishonor to be prohibited or assumes that from a son's perspective, such a father must be a sinner, whom a son is not required to honor.

Rav Sofer connects the case of suing a rabbi to suing a father. If you may sue your father, even according to the Rambam, then you certainly may sue your rabbi. Rav Sofer later found that the *Sheyarei Kenesses Ha-Gedolah* (*Yoreh De'ah* 250:4) equates the respect of a rabbi to that of a father in the context of a lawsuit. Rav Sofer sees this as supporting evidence that since you may sue your father, you may sue your rabbi.

---

131. He argues that this cannot be a case in which the father brought the lawsuit against the son. If it was, then the father chooses to take the oath and of course the son need not worry about obligating his father in any type of oath. The limitations mean that the son brought the lawsuit.

V. Beyond the Law

Rav Sofer adds two more points that make this series of responsa particularly interesting. Rav Sofer's correspondent was disappointed that he did not receive a prohibitive response. He clearly wanted to hear that this student/son-in-law was violating the law. Rav Sofer chided his correspondent for being blind to his own biases, to what must have been his personal friendship with the rabbi in question. Rav Sofer tells the story of Rav Yehoshua Falk, the sixteenth-century author of the *Sema* (*Sefer Me'irat Einayim* on the *Shulchan Arukh*), who went to court to argue his own case. The judges pointed out that he personally, in his own commentary, had discussed such a case and ruled against his own position. We can all be blinded by bias.

However, Rav Sofer also addresses the student who wanted to sue his rabbi/father-in-law. Clearly, the student felt angry and hurt by his teacher's actions. Is preventing the financial loss really worth the personal loss he would suffer, not to mention the desecration of God's name when a Torah student sues his father-in-law rabbi? What is technically allowed is not always appropriate. *Tehillim* says (Ps. 119:82): "The Torah of your mouth is better to me than thousands of gold and silver." Therefore, he should—not must but should—allow his anger to subside and try to find a compromise.

Rav Sofer suggested that an independent Torah scholar hear both sides of the case to determine whether a lawsuit is appropriate. If it is, the student should go forward (but this scholar may not serve on the court after hearing the case in advance). In this way, a student who suffered serious damage will still have recourse but one who is at fault or who fell victim to a misunderstanding will not create the spectacle of suing his rabbi father-in-law.

Rating Your Rabbi

I. Judging the Judge

Finding the perfect rabbi is an exercise in futility because every person has a unique combination of skills. A rabbi is in the right position when his skills match the needs of most of his congregants. However, those within his community with other needs, who do not fit in with the majority and may wish to look elsewhere for rabbinic services,[132] need the tools to find the right rabbi for them. These tools can be incredibly beneficial to diverse Jewish communities or they can be destructive to careers, rabbinic authority and organized religion in general. The key lies in maintaining a healthy balance between the rights of consumers to receive the best treatment and the rights of service providers for a fair evaluation.

Israel's 2016 Tzohar Law allows people to choose among authorized rabbis across the country for some official Rabbinate services, rather than limiting them to the rabbi of their city. They are customers who wish to use the rabbi who serves their needs best. When the bill was proposed in 2014, Itim, a communal advocacy group that has at times taken a very antagonistic stance toward the Israeli Rabbinate, launched a web app with which the public could rate rabbis and share their experiences. I never saw Itim's app and cannot evaluate it. Instead, I will discuss the concept

---

132. I address here a reality, not necessarily a practice that I approve. See above, "The Decline and Fall of Rabbinic Authority."

in general. Let me reiterate that what follows is not a description nor an evaluation of Itim's app.

Rav Aaron Levine (20th-21st centuries, U.S.), in his *Case Studies in Jewish Business Ethics*[133] (pp. 280-303), discusses the halakhic considerations of student evaluations of teachers. I believe that his discussion can be directly related to the issue of rating a rabbi, with perhaps one additional consideration. An important difference is that teachers' employers support the evaluation process and may even require a self-appraisal. With rabbis, it is unclear how the Israeli Rabbinate will react to these reviews or whether the rabbis will be forced to complete self-appraisals or respond to the customers' reviews. Therefore, what follows is my own summary of many of the issues Rav Levine raises as I believe they apply to this situation. The reader would do well to consult Rav Levine's full discussion.

1. Fair Warning
The first point is that rabbis offer services—those who use those services are customers. Customers deserve to know in advance about defective service providers. If a rabbi consistently mistreats people or overcharges them, customers have the right to be warned. This is not inherently *lashon hara* but, quite the opposite, a mitzvah of saving people from harm ("You shall not stand idly by your neighbor's blood, *lo sa'amod al dam rei'ekha*," Lev. 19:16). If a rabbi rating service appropriately allows future customers to avoid poor service, then it potentially fulfills an important mitzvah—but only if done right.

2. Bias
Let's discuss how to do it right. The first concern is bias. A major problem with most online rating services is that they lack quality

---

133. Hoboken, NJ, 1999.

control. Anyone with a grudge can leave a negative review. As we know, public figures accumulate enemies quickly, usually regular people who are somehow irked but sometimes mentally disturbed people. A proper rating service must filter complaints so that (1) only actual customers with experience can review the service and (2) reviewers are honest and do not display a bias. This can be realistically accomplished, as we will discuss.

3. Relevance

Another concern is relevance. The rating service must address only issues that are relevant to prospective customers. They cannot turn into general complaint forums about the service provider unrelated to the actual service. Nor should unusual demands be portrayed as standard service. If the service provider is asked to do more than usual and fails, the review must include that information rather than simply saying that he failed.

4. Purpose

Additionally, the information should only be provided to prospective customers. Reviews should not become what Rav Levine calls "a matter of curiosity and entertainment" (p. 286). Reading rabbinic reviews can easily become sport, or even worse, in the hands of an unsympathetic media.

5. Timeliness

Hopefully, customer reviews encourage service providers to improve. If so, old reviews should be removed. It is not clear how frequently this must be done but it seems improper to rate a rabbi today based on how he performed ten years ago. A review service should make appropriate measures to ensure that service providers are not punished for old mistakes.

6. Balance

Additionally, the perennial problem of customer reviews is that the unhappy customer complains much more than the satisfied customer praises. This creates an imbalance in the reviews. Rating services must make an effort to obtain a balanced portrait of the service provider.

7. Respect

Finally, all reviews must be written respectfully and constructively. Nastiness and sarcasm detract from the seriousness of this exercise. This rating service is specifically intended to harm people's livelihood and should be undertaken with the fear that a mistake can damage either the customer or the service provider.

Related to this, although not present in Rav Levine's case, is *kevod ha-Torah*, respect for the Torah, its students and its teachers. Rabbis, by their very position, deserve respect. Constructive criticism is appropriate but it must be solicited, provided and—if need be—publicized in a respectful manner. Rabbis should not be above criticism, even strong criticism, but they still deserve to be treated with respect.

II. Proposed Service Terms

The wrong solution is refraining from soliciting customer reviews. That fails to achieve the important goal of warning future customers and also deprives service providers of important feedback that can help them improve. What follows are suggestions based on the above discussion:

1. A rating app of rabbis should allow customers to enter their feedback but requires their submitting identifying information that includes how they received the service and what it was. The service must assure reviewers of confidentiality.

2. The review should consist primarily of yes/no or multiple choice questions that directly reflect the service provided, although a free-form comment must also be allowed so the customer can explain his specific circumstances.
3. The feedback is reviewed by a committee looking to weed out unfair ratings.
4. The free-form reviews are edited for language to ensure they are serious and constructive.
5. Reviews are actively solicited from all customers, those with positive and negative experiences, to ensure balance. Indeed, if this review service becomes popular, rabbis should be told to encourage happy customers to fill out a review. Presumably, the unhappy customers will register their complaints without prompting.
6. The rating app requires prospective customers to actively request reviews of specific rabbis they are considering using. There should be a request feature rather than automatic availability of information on every service provider. While this will be easily undermined by malicious journalists, it puts the burden of *lashon hara* on the journalists and not the organization providing the rating service.

These are my suggestions. I'm interested in hearing what others have to say about developing a positive way of reviewing rabbinic services. I suspect that any such service will be designed in a way that diminishes rabbinic respect. Therefore, I hope that this discussion remains theoretical only.

Retreating From Community: House Minyanim

People arrange a *minyan*, a prayer service, in their home to accommodate someone sick, elderly, or otherwise unable to attend synagogue. When I was a teenager, we had a Shabbos evening *minyan* in someone's basement because the mile-plus walk uphill to the nearest shul was, for many, too long to do twice on a Shabbos. But sometimes people attend a house *minyan*—effectively opting to abandon the community temporarily—out of sheer laziness or the desire to pray quicker and maybe a little bit earlier. A century ago, entrepreneurs would open "mushroom shuls" for the High Holidays in theaters, often praying while the theater was preparing for the next show and/or selling tickets.[134] Is praying in these alternative venues allowed?[135]

To answer this, we need to turn to an episode that occurred in St. Louis in 1951. The quickly growing Young Israel rented a social hall in a local hotel in which to hold its High Holiday prayers. The long-standing Beth Medrash HaGadol objected to this larger venue, which would draw many paying members from the larger and more

---

134. According to Dan Judson ("Mushroom Synagogues" in *The Jewish Week*, May 23, 2011), NY State's 1934 law against selling tickets to non-legitimate places of worship "effectively eliminated" the phenomenon. If so, why was Rav Yosef Henkin, in the responsum discussed below, complaining about them in 1952?
135. See also Rav Aryeh Lebowitz, "House Minyanim," *Torah Musings*, March 12, 2014.

established synagogue, and brought the issue to the attention of Rav Menachem Eichenstein, the Orthodox Chief Rabbi of St. Louis. Rav Eichenstein wrote a responsum forbidding the Young Israel from holding prayers in the rented hall. He sent this responsum to leading authorities who replied with their own responsa, generally agreeing with his conclusion. Among the illustrious respondents were Rav Yonasan Steif, Rav Yosef Eliyahu Henkin, Rav Bentzion Meir Uziel, and Rav Moshe Feinstein. The exchange of letters takes up the first section of the March 1952 issue of the rabbinic journal *Ha-Pardes*,[136] and was republished in the 1955 jubilee volume for Rav Eichenstein, titled *Berakhah Li-Menachem*.[137]

I. Praying at Home And at Shul

The Gemara (*Berakhos* 6a) quotes the following: "Abba Binyamin says: A person's prayer is only heard in a synagogue as it says, 'To hear the singing (*rinah*) and the prayer (*tefillah*)' (1 Kings 8:28) — the place of singing should be the place of prayer." Rabbeinu Tam (12th century, France; Tosafos, *Avodah Zarah* 4b, s.v. *keivan*) explains that if you pray alone but at the same time as the prayers in the synagogue, then your prayer is at a middle level—not rejected. But when you pray in a synagogue, your prayer is always at a higher level—heard. Similarly, Rambam (12th century, Egypt; *Mishneh Torah, Hilkhos Tefillah* 8:1) writes that you should always go to a synagogue. *Lechem Mishneh* explains that Rambam is ruling that even if you have to pray without a *minyan*, you should pray alone in a synagogue. This would seem to render a house *minyan* less than ideal.

The Talmud Yerushalmi (*Berakhos* 4:4) quotes R. Yochanan as saying that someone who prays in his home is as if he is

---

136. http://hebrewbooks.org/pdfpager.aspx?pgnum=5&req=12648&st=
137. http://www.hebrewbooks.org/43841

surrounded by iron. R. Yochanan seems to be saying that it is good to pray at home. The Yerushalmi challenges this from the saying of R. Chiya in the name of R. Yochanan that you must pray in a place designated for prayer, i.e., a synagogue. According to R. Yochanan, is praying at home good or bad? The Yerushalmi answers that one saying refers to praying with a congregation and the other refers to praying alone. *Pnei Moshe* (ad loc.) explains that if you are praying alone, without a *minyan*, you should pray at home in solitude to improve your concentration. However, the *Gilyon Ha-Shas* (ad loc.) points out that this interpretation contradicts the ruling that you should always pray in a synagogue, even without a *minyan*.

Rav Uziel explains the Yerushalmi's resolution in the opposite way. A *minyan* can pray in a private house and be confidently surrounded by iron. However, an individual, praying alone, must pray in the synagogue. The Rif and Rosh quote R. Yochanan as saying that a person's prayers are only heard in the synagogue; therefore you must pray at the time that a *minyan* is praying. Rav Uziel explains that if an individual prays at home but at the same time as the *minyan* in synagogue, it is as if he prays with the *minyan*. With this, Rav Uziel explains the Rambam in a different way than the *Lechem Mishneh* quoted above. Rambam (ibid.) writes that you should always try to pray with a *minyan*, if possible, and that you should go to the synagogue in the morning and evening because prayer is only heard from the synagogue. The first part, Rav Uziel explains, refers to a *minyan*, which can pray anywhere. The second refers to someone praying alone, which preferably must be done in a synagogue.

Based on the opinion of Rav Yechezkel Landau (18th century, Austria; *Tzelach, Berakhos*, ad loc., s.v. *ein*), Rav Eichenstein explains the Yerushalmi differently—that both cases refer to prayer without a *minyan*. If a *minyan* is in the synagogue but has finished prayers, you should pray in the synagogue alone because you are still with a congregation. But if the synagogue is empty, then pray at home without fear, as if you are surrounded by iron.[138]

According to Rav Eichenstein and the sources he quotes (Rav Landau and the *Lechem Mishneh*), you have to pray in a synagogue if possible, which rules out house *minyanim* as a regular option. According to Rav Uziel, you can pray anywhere with a *minyan*. Of course, this is all about the best practice. When you cannot attend synagogue, as a temporary situation, you still have to pray and may gather a *minyan* almost anywhere.

II. Other Places

Rav Uziel adds that every community must establish a permanent place for prayer. While temporary prayer with a *minyan* is allowed elsewhere, permanent prayer must take place in a designated area. Rav Uziel quotes *Yoma* (9b), which says that the first Temple was destroyed because it was used for two things—worship to God and worship to idolatry. While idolatry is certainly a terrible sin, the focus of the Gemara on the dual usage of the Temple implies that any other usage is inappropriate. The Temple, and a synagogue, must be designated solely for divine worship.

People are obligated to build a synagogue. The *Shulchan Arukh* (*Orach Chaim* 150:1) rules that townspeople can force each other to build it. Rav Uziel quotes the Chida (18th century, Israel) in *Machazik Berakhah* (cited in *Sha'arei Teshuvah* 90:4) who says in the name of *Malki Ba-Kodesh* that someone who prays with a *minyan* in a house is not called a bad neighbor (see *Berakhos* 8a). However, he has not fulfilled the obligation to build a synagogue unless the place where they pray is a permanent place of holiness. Rav Henkin (in his responsum, later published as *Gevuros Eliyahu*, vol. 1, no. 24, sec. 5) writes similarly, based on his own

---

138. Surprisingly, Rav Eichenstein quotes an interpretation offered by Prof. Louis Ginzberg, although he proceeds to disagree with it.

understanding. Therefore, praying in a living room or a basement used for other things is inappropriate on a permanent basis. If you want to have a *minyan* in your house, you have to designate that area solely for prayer.

However, another consideration is praying in a place where frivolities and even sins take place. *Taz* (17th century, Poland; *Orach Chaim* 154:1) rules that you may not rent a room for prayer if the room above it is unclean. Doing so shows disrespect to the prayer. Rav Eichenstein explains that "unclean" refers to spiritual, as well as physical, uncleanliness. Rav Eichenstein quotes Rav Moshe Schick (19th century, Hungary; Responsa, *Orach Chaim*, no. 7), who rules that you may not turn an animal pen into a synagogue because it shows disrespect to the mitzvah of prayer. Disrespect of a mitzvah is biblically forbidden, as we see in Shabbos (22a) regarding the biblical commandment to cover the blood of a slaughtered animal. We are not allowed to push dirt over the blood with our feet, because that would be disrespectful to the mitzvah.

Rav Moshe Feinstein (in his responsum later published as *Iggeros Moshe, Orach Chaim*, vol. 1, no. 31) quotes the *Ba'eir Heitev* (151:1) in the name of Rav Eliyahu Mizrachi as saying that a synagogue does not lose its holiness if someone sins it. In that case, a communal functionary had consorted with a young lady in the synagogue. Despite the desecration, the synagogue's holiness remains intact and may continue being used for prayer. Rav Feinstein offers suggestions why that is true but points out that the question assumes that generally we should not pray in a place where sins take place.

Rav Yonasan Steif adds that the first verse in *Tehillim* says: "Blessed is the man… nor sits in the seat of the scornful." Even when the sinful activity has ended, we may not sit in their seats and certainly not pray there.

III. Conclusion

Most house *minyanim* are not held in a room where blatant sins take place. However, they may be held in a room of frivolity, for instance a living room with a television. One can debate whether that is an appropriate place for prayer. However, it is not an appropriate place for ongoing prayer, such as a weekly *minyan*. That should be held in a place designated for prayer. Of course, these rules are such that extenuating circumstances allow for exceptions. If the synagogue is very far away, and many people may refrain from praying with a *minyan*, or if someone sick or elderly cannot attend synagogue, there may be room for leniency. In such cases, you should consult a rabbi.

Rav Eichenstein mentions at the end of his responsum in the 1952 journal that the Young Israel accepted his ruling and acted accordingly. In the 1955 version of the responsum, published in Rav Eichenstein's jubilee volume, he added that the Young Israel had since bought a large building which has plenty of room for the congregants. Rav Eichenstein concludes with a prayer that the Young Israel continue to grow in size and to influence the youth to follow the path of the Torah. Rav Eichenstein also noted that while he prohibited the Young Israel from renting the hall, he denied that the Beth Medrash HaGadol had any claims against the other synagogue for taking away members. People can choose to attend whichever synagogue they want.

Conversion Guidelines, Transparency, and Accountability

I. Three Paths to Distrust

The Orthodox Jewish community is currently experiencing a devastating lack of confidence in its leadership.[139] The seemingly ceaseless scandal after scandal, headline after headline, have taken their toll. If we can't trust the leadership, how can we continue as a community? There are three things we need to consider.

First, look beyond the four cubits of our community. The distrust in leadership is a global phenomenon. This should make us think, ask questions to which I do not claim to have the answers. Is there some poisonous leadership attitude in the general culture that has infected all segments? Maybe our culture gives leaders a sense of invincibility that allows them to take advantage of their situations. Or maybe the culture of celebrity and corporate superstar provides those in possession of leadership skills an attitude of entitlement.

The media culture certainly contributes to our distrust of leadership. The emphasis on scandals, even the creation of misdeeds out of what may otherwise be called misjudgment, affects all of us. Additionally, much of our communal conversation can be partisan, pitting one group against another, creating enemies who seek to knock each other down rather than discuss the issues.

---

139. This essay originally appeared in *The Jewish Link of New Jersey*, July 16, 2015.

Second, what would we do without leaders? How would we be able to function? We can certainly muddle through for a while but at some point, we would flounder and cease functioning. Shuls need rabbis. Communities need institutions which need senior management. We can limit the roles of these leaders; we can turn rabbis into sermonizers and teachers rather than role models and communal guides, which has already happened in some places; we can turn the heads of communal institutions into middle management, rather than senior leadership. We can do all that but, in turn, we will deprive our community of strong leadership. Maybe that is worth the price but the decision and its repercussions are part of a discussion we need to have before going down that path.

Third, what can we learn from the general culture? What techniques have been developed in corporate America, for example, to maintain leadership while curbing abuses? There are management consultants who specialize in governance, the careful balance between leadership and responsibility. Yet, as we consider applying any of these techniques, we also have to wonder how successful they have been in curbing abuse of power. From what I can tell, powerful people still abuse their roles, well beyond the confines of the Jewish community.

II. Encouraging Good Leadership

We, as a community, must be able to tolerate leadership mistakes made in good faith. We can live with good people who cannot see and know everything and therefore make decisions that, in retrospect, were wrong. We can even live with people who sometimes make bad decisions. But we dare not tolerate evil. We cannot allow into leadership positions people who lie, steal, or abuse.

We, laypeople and leaders of the Jewish community, need to enable good leaders while curbing their power to prevent abuse.

There are two keys to this task: transparency and accountability. If we are ever to regain faith in our leaders, these two words need to be the motto of the Jewish community.

Transparency is about clarifying expectations and allowing others to review progress. "And you shall be clear before the Lord and before Israel" (Num. 32:22) is an important principle in *halakhah* that demands extra measures of communication to avoid misunderstanding. When there is greater mistrust, there is greater need for transparency to regain that trust. Sometimes real-life situations are ambiguous. Transparency offers clarity on what is allowed and what is not; it prevents abuse. Leaders need to prove to the community with action, not just words, that they deserve trust. And with greater transparency comes greater accountability—we will be able to see mishandling and stop it.

The Torah administers punishment for multiple reasons. One is recompense, payback for the damage. Another is removal of evil from the community ("and you shall remove the evil from Israel"). Another is to serve as a deterrent for future misbehavior ("and all the people shall hear and fear and no longer act presumptuously" — Deut. 17:12-13). Accountability not only punishes people who do wrong, it prevents people from taking the fateful step over the sometimes gray line into abuse of power. Fear is an important motivator, especially in ambiguous situations.

A few years ago, the Rabbinical Council of America (RCA), of which I am a member, released recommended changes to its conversion protocols after a scandal and a lengthy evaluation process. These changes, and the process underlying them, broke new ground and showed us the direction Jewish communal organizations need to take. It's time for change; the RCA is leading the way.

III. Rabbinic Wild West

I moved to Brooklyn in 1994. At the time, the Orthodox Union had recently announced that it would no longer accept the kosher supervision of the Vaad HaRabonim of Flatbush. This local rabbinic organization had no official standards and instead allowed individual rabbis to set their own standards. In other words, customers had to ask a lot of questions in order to find out what they were getting. Effectively, this type of kosher supervision was a Wild West situation, with every sheriff making his own law, or at least his own legal decisions.

This system was a remnant of the chaos that was kosher supervision in the late nineteenth and early twentieth centuries. It allowed for rabbinic independence—certainly an important value—but also rampant fraud and corruption. When the kosher supervision agencies began setting standards, they offered transparency and consistency while dramatically decreasing fraud and corruption (completely eliminating fraud and corruption is a nice goal but let's not hold anyone to an impossible standard). It is still common to hear complaints about the kosher supervision agencies and some of these complaints are valid. But they pale in comparison to the fraud and corruption of the Wild West system of kosher supervision. The Vaad HaRabonim of Flatbush has since changed its kosher supervision policies and restructured and rebranded the kosher organization as Vaad HaKashrus of Flatbush, which is widely respected locally.

Prior to 2007, the Wild West system reigned in Orthodox conversions to Judaism. Back then, the RCA and its affiliated *beis din*, the Beth Din of America (BDA), would certify specific conversions if asked, only after investigating the details of the conversion after the fact. Beginning in 2007, the RCA established a system by which conversions would be systematically approved by following the Geirus Policies and Standards (GPS). GPS was intended to standardize the process, to allow for an alternative to the Wild West model.

After one of the GPS leaders was convicted of grossly abusing his power, the RCA poured resources into reevaluating its GPS guidelines. The results show marked progress toward transparency and accountability. Rabbis are required to provide details of the process in advance; prospective converts are provided guidance beyond their rabbi's control; complaints are taken seriously and investigated.

In the end, though, the proof will be in the implementation. Will the guidelines be enforced? Will rabbis be held accountable for failing to follow the rules? Slavish adherence to rules creates an unwieldy bureaucracy. Abandonment of the rules creates a Wild West situation. Our communal institutions need to learn from the RCA's current efforts. Transparency and accountability are difficult to implement because they require relinquishing managerial freedom. But if our community is to have the leadership it deserves, it needs to demand transparency and accountability.

Conversion Control In Israel

In 2015, a number of leading Religious Zionist rabbis announced that they would open a private conversion court.[140] After years of trying to change the laws, attain the position of Chief Rabbi and negotiate with the Chief Rabbinate, Rav David Stav, Rav Nachum Rabinovich, and others decided to proceed without the Chief Rabbinate. This scandalized some of their colleagues, leading to public denouncements and confrontations. What is this all about?

I. Ideology and Politics
Two simultaneous issues are being debated here, one ideological and the other halakhic. For decades, the Chief Rabbinate has been summarily ignored by Charedi and secular Israelis, except reluctantly when required by law. The primary constituency of the Chief Rabbinate is the Religious Zionist community, which can roughly be broken into moderate (Dati Leumi) and stringent (Chardal) factions.

Recently, Charedim (appear to) have taken control of the Chief Rabbinate, including the positions of Chief Rabbi, religious judges, and many bureaucratic roles. Their decisions largely do not reflect the religious sensibilities of Religious Zionists. In turn,

---

140. This essay originally appeared in *The Jewish Link of New Jersey*, August 20, 2015.

the Religious Zionist public is increasingly looking to its leading rabbis, rather than the Chief Rabbis, for spiritual and halakhic guidance. In other words, the Chief Rabbinate has lost its main constituency. The cynical among us may claim that this was a Charedi plot to destroy the Chief Rabbinate.

Currently, the Chief Rabbinate's main roles are kosher certification, conversion, and marriage. Charedim have their own private kosher certifications, marriage registrars, and conversion courts. Religious Zionists (Dati Leumi) have experimented with private kosher certification and non-Rabbinate weddings. The next step was a private conversion court. Critics, particularly among leading Chardal rabbis, charge this initiative with significantly chipping away at the authority of the Chief Rabbinate. What will be left for the institution if Religious Zionists undermine its remaining authority with private initiatives?

While this is certainly a political argument, it is primarily ideological. Religious Zionists, particularly among the Chardal, see the Chief Rabbinate in messianic terms. We pray three times a day in the *Amidah* for the return of the centralized religious judicial system. The Chief Rabbinate is not the fulfillment of that prayer but its precursor. It represents a step in the flowering of the Redemption. Seen in those terms, undermining the Chief Rabbinate is forestalling *Mashiach*. The better strategy is to improve the Chief Rabbinate.

The rabbis instituting this change can counter that this, alone, will not undermine the Chief Rabbinate; the Rabbinate has already fallen, we just need to realize it; or that their well-publicized efforts to reform the Rabbinate from within have failed and this is their attempt to force reform from without. Alternatively, perhaps they reject the messianic view of the Chief Rabbinate and take a pragmatic approach. Maybe they believe that if the institution serves the entire Jewish people, it can do wonders. However, if it fails in its purpose then it should be replaced by other mechanisms to serve the public. Those are the political-ideological issues. There is an additional halakhic element to the debate.

II. Converting Minors

As I understand it, the new conversion court was supposed to serve only children with Jewish fathers but gentile mothers who attend religious public schools (although some critics worry that this court will open the door to other, more liberal courts). These rabbis believe that a child can be converted to Judaism without accepting the commandments. Nearly 20 years ago, Rav Nachum Rabinovich wrote a responsum on the subject so his view is easily confirmed (published as *Siach Nachum*, no. 68).

The basic problem with converting a child is that children are halakhically incapable of accepting on themselves an obligation. While this is obvious regarding infants, it applies equally to anyone who has not reached maturity. How can a child convert to Judaism when acceptance of commandments is a fundamental element of conversion? How do adopted babies become Jewish?

The Gemara (*Kesubos* 11a) states that a child is converted with the intent of the court. Effectively, the officiating rabbis stand in the place of the individual converting (I am being imprecise because there are competing interpretations of this talmudic statement). The Gemara continues that since I can give you something that benefits you without your knowledge or acceptance, a court can confer Judaism on a child without his (legally accepted) knowledge. The issue then turns on when becoming Jewish is a benefit and when not. If the child will likely violate Shabbos and eat non-kosher as an adult, does the probable divine punishment render the conversion a detriment to the child?

This rose to the fore in 1864 when Rav Bernard Ilowy of New Orleans sent a halakhic query to Europe: Can a *mohel* circumcise the son of a Jewish father and a gentile mother? Two great European rabbis debated the issue. Rav Tzvi Hirsch Kalischer (19th century, Germany) permitted circumcising and converting the baby to Judaism even though the child will not observe the Torah. Rav Azriel Hildesheimer (19th century, Germany) argued at length to forbid (see *Responsa Rav Azriel*, vol. 1 nos. 229-230).

Subsequent authorities generally follow one of three positions regarding converting a child whose parents are not mitzvah-observant:

1. You can only convert a child if he will most likely observe the commandments. Significantly, Rav Avraham Kook (19th-20th centuries, Israel) followed this approach (*Responsa Da'as Kohen*, nos. 147-149).
2. You can convert a child if he will probably observe the commandments. For example, if given a Jewish education, there is a good chance he will begin observing Shabbos and keeping kosher, then the conversion is a benefit. Rav Joseph Soloveitchik (20th century, U.S.) followed this approach (*Nefesh Ha-Rav*, p. 245).
3. Merely becoming Jewish is a benefit, regardless of whether the convert becomes observant. While this will not help adults, who must accept the *mitzvos* in order to convert, it permits conversion of a child who must only obtain a benefit for the court to act on his behalf. Rav Moshe Feinstein (20th century, U.S.) seems to have accepted this approach (*Iggeros Moshe, Even Ha-Ezer* 4:26:3).

Rav Nachum Rabinovich (contemporary, Israel) follows this third view (as did Rav Shlomo Goren). Additionally, since these children are in religious schools, there is a chance that they will become observant. More importantly, since they socialize with their schoolmates as peers, they may find their life mate in school. These conversions prevent intermarriage. This is significantly different from the question previous generations faced—converting the child of an intermarriage which would facilitate, perhaps even encourage, intermarriage.

However, most of today's critics are students of Rav Kook's disciples and, given his strict view, they understandably disagree with this leniency. They also point out that these converted children are part of the Russian-Israeli community and may very likely marry a non-converted child of a gentile mother. These conversions may actually increase intermarriage, at least until and if the new conversion activity becomes widespread.

Ultimately, we are dealing with great rabbis debating an important communal issue. Regardless of where you stand, it should be recognized that both sides are acting with halakhic support and the intent to improve the Jewish community.

CHAPTER 5:

COMMUNITY

A community is a being unto itself, with unique traits and characteristics. It is also a group of individuals whose interactions can include friction and confrontation. In order to thrive, a community must navigate through these difficult sitations successfully. In this chapter, we explore different interpersonal challenges that have facced the Jewish community and how the community has tried to address them.

Why Are There Jewish Denominations?

I. Movements in Judaism

Judaism's response to modernity over the centuries has been one of constant change, sometimes small and sometimes large.[141] As attitudes shifted, movements developed. Reform broke from what would later be called the Orthodox mainstream. Conservative broke from Reform. Reconstructionist broke from Conservative. Traditional broke from Conservative. As the Passover song goes, *Chad gadya, chad gadya.*

Why does such a small nation continue to split into smaller pieces of a shrinking pie? I am certain that historians have more insight than I, but allow me to make a simple observation. Aside from basic human nature, there is an important political aspect to the splits. A denomination—a movement—remains viable only when its members care what each other think, when they are willing to listen and respond to one another's concerns. Compromise is the Scotch Tape of unity, clumsily but effectively keeping loose pieces from falling off. When we stop caring about how our colleagues and neighbors react, when we act unilaterally on the most contentious issues, we implicitly create new movements that are only formalized over time.

---

141. This essay originally appeared at Forward.com, Nov. 18, 2013, and is reproduced with permission.

Jonathan Sarna, in an essay[142] discussing a letter published in *Haaretz* from mainstream Orthodox rabbis rejecting recent developments in Open Orthodoxy,[143] astutely sees the letter's historic significance but misses one important—perhaps the most important—element. Sarna correctly notes that the Rabbinical Council of America, an important rabbinic body of Orthodox Judaism today, was itself subject to denunciations from the right in 1938, when it was first founded; however, he could have added even more historical context. Strongly worded objections have a long tradition in the Orthodox community, and for a very good reason.

II. Objections in Judaism
A loosely held movement like Orthodoxy is counterintuitively united by denunciations. As we adapt to changing circumstances, as we test new ideas and practices, we sometimes incorrectly misread our co-religionists' views. Public objections when private conversations fail—sometimes even harsh denunciations like that *Haaretz* letter—are wake-up calls to change direction for the sake of unity. They are uncomfortable, embarrassing and sometimes ugly, but they work. Many have commented that the messy eighteenth-century fight between Chasidim and their opponents ended because the Chasidim moderated their excesses in response to opposition. They stopped acting unilaterally and increased the priority of unity.

Sometimes, of course, there are divisive issues that are more important than unity. There are limits to our ability to compromise, issues that are close to our heart and key to our purpose, but for which we pay a heavy price.

---

142. "Why is Orthodoxy Packing Up Big Tent?" in the *Forward*, November 6, 2013.
143. https://orthodoxrabbis.wordpress.com/2013/10/30/statement-on-open-orthodoxy/

III. Objections to Open Orthodoxy

In 2010, the RCA issued a unanimous statement in opposition to the ordination of women as rabbis, regardless of what title they were given.[144] In 2013, Yeshivat Maharat graduated three *maharats*, women rabbis, who have now been employed by four synagogues. Yeshivat Maharat, founded by Rabbi Avi Weiss and housed in his synagogue along with his Yeshivat Chovevei Torah, is a cornerstone of Open Orthodoxy. Also in 2013, the Jewish Orthodox Feminist Alliance convened a conference on the *agunah* problem, concerning Orthodox women whose husbands do not grant them a religious divorce. Key speakers advocated reviving a long-dormant proposal—many times denounced by leading rabbis—that would effectively reinterpret the Talmud so that troubled marriages could be annulled without the husband's permission.

Despite the strongest objections from mainstream Orthodoxy, Open Orthodoxy has chosen to strike out unilaterally in many ways that other rabbis find discomfiting. For members of the movement, principle has clearly trumped unity. These are actions that therefore threaten to splinter the Orthodox movement.

IV. Moderation for Unity

The letter in *Haaretz*, which was issued by individual rabbis, was in response to Rabbi Asher Lopatin's op-ed declaring his widespread support in mainstream Orthodoxy. The letter might seem like a denunciation of Rabbi Lopatin or even a threat, but it is actually a call for unity. And that is what Sarna's essay overlooks. The letter ends by asking the leaders of Open Orthodoxy to reconsider their unilateral actions. It is a request that they try to find some kind of common ground with the rest of Orthodoxy and not disregard the principles that matter most to their fellow rabbis.

---

144. The RCA issued an even stronger resolution in 2015.

There remains now only the question of whether these Open Orthodox rabbis will start acting like members of a movement who care how their colleagues will react or whether they will go off on their own, acting unilaterally and creating their own movement.

Secession

July 28, 2016, marked 140 years since the Prussian government allowed Jews to secede from the general Jewish community in order to establish separatist, Orthodox communities. Is it a day to celebrate? It depends whom you ask. Rav Samson Raphael Hirsch (19th century, Germany) famously championed *Austritt*, secession, even appealing to leading Hungarian rabbis like Rav Moshe (Maharam) Schick (19th century, Hungary) for support. Rav Azriel Hildesheimer (19th century, Hungary-Germany), who led the modern wing of Hungarian Orthodoxy before leaving for Berlin in 1869, supported *Austritt* as well, but in a different way than Rav Hirsch.

These two personalities—Rav Hirsch and Rav Hildesheimer—represent two different ideologies. Rav Hirsch was an innovative Torah thinker and powerful apologetic writer who successfully built a community of committed laypeople, people who were part of the modern world while remaining staunchly religiously conservative. His movement was called *Torah Im Derekh Eretz*, by which he meant Torah and culture, worldliness.

In contrast, Rav Hildesheimer was a Torah giant whose responsa and talmudic commentaries made an impact on subsequent Torah literature. No less a Charedi figure than Rav Elazar Shach praised Rav Hildesheimer's Torah insights in a 1976 approbation to the latter's novellae on the Talmud, published from manuscript. Rav Hildesheimer, whose students joined him in the traditionalist scientific study of Judaism, was among the greatest figures of *Torah U-Madda* in history. I find it very telling that Rav Hildesheimer's insights into the weekly Torah reading, published at the end of his second volume of responsa, lack any methodological innovation. In style and approach, they are completely traditional, even uninspiring. In contrast, Rav Hirsch's Torah commentary was groundbreaking, combining careful textual readings with thoughts on Jewish philosophy and theology. Rav Hildesheimer's Torah was a traditional Torah while Rav Hirsch's was a new Torah for a new age. But in addition to that traditional Torah, Rav Hildesheimer supported and engaged in new types of academic studies which Rav Hirsch strongly opposed. The two joined forces on certain initiatives but from different perspectives.

In 1873, the Prussian government passed a law allowing Christians and Jews to secede from their religious communities if they renounced their membership in those religions. Both Rav Hildesheimer and Rav Hirsch had joined with other Jewish figures in lobbying for an amendment to this law, allowing Jews to secede from the official Jewish community and establish separate congregations for reasons of conscience. On July 28, 1876, this amendment was signed into law[145] by the king, enabling Orthodox Jews to secede from Reform-dominated communities.[146] Already in 1869, Rav Hildesheimer led a segment of the Berlin Orthodox community (Adass Jisroel) into secession from the main Berlin Jewish community, but until the 1876 change in law, Adass Jisroel members still had to pay a tax to the Jewish community from which they had seceded.

---

145. It is unclear to me whether this was an amendment to an existing law or a new law.
146. On this, see Jacob Katz, *A House Divided* (Hanover, NH, 1998), ch. 22.

Prof. David Ellenson (*Rabbi Esriel Hildesheimer and the Creation of a Modern Jewish Orthodoxy* (Tuscaloosa, AL, 1990), pp. 87-88) writes:

> Throughout this struggle [to pass this amendment], Hildesheimer both supported Hirsch and urged passage of this law.... Hildesheimer's activities on behalf of Orthodox secession from the general Jewish community took other forms. In 1876 his former student Israel Goldschmidt was offered the position of community rabbi in Frankfurt. Hildesheimer wrote to him in February, encouraging him not to accept the position. There were several reasons for this decision... but it is clear that a major one was that he did not want to weaken the *Austrittsgemeinde* (Orthodox secessionist community) in that city. Goldschmidt heeded his teacher's advice and turned down the proffered position. Indeed, a year later Hildesheimer offered similar advice to his outstanding and beloved pupil Marcus David Horovitz, who had been invited to become the Orthodox rabbi of the general Jewish community in Frankfurt. Horovitz defied his teacher's counsel, but Hildesheimer's advice nonetheless indicates his wholehearted commitment to the concept of Orthodox secession, when necessary, from the larger Jewish community....
>
> [Regarding the Frankurt secession debate, Hildesheimer wrote to Lippman Mainz in support of secession.] Hirsch was right to secede from the general Jewish community, and in Hildesheimer's view, Mainz was wrong to oppose Hirsch on this issue.

Prof. Adam Ferziger adds some nuance to the evaluation of Rav Hildesheimer's view. In his *Exclusion and Hierarchy: Orthodoxy,*

Nonobservance and the Emergence of Modern Jewish Identity,[147] he writes:

> However, [the Berlin separatist community] developed a far less rigid perception of communal separation than that espoused by Hirsch and his followers. According to popular legend, when the *austritt* law was passed, in Frankfurt the Orthodox proclaimed, "Blessed are we for having been granted the right to secede," while in Berlin they lamented, "Woe unto us for having reached the point of secession"....
>
> The differences between Berlin and Frankfurt separatist Orthodoxies were not limited, however, to a less antagonistic stance on the part of Berliners toward the non-Orthodox community. Rather, unlike the Hirschians, when it came to issues that were of common interest to all Jews, the Adass Jisroel community and its leaders were willing to work together with other Jews. Hildesheimer, who set the tone for the Adass Jisroel community, cooperated with non-observant Jews in a variety of ways. Within his own locale, he was willing to join with non-Orthodox rabbis and even the leaders of the Berlin *Gemeinde* in order to fight anti-Semitism.... He was directly involved in setting up welfare and educational institutions to serve refugees from Eastern Europe. In this capacity, Hildesheimer, unlike many of his Orthodox colleagues, was willing, once again, to work with non-Orthodox Jews—even ones with whom he had sharp ideological differences or whose lifestyles were antithetical to the religious values he held dear....
>
> In all of the examples of cooperation with the nonobservant described here, the Hirschian separatists

---

147. Philadelphia, PA, pp. 151, 153-154.

were extremely critical of the Berliners. As far as the Frankfurters were concerned, any cooperation with non-Orthodox Jews in an organized framework was tantamount to legitimizing their religious ideology and lifestyle.

I believe there are many parallels between Rav Hildesheimer's approach to interacting with non-Orthodox leaders and organizations, and Rav Soloveitchik's approach, many decades later in America, of distinguishing between internal and external matters.[148]

And in answer to my initial question, according to popular legend quoted by Prof. Ferziger in the above passage, Rav Hirsch and his followers in Frankfurt might wish people a happy *Austritt* day. Rav Hildesheimer and his Berlin congregation would probably consider it a sad day, when Orthodoxy was forced out of the general Jewish community.[149]

---

148. On Rav Joseph Soloveitchik's attitude, see Rav Bernard Rosensweig, "The Rav as Communal Leader" in Rav Menachem Genack ed., *Rabbi Joseph B. Soloveitchik: Man of Halacha, Man of Faith* (Hoboken, NJ, 1998), p. 245ff.

149. For more on Rav Hildesheimer, see my "Rav Hildesheimer's Response to Ultra-Orthodoxy" in *Hakirah* 24 (Spring 2018).

Crossing Denominational Lines

Limmud is a conference, originally in England but replicated around the world, in which Jewish teachers across the denominations lecture on a wide variety of Jewish subjects.[150] For years, Orthodox rabbis have debated whether to attend and teach. In my opinion, there must be an Orthodox presence there but there also needs to be an Orthodox refusal to attend. In 2014, the newly appointed British Chief Rabbi Ephraim Mirvis made news by attending Limmud. While it is widely understood (although unconfirmed) that attendance was an unofficial precondition for the office of chief rabbi, thereby guaranteeing that whoever was appointed would attend, the appearance of so important an Orthodox figure at Limmud generated controversy. Rightly so; his appearance was important and so was the controversy.

I. Honoring and Legitimizing

I see three main issues with attending Limmud. The first is the legitimacy given to the non-Orthodox teachers. Personally, I would be honored to speak at an event where the Chief Rabbi is speaking. My name appearing on the same list as his would mean—to me and to the whole world—that I have made it to the big league, that while I may not have his title, his scholarship, or his talents, I am

---

150. This essay originally appeared in *The Jewish Press*, February 6, 2014.

still at least within spitting distance of one of the most important rabbis in the world. In reality, I am not in that league and have not appeared with him. But, speaking personally, doing so would give me great honor.

I do not believe that the Chief Rabbi, or any important Orthodox figure, should be granting that honor to someone who does not share our core beliefs about Torah, regardless of denominational affiliation (affiliation is much less important than beliefs and practice). A non-believer, or for that matter an unrepentant sinner, should not be raised on an Orthodox pedestal (see *Arukh Ha-Shulchan*, *Yoreh De'ah* 243:4). The Chief Rabbi represents the Torah. His honor is the Torah's and the people whom he honors are the people whom the Torah honors.

I recognize that I am unfairly picking on the Chief Rabbi. Please keep reading to see a fuller picture.

II. Non-Orthodox Teachers
Additionally, if Orthodox rabbis widely embrace Limmud, the Orthodox laity will follow in large numbers. Of course, some will come regardless. But when the Orthodox leadership encourages attendance—whether explicitly or implicitly—many more will come. The nature of Limmud is that presenters represent a broad spectrum of Judaism. Many, currently most, base their teachings on beliefs that Orthodox Jews consider heresy. They will speak about the human authors of the Torah, the bias of the Sages, the immorality of *halakhah* and choosing whether to follow even basic biblical laws. Some will do this directly and some only in passing. Even the most sensitive and sincere teachers will often incorporate their non-Orthodox attitudes within their teachings. The most innocuous subject may include subversive theological ideas, often unintentionally (see Rema, *Yoreh De'ah* 153:1; *Chelkas Mechokek*, *Even Ha-Ezer* 22:6).

If the Orthodox leadership permits attendance at Limmud, they will effectively be permitting Orthodox Jews to study Judaism under non-Orthodox teachers. They will be encouraging the spread of heresy among the faithful. Of course, many Orthodox Jews will be able to intellectually deflect these foreign assumptions and beliefs, perhaps even growing stronger from the challenge. But ideas have wings; they excite and inspire. This is especially true when the intellectual match is uneven, when the non-Orthodox best and brightest are teaching the Orthodox not-so-best and not-so-brightest. There is a risk, a very real risk, that some Orthodox Jews will become enchanted by the passionate spokespeople of non-Orthodox Judaism.

I am not saying that non-Orthodox scholars have nothing to teach us. Quite the opposite. They offer a fresh perspective that will take us out of our comfort zones and force us to look anew at well-worn texts. It is precisely because they have much to teach us that we have to be very careful about the unconscious and insidious desanctification of sacred texts.

When the Chief Rabbi attends Limmud, or when *roshei yeshiva* or yeshiva presidents attend, and their actions are widely publicized, they are effectively permitting the Orthodox masses to go. They are saying that there is nothing wrong with studying under non-Orthodox teachers. Come, hear the Chief Rabbi speak, and while you're here you must attend this session on this topic that interests you taught by a bare-headed Reform rabbi who neither observes Shabbos nor *kashrus*. Or worse, by a yarmulke-wearing Reform rabbi who observes Shabbos and *kashrus* but will teach that you do not have to.

III. Unity and Outreach

On the other hand, the Orthodox impact on the non-Orthodox attendees can be enormous. Sitting together as friends breaks down misconceptions on both sides and promotes communal unity. When the Orthodox refuse to attend, the non-Orthodox are insulted, with untold consequences on the individual and communal level. And when the Orthodox engage the non-Orthodox on a personal level, extended families are reunited and broader communities are joined in harmony (and *yeshivos* are funded).

There is an additional element of outreach. Many non-Orthodox Jews have never met a refined and intelligent Orthodox Jew. They expect Orthodox Jews to be socially and intellectually backwards. The impact of this type of interaction has brought many people to Orthodoxy, including non-Orthodox rabbis. This is particularly true when an Orthodox scholar teaches, offering an intelligent and compelling worldview. There is great outreach potential at Limmud. An Orthodox rabbi has the unique opportunity to teach an audience thirsty for knowledge and often unaware of basic traditional texts and concepts.

I am not suggesting that an Orthodox rabbi scan the audience, targeting those most vulnerable. When an Orthodox rabbi gets up and speaks intelligently, he has already broken down barriers. When he sits and shmoozes with his neighbors, he has changed perceptions. And if he inspires his audience with a particularly good lecture, he has drawn people closer to Orthodoxy. All I am suggesting is that an Orthodox scholar do his best teaching job and that alone will frequently accomplish wonders.

IV. Golden Mean
The Chief Rabbi's attendance at Limmud probably helped dozens return to Jewish observance as *ba'alei teshuvah*, even if not immediately. He stole the show, breaking down barriers and drawing people closer to traditional Judaism.

The question is how to balance this incredibly positive impact with the competing concerns. I suggest, as a theoretical proposal and not practical guidance, that, absent the crushing pressure the Chief Rabbi faced, only Orthodox scholars who are not in prominent positions attend Limmud. When they are not high profile figures, they will not attract the attention and offer the legitimacy that is so problematic. Few will say that since the assistant rabbi of some synagogue taught at Limmud, I may attend as well. Of course, some Orthodox people will go, but they are the people who would go anyway. And those Orthodox teachers who attend should not actively encourage laypeople to go; they might even privately discourage attendance.

Their role is not that of a trailblazer, clearing the way for others to follow, but as ambassadors of Orthodoxy. Their goal is to participate, make friendships, and teach their hearts out. In this way, the dangers of legitimization and permission are largely mitigated while the benefits of participation are maintained. Perhaps this is an appropriate recipe for Limmud success.

Will Charedi Ideology Change?

I. Three-Step Solution

Helping those who are suffering is a natural instinct and a religious imperative. Yet accomplishing this assistance on a societal scale is frustratingly elusive. We live in the most prosperous society in history yet we have millions of starving people in our midst. In a provocative essay in *Commentary* magazine, Arthur C. Brooks, president of the American Enterprise Institute, proposes a conservative agenda to fight poverty that resonated with me.[151] In it lie the key principles to solving the rampant poverty that currently plagues the Israeli Charedi community.

Brooks sets three prongs to his approach: transformation, material relief, and opportunity. You cannot save people from poverty if they are morally or ideologically incapable of escaping it. We must give them the tools to take responsibility for their own wellbeing, often but not necessarily through religious means.

We must also provide material relief. You cannot start a business without capital. You cannot even think of starting a business without food. The "safety net" is a crucial part of saving people from literally dying of starvation in the streets. No society should allow such suffering.

---

151. "Be Open-Handed Toward Your Brothers" in *Commentary*, February 2014.

And finally, no one can escape poverty without employment opportunity and the training necessary to work productively. Education is the key to escaping poverty. Those who cannot communicate effectively or perform basic business tasks will not be able to find jobs.

II. Meaningful Change

How does this relate to the Charedi community in Israel? Material relief is provided by the government in abundance, even if in significantly decreasing amounts due to budget cuts. But is this welfare designed to increase or decrease dependence? I don't know. Welfare should be designed to encourage, not discourage, job training and employment. While the unemployable cannot be abandoned, those who can work must be financially encouraged to leave the welfare rolls.

While material support in some sense exists, the other two principles are lacking. Charedim receive pitifully little secular education, which prevents many (but not all) from escaping poverty. Perhaps most importantly, Charedi society in Israel looks down on employment, considering lifetime study the ideal. Without ideological transformation, without an attitude that economic self-sufficiency (through divine beneficence) is the ideal, many people will be unable to successfully support their families.

Battling Charedi poverty requires changing emphases in Charedi ideology. This is not something outsiders can do. It can only come from the inside, whether from the top down (i.e., rabbinic fiat) or through grass roots, through an uncontrollable attitudinal shift of the populace. Education reform will accompany that ideological change.

As someone who believes that the Torah places a high value on gainful employment, I hope the leading Charedi rabbis will take the lead in this necessary ideological shift. I have been waiting many years for it to happen and maybe the time will come soon. The other possibility, the grass roots shift, will prove uncontrollable and almost certainly will also include other ideological changes that may be less theologically orthodox. Only time will tell.

Why We Fight

I. Endless Debate

The Jewish community seems constantly engaged in battle. Aside from the normal friction that is part of any group dynamic, we also experience prolonged and bitter ideological conflicts. The Left insults the Right, and vice versa. Some Orthodox groups denounce the Reform movement, and vice versa. One group rejects another's kosher supervision and that group rejects the first's treatment of converts. And so on and so on.

The discord is frustrating and exhausting. These are good people with good intentions, all trying to do the right thing. Yet they fight with a stubbornness that continues to disappoint our desire for harmony. Why can't we all get along? A community divided against itself cannot stand. Why can't we put our disagreements to the side and focus on the many areas on which we agree? Perhaps there is another way to look at this, a perspective in which this phenomenon is something for which we should be grateful.

The Mishnah (*Avos* 5:21) says that a dispute that is for the sake of Heaven will endure. Shouldn't it be the opposite? If people are truly sincere, they should be able to resolve their differences. Their disagreement should not endure. Yet the Mishnah states that it will last. I found an answer while reading Hillel Halkin's recent biography of Vladimir Jabotinsky, the famous Zionist leader.[152]

---

152. *Jabotinsky: A Life* (New Haven, CT, 2014).

In the early twentieth century, when Zionist activity was at its pre-State peak, Jabotinsky was a passionate advocate of armed defense. He envisioned Jews fighting for their rights by establishing local self-defense patrols and an active underground army in British-controlled Palestine. His movement, the forerunner of the Likud party in Israel, determinedly sought broad representation, if not domination, in the World Zionist Organization. This put Jabotinsky in direct competition with David Ben-Gurion, whose party ultimately won control.

II. Zionist Discord
What struck me while reading this account was the level of vitriol in this dispute. These two great leaders, both of whose goal was establishing a Jewish homeland in Israel, harshly denounced each other's ideas. Not only was the rhetoric heated but there was actual physical violence. Halkin writes (p. 181):

> Groups of demonstrators interrupted and heckled both men. Violent brawls were frequent. In Warsaw, Ben-Gurion was attacked with Revisionist stink bombs and bricks; in Brisk, Jabotinsky was stoned by a Labor Zionist mob. The level of invective was fierce. Jabotinsky called the Zionist Left "lackeys of Moscow." Ben-Gurion referred to him as "Vladimir Hitler"....

Why the nastiness and infighting? Jews are a tiny minority in the world and, among them, Zionists are a small group. These disputants all agreed on so much yet they magnified their differences, dwelling on the areas of dispute rather than points of convergence. Why couldn't the Zionists get along?

III. Passionate Disagreement

We need to look deeper. Rather than focusing on the disputes, we need to think about the reason for the disagreements. Certainly, there was an element of personality but I think the primary reason is simple: they cared. Both Ben-Gurion's and Jabotinsky's followers cared deeply about their Zionism. The stakes were very high—a Jewish homeland—and these people were so involved, had so much of their being invested in these issues, that they magnified every point of disagreement. Their conflicts were not due to a lack of care for other Jews but because they cared so much. Passion, not stubbornness, is the basis of ardent ideological debate.

So too, today, the people who fight care just as much as the Zionists of yesteryear, even if they are less violent. Passion seeds our disputes. We care so much about our issue that we see loss as failure with profound consequences. Whatever the issue is—education, Torah, equality—we embrace it with such passion that this leads to discord. We fight because we care.

To some degree, we should be happy about this. No, I don't like nasty rhetoric, denunciations, or fistfights, and I am certainly not calling for more of them. However, I see infighting as a sign that we can overcome the greatest threat to Judaism today. Some see intermarriage as the primary enemy of Jewish continuity. Others see Jewish illiteracy as the culprit. I believe it is apathy.

Too many people simply don't care enough about Judaism to even make an effort. At most, they identify as a Jew, some only when it is necessary or convenient. And even those who identify as Jews are often so distracted by media, so glued to their screens, that their Judaism is only a passing thought. People who fight about Judaism care about it. Those who debate the most ferociously about Jewish ideology are those who care so deeply about it that they have intertwined these issues with their own identity.

We need more people who care deeply about Judaism. We are losing souls to apathy. Thank God, we still have some fighters left among us. They are the future of Judaism.

The Agunah Debate Continues

Ideas are important, especially when put into practice.[153] Legal theories can change the world. Debates over legal theories can impact the community and well beyond, even before the ideas are implemented. I believe that in the latest debate over rabbinic action on behalf of *agunos*, a key point has been misunderstood.

In 2015, Rav Hershel Schachter published a public letter to rabbis, strongly advising them against relying on rulings of the International Beit Din for Agunot.[154] Among his arguments was that a responsum by one of this *beis din*'s judges was "mistaken from beginning to end."

I. *Get Zikkui*

Rav Schachter was referring to a paper presented by Rav Simcha Krauss on December 25, 2014, in a public discussion with Rav Jeremy Wieder and Prof. Chaim Saiman (neither of whom agreed with Rav Krauss). Rav Krauss argued at length that a *beis din* can give a *get* to a woman on behalf of a recalcitrant husband even if he objects (called a *get zikkui*). Indeed, this is a radical claim that provides a solution to the plight of the *agunah*. Rav Wieder strongly

---

153. This essay originally appeared in *The Jewish Link of New Jersey*, September 8, 2015.
154. "Advising Against the Use of the International Beit Din: A Translated Letter From Rabbi Hershel Schachter, Shlita," *Jewish Link of New Jersey*, September 3, 2015.

critiqued this paper. Likewise, Rav Schachter argued that this approach is not only unprecedented but also completely mistaken.

Rav Krauss stated, in a response, that he presented two recent precedents to Rav Schachter, who was unaware and uninterested.[155] In fact, Rav Schachter was correct that neither case serves as a precedent for Rav Krauss' proposal. The portrayal in Rav Krauss' letter of Rav Schachter as uninterested and unaware, or at least that perception which was felt by many readers, is strange—given Rav Schachter's encyclopedic knowledge and interests—and unfair, as we will soon see.

But first an important point. Rav Krauss' responsum represents only his own view and not that of the *beis din*. Other judges on the court may feel differently and rule against this proposal. Nor has this proposal been acted upon. However, as the leading judge of the *beis din* and its driving force, Rav Krauss' opinion on this radical proposal to solve the *agunah* problem is highly relevant.

Additionally, before we address the specific issue under concern, let us also note that Rav Krauss personally criticized harshly another proposal to solve the *agunah* problem. When Rav Emanuel Rackman initiated his Bet Din Tzedek L'ba'ayot in 1998, *The Jewish Week* quoted Rav Simcha Krauss as saying, "This has nothing to do with right-wingers and left-wingers but with the integrity of *gittin* (religious divorces).… I will not make a joke of the halakhic system and that is what is happening here." These are weighty matters that bring out passion and concern, both by Rav Krauss and Rav Schachter.

II. Precedents

Rav Krauss cites two precedents for his *get zikkui*. This first is a relatively recent ruling of a *beis din* in Safed about a vegetative

---

155. "Response to Rav Schachter's Criticism of the International Beit Din on Torahweb.org," *Jewish Link of New Jersey*, September 3, 2015.

or near-vegetative man on whose behalf the court gave a divorce to his wife. This ruling was roundly criticized, particularly by Rav J. David Bleich in an exhaustive 73-page article in the journal *Tradition* (48:1, Spring 2015). Regardless, the ruling does not serve as a relevant precedent because in that case, the husband was not objecting. Rather, he was unresponsive for medical reasons. Rav Krauss' case, in which the husband openly protests the actions on his behalf, takes the matter much further.

The second precedent is a responsum by Rav Shalom Messas, written shortly before his passing in 2003 and published in Volume 4 of his *Responsa Shemesh U-Magen*. The issue was a hotly contested divorce case in Brooklyn, ugly on more levels than is usual for a divorce. A Brooklyn *beis din* permitted a woman to remarry without a *get*, causing a rabbinic controversy. The question was sent to Rav Ovadia Yosef, who passed it on to Rav Messas. This is not the place to discuss the entire controversy, including the many rumors and accusations. The only relevant issues here are the facts and arguments in Rav Messas' responsa, which I believe support Rav Schachter and not Rav Krauss.

III. *Shemesh U-Magen*

In *Responsa Shemesh U-Magen* (vol. 4, no. 100), Rav Messas explains the facts presented to him. In 2001, a young American Charedi woman married a man she thought was a normal Charedi man, with plans to be supported by her parents for four years while he learned in *kollel*. After a year and a half, she learned that her husband had been consistently stealing from her sister's brother-in-law, to which he confessed in (secular) court. The wife also learned that her husband frequented prostitutes, and therefore she demanded a divorce. A *beis din* in Jerusalem ruled, without the husband's presence at the proceedings, that he can be forced to give her a *get*. The husband then disappeared and his family demanded millions of dollars from the wife's family, threatening violence if the husband was physically coerced to give a *get*. The Brooklyn *beis din* provided testimony from a Johannesburg *beis din* that the husband had frequented prostitutes even before the marriage, as well as results of an investigation indicating that he took drugs and violated the laws of Yom Tov and *kashrus*.

Therefore, the woman requested annulment of her marriage since she never agreed to marry a man who frequents prostitutes. Such a man may not have marital relations because of concerns he may transmit AIDS (presumably HIV) to his wife. If she had known that she could not consummate her marriage without entering this life-threatening danger, she would never have married the man. This is quite a surprising argument on many counts, which is why it led to a rabbinic controversy. For our purposes, we will only discuss Rav Messas' analysis.

Rav Messas objects to outright annulment. While it is true that Rav Moshe Feinstein annulled marriages in this way, Rav Messas considers this a minority opinion. However, he will annul a marriage if there is also another reason to be lenient. In this case, he notes that when there is danger to the woman, this constitutes an additional reason for leniency. Therefore, since there is no possibility of obtaining a *get* from the husband, he ruled that the marriage can be annulled.

Rav Messas then adds that, "as a mere stringency" (*chumra be-alma*), it would be best ("*mah tov u-mah na'im*") for the court to give a *get* as the agent on behalf of the husband. While he would permit the woman to remarry without a *get*, Rav Messas suggests that a *get zikkui* be given as a stringency.

Importantly, Rav Messas adds that all this requires the consent of Rav Ovadia Yosef.

IV. Analysis

Not only doesn't this ruling support Rav Krauss' proposal, it bolsters Rav Schachter's argument. Rav Krauss proposed giving a *get* on behalf of a husband who objects. In this case, the husband had disappeared and was not directly objecting. That is an important difference. Rav Krauss wants to take this a step further.

But more importantly, Rav Messas only offered this suggestion as a "mere stringency." He had other arguments to permit annulment that, in his view, were entirely sufficient without this stringency. There is no indication that Rav Messas would permit ending a marriage merely by *get zikkui*.

And finally, Rav Schachter's main objection was the initiation of radical solutions without the approval of leading rabbis. Rav Messas shared that concern and therefore conditioned his ruling on the consent of Rav Ovadia Yosef. Like Rav Schachter, he insisted on the review and approval of a leading expert. Note that, at the time, Rav Messas was approaching the age of 90 and had served as a rabbi since the age of 36. Yet he recognized that difficult decisions on such matters require expertise and at least a modicum of consensus. That is Rav Schachter's point.

V. Continuation

But the matter continues in the next responsum (no. 101). A week and a half later, Rav Messas published a responsum explicitly retracting his ruling based on new information. The husband's father came to Rav Messas and proved with laboratory results that his son does not have HIV. He said that his son was "missing" because he was in jail over the theft, and that the testimony from the Johannesburg *beis din* was taken from inadmissible witnesses. Based on this, Rav Messas retracted his entire ruling and demanded a new *beis din* case on the divorce.

Significantly, this second responsum contains an addendum from Rav Ovadia Yosef rejecting the original ruling even without the new evidence. In other words, Rav Messas conditioned his original ruling on the consent of Rav Yosef, which was not forthcoming. This is in addition to Rav Messas' retraction based on new evidence.

All this is hardly precedent for a new and radical solution to the *agunah* problem. The communal problem of the *agunah* can only be solved through consensus. Permitting a woman to remarry under questionable circumstances irresponsibly threatens her and her future children with tragic consequences, effectively turning a bad situation into an even worse situation. As we have seen above, there are sometimes solutions for difficult cases. Other times, the hands of the judges are tied. In those cases, creative paths are available to legitimately convince the husband to willingly give a *get*.

The Convert Problem

I. The Problem
While Israeli rabbis and politicians debate conversion standards,[156] afflicting many converts with confusion and difficulty during this transitional period, a local problem of greater personal significance recedes to the background. Rav Gedalia Dov Schwartz, senior rabbinic judge of the Chicago Rabbinical Council and the Beth Din of America, tries to tease that problem out of hiding and eradicate it with his 2011 booklet, *Loving the Convert: Converts to Judaism and Our Relationship With Them*.[157]

The Orthodox community, particularly in metropolitan areas, is quite homogeneous. The differences between people and sub-communities are generally quite minor. Converts, by dint of their non-Jewish backgrounds, are different. The few Jews who do not like people who are different will automatically dislike converts. Many others, though, may unintentionally make converts feel uncomfortable and even unwanted. A resulting feeling of rejection can be devastating to some converts.

II. The Solution: Part 1
The solution to this problem is two-pronged. The first is education of the greater Orthodox community. In this booklet, Rav Schwartz

---

156. See above, "Conversion Control in Israel."
157. Published by the Chicago Rabbinical Council, 2011.

takes on that task. *Loving the Convert* contains four sections. The first part, consisting of chapters 1-4, delineates the halakhic and hashkafic obligations of sensitivity to converts. Not only must we love them and pray for them three times a day, we must be extra careful to avoid offending them. In many ways, converts lack the typical support system in the Jewish community.

The second part of the booklet contains personal statements from converts about the difficulties they have encountered joining the Orthodox community. The third section examines halakhic issues related to converts, such as whether he may become a yeshiva dean (yes) or recite *Kaddish* for his deceased gentile parent (yes but only occasionally). The fourth part contains the Hebrew endnotes and extensive primary sources for the first and third parts.

Initially, the second section of the booklet seems out of place. Why would a prominent halakhic authority include the emotional words of laypeople in his work? However, when writing about the need to embrace converts, he clearly saw a need to point out both their sensitivities and the areas where our community needs work.

III. The Solution: Part 2

I mentioned earlier two elements to solving this problem. The first is educating the community. The second, not addressed in the booklet, is educating converts. They have to understand that a community that strives for closeness and closed-ness, a tight-knit society that builds a wall to the secular world (of varying heights, depending on each community), will present obstacles to joining. We will ask personal questions about your upbringing; we will play Jewish geography; we will treat you like family.

You may find this invasive, especially when some people are overly nosy. You may feel uncomfortable because you don't have what you think are the "right" answers. You may not want to reveal your life's story to strangers or at every Shabbos meal you attend. Just remember that this is not a unique experience for converts. *Ba'alei teshuvah* and people with unusual backgrounds—foreign accents, small-town upbringing—face the same challenge.

You have to learn two skills. The first is blending in. Even those whose racial characteristics preclude fitting entirely into the American Orthodox community can blend in with their behavior. If you dress, speak and act like a member of the community, you will find you are treated much more like a member. You also have to learn how to deflect questions you don't want to answer. In a perfect world, no one will ask you rude questions. Until then, have answers ready like "Someday I'll give you the whole story" or "It's a long and private story." You can prepare joke answers or change the subject.

IV. Conclusion

It is hard for a community leader to acknowledge a societal problem. I salute Rav Schwartz for also trying to solve it, even partially, through education. I'm not holding my breath until we eradicate rudeness. However, raising awareness can at least mitigate the problem and encourage others to reach out to those among us who feel vulnerable and rejected.

Why Orthodoxy Needs Its Left Wing

I. The Fringes of Orthodoxy

When I was a non-religious teenager exploring Orthodoxy, I was looking for something different.[158] I had no need for a religion that supported the values I had absorbed from popular culture because I could get that elsewhere. However, I was not going to join a religion from another planet. I needed to be able to relate to a new community in order to join it. This common experience presents an outreach challenge to the Orthodox Jewish community. In recent decades, society's values have moved in radical directions, sharply diverging from Torah values. How can a community actively attract newcomers while retaining its integrity?

We desperately need to teach our children traditional values, to impart to them the ageless wisdom of the Torah. Yet, values contradictory to the Torah seep into our lives from all directions. This difficulty is compounded because we believe that sometimes we can learn important lessons from secular society. When do we fight the influence and when do we embrace it? We constantly walk this tight line, praying that our children maintain the balance and continue this tradition into the next generation. The vexing problem of our day is ensuring that continuity. Part of the solution—the way I entered the Orthodox community—is through Jews on the fringes of Orthodoxy.

---

158. This essay originally appeared in *The Jewish Link of New Jersey*, February 25, 2016.

Some people on the fringes of Orthodoxy accept the new values of general society but observe traditional Judaism and believe its basic truth claims. They remain upstanding members of the Orthodox community yet look at the world through what I, on the right, see as secular eyes. Despite the non-traditional aspects of their value system, these Jews play an important sociological role in the Orthodox community.

II. Critiquing the Left

A quarter century ago, Rabbi Jonathan Sacks (contemporary, England) offered a precise description of this group on the fringes. In *Arguments for the Sake of Heaven*[159] (pp. 195-199), he refers to Modern Orthodoxy in a narrow sense, which he proceeds to describe and reject. If Lord Sacks rejects it, this cannot be what most people today call Modern Orthodoxy since he is widely considered one of Modern Orthodoxy's current thought leaders. Rather, it is a movement whose "major spokesmen have been Emanuel Rackman and Eliezer Berkovits, and, more recently, Shlomo Riskin and David Hartman; more radically still, Irving Greenberg." These thinkers "attempt to locate modern consciousness within tradition."

Rabbi Sacks discusses the reasons he rejects this approach: "Judaism, I believe, is far less compatible with modern consciousness than [this group] has suggested. Nor is Halakha as open to change as some statements within the tradition might lead one to conclude. There is a difference between the wide powers theoretically available to a Jewish court of law and the much narrower precedent of how those powers have actually been used. Nor can it be taken for granted that everything that can halakhically be permitted, ought halakhically to be permitted." Rabbi Sacks proceeds to elaborate this last point at greater length.

---

159. Northvale, NJ, 1991.

III. The Orthodox Bridge

However, he sees an important role for this group on the fringes of Orthodoxy. It "provides a bridge between Orthodoxy itself and Conservative and Reform Judaism and Secular Zionism. Such a bridge must be found if Orthodoxy is once again to become the faith of the entire Jewish people."

When most Jews accept the values of general society, mainstream Orthodox Jews have difficulty engaging with them intellectually. Our starting points are so different from theirs, our basic judgments of right and wrong so dissimilar, that meaningful conversation often ends before it begins. When we express concerns over abortion or assume that marriage must be between a man and a woman, we speak from a place so far from the average American that we struggle to communicate. While we can still reach many, as evidenced by the success of outreach professionals, we cannot reach those who automatically tune us out for the sin of being politically incorrect.

Orthodox Jews on the fringes serve as a bridge. They can convey the beauty of Shabbos without turning people off on issues of basic values. They can bring people to a kosher Pesach *seder* without awkwardly sidestepping conversations on the burning political and social issues of the day. Many non-Orthodox Jews will feel more comfortable engaging with a Jew who does not seem primitive for rejecting what they believe is the consensus of decent, educated people.

This rings true to me. In my youth, I initially bonded with Orthodox teenagers on the fringes of observance because we had much in common. At the beginning of my journey, they broke down a barrier for me, allowing me to look more closely at a world that I would otherwise have dismissed as completely unrelatable. Additionally, the bridge goes in the other direction. Mainstream Orthodox Jews engaged in a spiritual struggle can find something of a safe harbor in the fringe groups without fully leaving a life of Torah observance.

IV. The Left as an Obstacle

Yet a bridge must stand firmly on both sides of the river. In 1991, Rabbi Sacks could refer to the group now called Open Orthodoxy as a force for outreach. However, as he points out, in order to belong to the community of Orthodox conversation, you have to accept the broadly defined revelation of Torah, the sanctity of the Bible and Talmud. Lately, a variety of vocal members of Open Orthodoxy have denied aspects of this revelation, whether by embracing biblical criticism or extensive talmudic criticism or by rejecting the halakhic process emerging from the Talmud. Additionally, Open Orthodoxy is starting to sharply diverge in practice from mainstream Orthodoxy. In particular, egalitarian prayer services of various types and employment of women rabbis serve as a growing behavioral barrier between Open Orthodoxy and the mainstream.

Furthermore, for a number of years, Open Orthodoxy has been challenging mainstream Orthodoxy on its core values and beliefs. Transmitting those traditions is the primary challenge Orthodox Jews encounter in these difficult times, when we face the seemingly insurmountable obstacle of popular culture. Rather than a group on the fringes of Orthodoxy, Open Orthodoxy has become part of the greatest hurdle the mainstream must overcome. In return, mainstream Orthodoxy has attacked Open Orthodoxy, further distancing the divergent group.

Mainstream Orthodoxy needs its critics and independent thinkers. It also needs a liberal wing on the fringes that deep down speaks the language of secular society. But that wing, in addition to accepting the same belief system, has to respect the core group and recognize, without attacking, the different values each side embraces.

IV. Returning to Unity

For decades, a great compromise kept a polite lid on disagreements. We believed we agreed on fundamental beliefs and, when it came to divergent values, we avoided discussing the issue and tried hard not to antagonize each other, despite the occasional ugly incident on both sides. In this way, the fringe did not pose a challenge to the mainstream's values.

Is it possible to return to a time when the right wing briefly grumbled at left wing innovations and moved on; and when the left sometimes held back in order to maintain its ties to the mainstream? When an innovative synagogue program was intentionally kept out of the media to avoid highlighting areas of conflict? When a radical initiative was rejected because it might cause division in other communities? When we did not mischievously read rabbis' weekly Torah insights seeking non-traditional teachings for which to criticize them?

I don't know. Orthodoxy needs a liberal wing. At a time when Jews are assimilating in disturbing numbers, Orthodoxy needs a bridge to non-Orthodox Jews and secular society. But it also needs to face its own formidable challenge of transmitting its beliefs and values to the next generation.

Leaving Modern Orthodoxy

I. Rising Career

Why would a leading Modern Orthodox rabbi join the Conservative movement at what seemed to be the height of his career? R. Harry Epstein (1903-2003) had impeccable Orthodox credentials. His father, Rav Ephraim Epstein, was the leading Orthodox rabbi in Chicago who also founded what would later be known as the Skokie Yeshiva, where the young Harry studied. Harry went on to RIETS in New York, which at the time did not have its associated Yeshiva College. He then traveled to Europe to study in Slobodka under his uncle, Rav Moshe Mordechai Epstein. After two years there, he moved to the land of Israel as one of the original ten students in the Hebron Yeshiva. He returned to America, attended Chicago University, and became a rabbi, first in Tulsa and then in Atlanta. Before leaving Israel, he obtained rabbinic ordination from his uncle, Rav Ya'akov Moshe Charlap, Rav Avraham Kook, and others. He subsequently obtained numerous graduate degrees. R. Epstein was a young Orthodox scholar with a solid yeshiva background and a university education.

After a brief stay in Tulsa, Oklahoma, serving the congregation which Rav Bernard Revel's father-in-law attended, Epstein moved to Atlanta, where he led Congregation Ahavath Achim, a synagogue facing a serious generational split. The older, Yiddish-speaking generation wanted an old time religion while the younger, American generation demanded a faith in accordance with the times. R. Epstein had the diverse skills to address both the older generation with his traditional yeshiva abilities and the younger generation with his college degree. He taught advanced Talmud and preached eloquently in English.

Worried about losing the younger generation, he slowly adopted accommodations for the more Westernized and less religiously committed population. He enjoyed great success, growing his synagogue into one of the largest in the country and becoming a spokesman for Judaism to the outside world, particularly with interfaith leaders. A scholar and a preacher, R. Epstein rose to a leadership position in American Modern Orthodoxy, serving on the executive committees of both the Orthodox Union and the Rabbinical Council of America.

II. Breaking Away
After World War II, with increased rabbinic immigration from Eastern Europe, R. Epstein sensed a rightward shift in Orthodoxy. Frustrated with the increased traditionalism and concerned for the future of American Judaism, R. Epstein joined the Conservative movement in 1954 at great personal price: his wife objected and his father ceased corresponding. Epstein was certainly not the only Orthodox rabbi to join the Conservative movement, although many today may be surprised by the denominational shifts. Why would a thoroughly Orthodox rabbi, steeped in texts and traditions from earliest youth, trained and ordained by the greatest educators and thinkers of the day, abandon Orthodoxy?

R. Epstein's biographer, Mark Bauman, in his *Harry H. Epstein and the Rabbinate as Conduit for Change*,[160] attempted to understand what drove R. Epstein to join the Conservative movement. R. Epstein was a proponent of progress within tradition.

---

160. Rutherford, NJ, 1994.

Concerned that Orthodoxy was increasingly uncompromising, "liv[ing] in the past and ignor[ing] American conditions," he felt that Judaism needed to continue evolving as a dynamic religion.

R. Epstein championed women's religious rights. He "advocated bat mitzvah, mixed seating, and participation in services" but "blanched at the idea of women reading from the Torah." He began a Friday night service at a time convenient for young people planning on attending theater afterward, introduced responsive and English readings into the prayers and established successful youth and adult education programs. He believed in accommodation in order to keep and attract new members, and religious evolution to meet the needs and reflect the values of the day. He advocated religious practice that was adjusted "in accordance with the times." He was a dynamic, popular rabbi who received great acclaim for his innovations. New generations demand new approaches, which are always applauded for their short term gains even if leading to long term assimilation.

III. Shifting Left

Surprisingly, Bauman does not consider Epstein's theology as a reason for his leaving Orthodoxy. Coming of age in the early 1920's, R. Epstein was a believer in progress. He accepted history as a form of continuous revelation, which Bauman connects to the thought of Zechariah Frankel. Epstein believed that "archaeology and biblical criticism supported the Bible as a book of parables" and more generally accepted the results of modern critical scholarship.

R. Epstein truly believed in the mission of the Conservative movement. He left Orthodoxy because his theology and practical plans did not match his Orthodox origins and training. And yet, later in life, R. Epstein expressed regret of his decision to join the Conservative movement. Bauman writes:

To the interviewer [Bauman] in the 1980s, the rabbi bemoaned the decision to join the Conservative ranks. Conservatism had become too nebulous. It lacked substance and was too willing to compromise fundamentals.

A movement devoted to pushing the envelope will continue pushing it indefinitely, both in practice and in theology. Innovations can only be kept at the margin when they are a sideshow, not when they are the main attraction. But when religion becomes about progress, it becomes nothing but progress. While people sometimes feel forced to make compromises, they do so out of a sense of need, not as an ideology. A principle of compromise is a lack of principle.

There are many points on the spectrum of Orthodoxy, many different ways of combining tradition and modernity. However, they all seek to operate within the mainstream traditions of Jewish law and thought. Harry Epstein left Orthodoxy formally in 1954, blaming it on a shift to the right. His agenda of religious accommodation and his theology of continuous revelation and biblical criticism placed him in the Conservative camp long before then. He had called his movement Modern Orthodoxy but realized that, while it emerged from the Orthodox community, it really was Conservative.

How Orthodox Is Open Orthodoxy?

Rabbi David Rosenthal published an expose on an emotionally charged communal issue.[161] The book's title, *Why Open Orthodoxy Is Not Orthodox*,[162] leads with his conclusion. To the author's credit, he places his agenda front and center. Are we, as a community, willing to entertain this painful accusation? We must give the issue due consideration, regardless of whether we ultimately accept or reject Rabbi Rosenthal's conclusion.

I. Boundary Setting

To a secular Jew, the boundaries of Judaism remain vague. After rejecting the traditional matrilineal definition, even Jewishness rests in ambiguity. Yet, secular Jews overwhelmingly reject Messianic Judaism from the tent of Judaism. Ironically, many of these Messianic Jews (somewhat inaccurately called Jews for Jesus, which refers to members of a specific organization) observe more Jewish ritual than the average Jew, keeping some version of kosher and the Sabbath. Yet, broad consensus exists that Jews who accept Jesus as their messiah have crossed a communal boundary that remains undefined. However, even if they cannot precisely define the red line of communal acceptance, these judgmental secular Jews accept that it can be crossed.

---

161. This essay originally appeared in *The Jewish Link of New Jersey*, July 7, 2016.
162. N.p., 2016.

Orthodox Judaism has stronger beliefs and practices than secular Judaism. Unlike the broader Jewish community, we reject atheism as theologically unacceptable and would reprimand an atheist rabbi who continues teaching in the name of Orthodox Judaism. If he doesn't believe in God, he isn't Orthodox and his teachings do not represent Torah or traditional Judaism. What purpose do we serve by declaring an atheist rabbi non-Orthodox? We prevent him from teaching his heresy to unsuspecting children and adults, who often lack the sophistication to differentiate between traditional and non-traditional beliefs.

Yet, do we want a community in which every rabbi is continually challenged whether he truly believes in God? We dare not allow a theological inquisition nor the suspicion and fear it evokes. We rightly assume that Orthodox rabbis and teachers believe in God unless otherwise indicated. And if they seem to reject God's existence, a senior community official needs to have a delicate, private conversation to determine whether they should be advised to find other career options. We cannot have atheist rabbis teaching in our shuls and yeshivas. But we also cannot spend our limited energy and resources on weeding out atheists from the rabbinate. We need to find a middle ground between blanket acceptance and relentless inquisition.

II. Balancing Unity

On the one hand, communal harmony must take its rightful place as a high priority. We are a small nation, and Orthodoxy is a minority within that minority. If we start rejecting atheist rabbis or the like, we will upset their supporters and split our community even further. Is it worth it? Does theological purity take precedence over communal harmony?

The answer must be that it depends. How serious is the deviation from tradition? How much communal disharmony will it cause? These must be carefully balanced by our communal leaders, those who are keenly sensitive to both the theological issues and the communal implications. But before they reach that decision, they need facts. Rather than deciding that Messianic Jews are Orthodox just because they look and act that way, leaders need to know what beliefs this group professes and how its members act outside the communal spotlight.

Rabbi Rosenthal's book does not address Jewish atheists or believers in Jesus. He discusses rabbis who proclaim their Orthodoxy while pursuing changes to religious beliefs and practices, which cannot be compared to the extreme cases of atheists and Messianic Jews. How radical are these changes? Rabbi Rosenthal's task is to provide that information. To some degree, this is an almost impossible job. How do you describe a movement that consists of individuals? Who is Open Orthodox? And since every person in a group has his own personal beliefs and practices, how can that group ever be described accurately?

III. Defining the Problem

There are two ways to do that. One is to conduct an extensive survey of Open Orthodox Jews and/or leaders to determine trends. This would be an expensive and difficult undertaking but would yield very important communal information. Rabbi Rosenthal takes a different approach. He presents and analyzes statements and actions by a broad cross-section of Open Orthodox leaders. He spends time on the movement's top leaders, some rabbis in its core and some on its periphery. In this way, he avoids defining the movement by its outliers while not ignoring them, focusing mainly but not exclusively on the core and top leadership. This is a dangerous path to take because many readers will take this as a string of personal attacks, generating sympathy for his "victims." In reality, Rabbi Rosenthal is analyzing their teachings, taking their words seriously as they surely intended.

One chapter that spoke to me is titled "Values." Rabbi Rosenthal attempts to demonstrate that Open Orthodox thinkers evaluate the Torah based on their own moral sense and, when they detect a conflict, choose their morality over the Torah. On the one hand, there is much to commend in this enhanced sense of morality. We live surrounded by great moral failures, in a way that is often shocking and depressing. But we must also recognize that moral sensibilities change with time. The lack of commitment to a Torah anchored in divine command is not only theologically wrong but a situation that quickly devolves into a religious free-for-all. As Rabbi Rosenthal documents, we can already witness this happening on the periphery of Open Orthodoxy. For example, one of the great moral challenges of our day is homosexuality. We already see steps within Open Orthodoxy to completely permit what an explicit Biblical verse prohibits. Right now we see the path already selected and the first steps taken by some. I predict that soon some Open Orthodox rabbis will be conducting gay weddings.

I do not agree with every step of Rabbi Rosenthal's interpretation and analysis. Rabbi Rosenthal, a Ner Israel graduate, is part of what I call the left wing of the Charedi world. His book includes a foreword by Rav Aharon Feldman, the *rosh yeshiva* of Ner Israel, an occasional critic of movements within and outside of Orthodoxy, such as messianic Chabad and Religious Zionism. Therefore, I read Rabbi Rosenthal's analysis critically, recognizing that he and I do not always share the same views. However, I find much of Rabbi Rosenthal's evidence compelling. Nothing speaks louder than facts but even facts can be distorted when context is omitted. Rabbi Rosenthal attempts to provide that context through his narrative, and he includes additional documentation and Internet links so readers can decide for themselves.

Sometimes we interpret the facts differently. For example, Rabbi Rosenthal quotes one senior Open Orthodox figure as doubting the divine origin of the Torah. That rabbi wrote that he believes that God wrote the Torah and therefore does not care whether, as a matter of historical fact, He actually did. While I agree that this rabbi's statement is incoherent, I believe it reflects confusion and/or poor writing, not necessarily heresy.

IV. A Necessary Conversation

If we accept Rabbi Rosenthal's premise that Open Orthodoxy lies outside of Orthodoxy, are we opening ourselves to similar accusations? As a Yeshiva University graduate and a Modern Orthodox Jew, I have personally been subject to similar accusations. However, I do not see how that matters. Even if I believe that someone else's judgment is wrong, I still must exercise my own best judgment. If someone considers my Religious Zionism theologically confused, does that mean that I should no longer care if my rabbi believes in Jesus? That conclusion is absurd. The proper response is to exhibit care and measure in our judgments. In that sense, this book raises important questions that must be considered by our own thought leaders. Many of these issues are highly nuanced, requiring expertise to evaluate. Thankfully, we have experts in our community and need to use their services properly.

Ultimately, this book will not serve to excommunicate a movement from Orthodoxy. It will alert the community to educate itself, to open its eyes and conduct its own investigation. This book is a call for awareness, pleading with the community to take notice of recent developments. Now that this book is widely available, ignorance is no longer an option. Community leaders will have to decide for themselves whether Open Orthodoxy is Orthodox.

All the Lonely People on Social Media

We are the generation that has seen the rise of the Internet and social media, and we are still experimenting with these new tools, learning what works and what doesn't.[163] I am a fan and avid user of social media but believe that we (myself included) have a lot of room for improvement in how we use it. There are many lessons we can explore about better usage, but I would like to focus on one, perhaps less obvious, aspect. A few years ago, a middle aged single woman submitted a letter to the editor of a local Jewish newspaper in which she guiltily admitted to experiencing profound sadness when seeing pictures on social media of other people's lifecycle events that she will never experience—giving birth, celebratng bar mitzvahs, marrying off a child, etc.

I had two simultaneous reactions to this letter. I understood her pain and saw how difficult it must be to witness other people enjoying a life that you so desperately want for yourself. However, I also wondered how people can be told not to share their joyous occasions. Isn't celebrating (and mourning) together an essential part of a community? If we keep those lifecycle events private out of respect for those who cannot experience that unique joy, we diminish the extent of the communal reach into our lives. Must we severely handicap the community to avoid offending others? The

---

163. This essay originally appeared in *The Jewish Link of New Jersey*, September 29, 2016.

answer to these two competing concerns, as with so much in life, lies in maintaining a careful balance.

The Evil Eye
Those steeped in Jewish cultural practice are familiar with the varieties of the phrase *kainainahara*, (mis)pronounced differently, depending on geographic origin. They all mean the same thing: "without *ayin hara*, the evil eye." What is the evil eye? The Talmud discusses it in a number of places. For example, someone who becomes wealthy must fulfill additional commandments in order to avoid *ayin hara* (Rashi, *Eruvin* 64b s.v. *ba'al*). Similarly, you are not allowed to stand at the edge of someone's unfenced field and stare at it because you might damage it through *ayin hara* (Rashi, *Bava Basra* 2b s.v. *assur*). Some understand *ayin hara* as a mystical method of inflicting damage. Rav Eliyahu Dessler (20th century, England-Israel; *Mikhtav Me-Eliyahu*, vol. 3 p. 314, vol. 4 p. 6) takes a non-mystical approach. He explains that *ayin hara* is the impact of causing someone else to be jealous. If you enjoy success publicly, others may wrongly be jealous of your good fortune. Causing their jealousy, even unintentionally, is in itself a religious failing that is punished with the damage of *ayin hara*.

The *Orchos Tzadikim* (13th century, France; ch. 14) writes similarly: "The early sages would pray, 'Do not let our jealousy be on others nor other people's jealousy on us.' Why would they pray about other people regarding this character trait and not other [traits]? This is the explanation: Many people cause others to be jealous and desire their fields. Therefore, people would pray about others, because maybe they were causing others to be jealous, and the Torah (Lev. 19:14) says, 'Do not place a stumbling block before a blind person.'"

Often, conspicuous behavior—driving a fancy car, making a lavish party—is intentionally designed to stir jealousy. Even when it is done for other reasons, the outcome is almost inevitable. If you cause someone else to become jealous, you are guilty of causing him to sin.

The *Orchos Tzadikim* continues: "Therefore, it is proper behavior for a man—and his wife and children—not to wear clothes that are overly nice or fancy. The same applies to food and other similar items. This is to prevent others from being jealous of him." Conspicuous consumption leads to unhappiness, jealousy, *ayin hara*. The Joneses, with whom everyone is trying to keep up, are religiously guilty of inspiring jealousy.

Appropriately Sharing

Presumably, the same applies to sharing pictures of our joyous occasions. If we cause other people jealousy, even unintentionally, we are guilty and risk the *ayin hara* consequences. However, stifling celebration is not the answer to other people's loneliness.

Rambam (12th century, Egypt; *Mishneh Torah, Hilkhos Yom Tov* 6:18) writes that the mitzvah of the joyous Yom Tov meal includes inviting the poor and others who need you. If you just eat with your family and ignore other people, your joy is an embarrassment. Rav Joseph B. Soloveitchik (20th century, U.S.) explained this Rambam as implying that true joy must be shared, must overflow to your community and particularly those who need help. If you keep your joy to yourself, you are not experiencing it properly.

Sharing our joyous occasions is an essential part of our celebration. However, we must do it in a way that spreads joy and not pain. Posting pictures and lifecycle events to social media is not sharing but informing, Internet lingo notwithstanding. When we Instagram our joyous occasions, we do not bring others into the celebration but merely show them that we are celebrating. Sharing is when people celebrate with us, enjoying themselves and enhancing the entire celebration. When we share modestly, within local standards of behavior without undue ostentation, we spread joy. When we inform, we risk upsetting others without sharing the joy.

A Turkish Community's Tax Revolt

Determining tax policy is a crucial government function. However, it also has a religious aspect. We like to think that life is about spirituality and principles but there is also an element of practicality. As Maslow taught us, we have to meet our basic physical and financial needs before we address our spirituality. To the rabbis, these financial needs are spiritual. Therefore, taxation is a religious issue when it concerns those who are financially vulnerable. This is always a concern but rises in prominence under times of stress. In the 1840's, following Ottoman tax reform, this issue nearly tore apart a Jewish community. One rabbi, a prodigious thinker and prolific writer, successfully took on communal leadership to defend the poor against tax reform run amok.

I. Talmudic Taxation

Jewish communities need money in order to operate. When Jewish communities are able to self-govern, they need to fund basic operations and also charitable works. The Talmud (*Bava Basra* 7b) discusses how to allocate fairly the taxes to raise this money. The conclusion, taken in conjunction with *Bava Kamma* (116b), is that taxes for life-saving measures are allocated among citizens individually based on risk; taxes for everything else are allocated based on wealth. Rabbenu Asher (*Rosh, Bava Basra* 1:22) explicitly applies this to Medieval taxation in the Jewish community. Nearly all taxes must be allocated according to wealth (not based on income and not equally).

This would seem to rule out a sales tax on necessities, such as kosher meat. Since rich and poor people purchase at relatively even levels, this tax would be fairly flat for all citizens. A poor person with a larger family might even buy more meat than a rich person with a small family. This regressive tax violates the talmudic rule for taxation.

II. The Tanzimat

In 1839, the Ottoman Empire began a massive modernization campaign (called the Tanzimat) that included tax reform. In the past, tax farmers collected for the government and kept a large portion for themselves. The government wanted to tax individuals, rather than communities, in a way that is more fair, more direct and more equal. The result was immediate chaos.

It took many years for the tax reform to succeed. At first, the government was unable to collect taxes without the experience and contacts of the tax farmers. Spreading the tax more evenly meant large populations receiving a much larger tax burden. In some places, local residents fought off the government's tax collectors. In other places, tax collectors continued their activity. The taxes included a head tax on non-Muslims, varying by wealth, and a 0.1% wealth tax.[164]

---

164. See Stanford J. Shaw, "The Nineteenth-Century Ottoman Tax Reforms and Revenue System" in *The International Journal of Middle East Studies* 6 (1975), 421-459; E. Attila Aytekin, "Tax Revolts During the Tanzimat Period (1839-1876) and Before the Young Turk Revolution (1904-1908): Popular Protest and State Formation in the Late Ottoman Empire" in *The Journal of Policy History*, 25:3 (2013), pp. 308-333).

III. The Izmir Compromise

The tax controversy in the Jewish community of Izmir, a large city in Turkey, unfolded in three stages.[165] In 1838, the Jewish community in Izmir was presented with a significantly increased tax burden. The community borrowed to pay this and other obligations but could not afford to pay its creditors. In 1840, community leadership decided to resolve this financial crisis by unilaterally reducing the debt by 25%, in exchange refraining from raising tax revenue from the wealthy members of the community for four years. Instead, they pushed the remaining tax burden onto a kosher sales tax on meat and wine. The existing sales tax was increased from 10 gold coins per measure to 34 coins, a staggering increase. Community leaders demanded that the rabbis affirm this agreement, forcing them to sign.

This tax burden was unbearable and people simply stopped paying any tax at all. For three years, the Jewish community hobbled along, collecting ad hoc taxes on wealthy individuals and borrowing, an unsustainable strategy.

Throughout those three years, the leadership argued over how to resolve the problem. Finally, in 1843, the community reached a compromise. Three representatives of the wealthy population, three representatives of the poor population and a seventh independent member sat together and quickly reached agreement. The sales tax was lowered to 20 gold coins, 10 for ongoing charitable needs plus another 10 to repay the community's debts. The sales tax would revert to 10 gold coins after the debt was paid. Community tax obligations to the government would be paid by a tax assessed on wealth. Before enacting this compromise, the community leadership had every rabbi in the city sign that they agreed with this decision and would not privately advise people to the contrary.

---

165. This entire episode is described in great detail by Rav Chaim Palaggi in his *Chukos Ha-Chaim, Choshen Mishpat*, no. 93.

IV. The Izmir Controversy

Three years later, in 1846, new community leaders found that the sales tax was insufficient to pay the community's debts. They inquired of the leading rabbis whether a temporary tax to resolve the past debt should be instituted as a sales tax or a wealth tax. That is when everything collapsed. People began challenging the validity of the compromise. The rabbis supported in writing both the original change and the compromise. Since the first was invalid, the second must be also.

The rabbis insisted that the great tax compromise of 1843 was legitimate, in contrast to the sham 1840 tax change that was forced on the public by communal leaders who coerced the rabbis to sign an agreement they believed contradicts the Torah. The high sales tax of 34 gold coins constitutes theft from the poor and devastates the community's impoverished population, including widows, orphans and Torah scholars. The lower tax of 20 gold coins is legitimate.

Many community members found this hard to believe and refused to pay the sales tax of 20. They insisted that any increase was unfair. If a tax of 34 was theft from the poor, so was a tax of 20. They insisted that the sales tax return to 10, which was all they would pay. To quiet the controversy, Rav Chaim Palaggi was enlisted to explain the rabbis' views on taxation. At the time, he served as the head of the city's religious court. He was aged 55, hardly an elder, although now he is known as an important figure in Jewish law.

Rav Palaggi revealed a hidden Torah literature that he had been compiling for years. Since the original change in 1840, he had gathered a consensus to topple the unfair tax that took full form in the 1843 compromise. At the time of the original change, when the local rabbis realized they would be forced to sign, they sent letters to rabbis in other cities and countries denouncing the compromise and declaring in advance that their signatures were coerced and nullified. Rav Palaggi also sent requests to great rabbinic courts in Israel and the Mediterranean area for evaluations of the tax. Unanimously, they denounced the high sales tax and encouraged opposition. Rav Palaggi wrote an encyclopedia of Jewish self-government, titled *Massa Chaim*, which includes the full correspondence as well as a number of his own polemics on the subject. While the book was only published in 1874, portions of it were clearly written in the midst of the tax controversy between 1840 and 1846.

V. Is a Kosher Tax Kosher?
The irony of the 1843 compromise was lost on no one. The compromise retained the key problem of the original change— the sales tax. If the Torah requires that taxes be assigned based on wealth, i.e., progressively, then any regressive tax like a sales tax on basic necessities should be forbidden. How could Rav Palaggi champion a solution that runs contrary to the Torah?

He explains at great length as follows.[166] First, before even discussing the sales tax, he points out that the community leaders had no right to reduce the debt by refusing to pay the community's creditors 25% of the debt. That constitutes theft from the lenders. Somehow, the community must find the money to repay its debts.

Rav Palaggi further documents that sales taxes have been used by Jewish communities for centuries. If the entire community agrees to it, then they implicitly forgive the imposition of what would otherwise be theft. Since everyone has to support charity, the sales tax on kosher food is the poor person's way of giving charity. Additionally, the community leadership examined the old debts and concluded that half were due to charitable works. That half of the old debts was funded from the sales tax to ensure that

---

166. *Chukos Ha-Chaim*, ibid.

the sales tax paid almost exclusively charitable works. Again and again, Rav Palaggi emphasizes that a sales tax can only be used to fund the community's services, which are charitable. Using it to pay for government charges is theft because those expenses must be paid based on wealth.

However, even the sales tax constitutes theft from the poor unless they receive more than they give. The allocation of charitable funds to poor individuals must offer sufficient support so that they can buy meat and pay the sales tax. In this way, they are supported by the community and fulfill their obligation to give charity.

VI. Doing the Right Thing
Some poor people—poor orphans and widows—are exempt from giving to charity. Therefore, Rav Palaggi ensured that poor orphans receive more than they give and instituted that widows receive a refund of their sales tax. In this way, the community avoids stealing from the poor.

In other words, the original change failed in the community's mission to support the poor. A regressive tax does not violate that mission as long as it does not interfere with the support of those who are most vulnerable.

Rav Palaggi adds another jab at the original change. The sultan had decreed that government taxes be paid as a wealth tax. The community leaders had placed the tax burden entirely on the sales tax. By doing so, they defied the sultan, a treasonous act contrary to the Torah. Even the head tax is commonly paid, by all the other non-Muslims in the city, based on wealth. This is what the sultan desires and everyone must follow these rules of the land.

The time when Jewish communities raise funds through taxes have long passed. People now have the right to choose to affiliate rather than an obligation to follow the community rules. However, the underlying principles of Jewish communal taxation can guide us in our policies and principles. First and foremost, we must care for the poor. Beyond that, society's focus on progressive taxation is not an absolute value. For centuries, Jewish communities funded charitable activities with sales taxes. On the other hand, allocation of sales taxes and other regressive taxes to non-charitable activities deserves condemnation. The least able should not bear the burden of non-essential government activities, even if they are important. I am far from an expert on U.S. tax policies but I suspect we have much to learn from Rav Chaim Palaggi's passionate defense of tax reform.

CHAPTER 6:

VALUES

Many leadership decisions address issues beyond black-letter law. They require direction, values, spirit of the law rather than its letter. Jewish philosophy often emerges from the law as the implied or underlying message. Even when it does not, it cannot conflict with the legal literature. Therefore, the values by which leaders guide the community must be informed profoundly by *halakhah*. In this chapter, we explore some recent hot button topics in the context of Jewish values, particularly as they emerge from Jewish law.

Gender Roles

Orthodox women continue to break down ritual barriers, or at least that is what we read in the Jewish media.[167] In reality, we continue to discuss women and public ritual and continue to avoid the real discussion.

There are two main issues: change and gender roles. Let us discuss the latter, which I think is crucial to understanding all the current debates. The traditional texts clearly discuss men and women as categories, as entire groups, even though individual men and women vary. People are unique but generalizations are utilized (see *Moreh Nevukhim* 3:32 that the Torah deals with generalizations and not exceptions). The Orthodox worldview, as evidenced by the most prominent literature of the past two centuries, has been that men and women inhabit different roles in Judaism. Women are the private, home-centered individuals and men are the public individuals. Women are more spiritual and connect to God with less ritual while men require more rituals. Rav Samson Raphael Hirsch (19th century, Germany; commentary to Lev. 23:43) writes:

> Clearly, women's exemption from positive, time-bound mitzvot is not a consequence of their diminished worth:

---

167. This essay originally appeared in *The Jewish Press*, February, 21, 2014.

nor is it because the Torah found them unfit, as it were, to fulfill these mitzvot. Rather, it seems to me, it is because the Torah understood that women are not in need of these mitzvot. The Torah affirms that our women are imbued with a great love and a holy enthusiasm for their role in divine worship, exceeding that of the man.

Rav Joseph B. Soloveitchik (20th century, U.S.) believed that men and women were given different inherent natures as part of Creation. He is summaried by Rav Avraham Besdin (*Man of Faith in the Modern World*,[168] pp. 84-85) as saying:

> Two humans were created who differ from each other metaphysically, not only physiologically, even as they both partake of Divine qualities. This contradicts the perverse notion that Judaism regards woman as being inferior to man. It also cuts away another false notion that there is no distinction between them in terms of their spiritual personalities. Two sexes were formed not only for propagative purposes, but they constitute existential originals. They differ in their psychical natures.

In particular, this emerges from the halakhic roles allotted to men and women. The Oral Torah teaches us that women are exempt from time-bound positive commandments. Men are obligated in various communal activities while women are exempt. Many explain that women are charged with the religiosity of the home, with the continuity of the family tradition. While the publicity-seeking atmosphere of Western culture only values the public role, and therefore places the synagogue at the center of religion, Judaism traditionally values the home over the synagogue, the private over the public.

---

168. Hoboken, NJ, 1989.

Rav Moshe Meiselman (Contemporary, Israel; *Jewish Woman in Jewish Law*,[169] p. 16), writes:

> The Jewish woman is the creator, molder, and guardian of the Jewish home. The family has always been the unit of Jewish existence, and while the man has always been the family's public representative, the woman has been its soul.

He writes later (p. 135):

> The inner dimension of striving is the essence of the Jewish heroic act, and woman was enjoined to develop this trait of personality to its highest degree. Thus, she was assigned the private role while man was assigned the public role.

Rav Joseph B. Soloveitchik devotes a chapter of his *Family Redeemed*[170] ("Parenthood: Natural and Redeemed") to discussing primarily the differences between motherhood and fatherhood. He writes (pp. 114-115):

> There is a distinction between mother's and father's mission within the covenantal community, since they represent two different personalistic approaches. Father's teaching is basically of an intellectual nature.... If the father cannot accomplish it all by himself, he must see to it that his child obtains the necessary instruction.
>
> However, Judaism is not only an intellectual tradition but an experiential one as well.... There is beauty, grandeur, warmth, and tenderness to Judaism.... Experiences are

---

169. New York, NY, 1978.
170. New York, NY, 2000.

communicated not through the word but through steady contact, through association, through osmosis, through a tear or a smile, through dreamy eyes and soft melody, through the silence at twilight and the recital of *Shema*. All this is to be found in the maternal domain. The mother creates the mood; she is the artist who is responsible for the magnificence, solemnity and beauty.

The current debate about women's position in Judaism is mainly (but not solely) about gender roles. Some wish to reject the worldview distinguishing between gender roles, either because they believe it does not accurately represent the Torah or because times have changed. This second argument is often made by pointing out that women can reach great heights in the secular world. Implied within that argument is that we must change religious gender roles because secular gender roles have changed. I find truth in the statement because women have accomplished a great deal in the secular world but I reject the conclusion because we should not change our religious values based on secular values. The first argument above—that separate gender roles does not truly represent the Torah's view—is, in my opinion, a false attempt at revisionism. I accept the writings of the leading Orthodox thinkers of recent times.

Once we recognize this underlying premise, we can understand the practical attitudes on the different sides of the debate. Righteous women can and always have accepted additional practices. They are exceptions to the general rules. As long as they are not attempting to change worldviews, they will face little opposition. Of course, there may be technical impediments; men sometimes face those also. But as long as they—both men and women—remain within traditional worldviews, they have leeway for personal experimentation, to find their own places within the community. That is why we can sometimes find unusual precedents in the past. Some women—Michal, for example—may have worn *tefillin*. Some may have been great Talmud scholars. Devorah was a prophetess. But they did not attempt to unravel traditional gender roles.

In the Charedi community today, we see some experimentation among women. There are Tehillim groups and Amen groups, among other new practices. They are usually quietly opposed by some rabbis but only mildly. Because these are not revolutionary attempts to change communal worldviews, they are left alone. Leaders have to prioritize their efforts to change the community. These are small issues, at most.

Today's challenge is beyond that. It is about changing the community's worldview. Make no mistake; the rhetoric is explicit. As such, it is not just about the technical issues, or about women wanting to fulfill extra commandments. It is about breaking down barriers, egalitarianism, changing gender roles. The ordination of women as rabbis is about enabling women to adopt men's roles, not about promoting the unique righteous women of our generation. The calling of women to the Torah is also about egalitarianism. Even if technically allowed within *halakhah*, which I believe neither prior examples are, they are certainly forbidden when done in order to change a Torah value. There is much more to Judaism than *halakhah*. We must follow not only the Torah's laws but also its worldview, its *hashkafah*.

There are moderate rabbis who believe women should be given more ritual opportunities. However, they are still committed to traditional gender roles, which puts them in a difficult position. They want to oppose revolutionaries but must use nuanced language so as not to oppose minor experimentation. This often leaves people wondering which side they are on. If they oppose women rabbis, why do they say that women should have leadership opportunities but not as rabbis? If they oppose women wearing *tefillin*, why do they say that the issue is complicated? I believe it is because they approve of individual women using their talents and spiritual accomplishments in ways that do not undermine the Torah worldview. Personally, I think these rabbis are wrong in their tactical approach and underestimate the confusion they sow by publicly allowing any experimentation. They are indirectly empowering those attempting to change the community's *hashkafah*.

People are unique and need to find their own places within Judaism, embracing both the Torah spirit and laws. But sincere individuals must not be used as pawns in an attempt to alter the Torah *hashkafah*.

What Does Modern Orthodoxy Stand For?

Being Modern Orthodox is more than just being "frum enough" or "frum but not too frum."[171] Some people don't like the term Modern Orthodox or use different names for various sub-groups. Be that as it may, a group has to stand for something or its existence is meaningless and its future doomed. That is why, for decades, Modern Orthodox leaders have been explaining its ideology. A friend sent me a few classic articles on the subject and I'd like to highlight some key quotes that help me define, at least partially, what Modern Orthodoxy means to me.

Rav Norman Lamm (contemporary, U.S.) wrote in "Modern Orthodoxy at the Brink of a New Century" (*L'Eyla*, April 1999) that: "Modern Orthodoxy shares with the Charedi world a total commitment to Halakhah, and melds this with a critical openness to the rest of the world." In his view, being Modern Orthodox requires being a fully committed Jew. You have to go to *minyan* three times a day, keep (full) Shabbos and observe all the other laws. Modern Orthodoxy is not about halakhic shortcuts or half measures.

Modern Orthodoxy adds to this committed life an openness to the world. Its adherents embrace science, literature, politics, and all the wondrous developments in culture. As Rav Lamm adds

---

171. This essay originally appeared in *The Jewish Link of NJ*, December 4, 2014.

in that article: "This is the way Judaism was meant to be lived—in the fullness of life, not only in a ghetto." In an article three decades earlier, "Modern Orthodoxy's Identity Crisis" (*Jewish Life*, May-June 1969), Rav Lamm wrote: "[I]t is our religious duty, our sacred obligation, to live the whole Torah tradition in the world, instead of retreating from a world in which there is literally no longer any place left to retreat to."

But note his limitation in the first quote above: "a critical openness." We have to carefully evaluate everything in life and particularly the elements of general culture we wish to embrace. We have great tools for evaluation—the Torah and tradition we have received through the generations. Only those elements of the general world that are halakhically and hashkafically acceptable should be embraced. We cannot allow our minds and our lives to be diluted by filth or misguided values.

R. Shlomo Riskin (contemporary, Israel) wrote in "Where Modern Orthodoxy Is At — And Where It Is Going" (*Jewish Life*, Spring 1976): "Our challenge must be to insure the fact that our youth derive its axiological standards from the Torah, and to adequately prepare them to extract the religious principles from the secular studies they pursue." Yes, we engage in the world, in society. We allow general culture into our homes but we have to make sure that our hearts and minds are guided by Torah. We can and must take the good from the world, but we have to filter out the bad ideas and attitudes, protecting ourselves and our children.

The Vilna Gaon (18th century, Lithuania) is quoted as explaining as follows the surprising statement of Mishlei (31:30): "*Sheker ha-chein ve-hevel ha-yofi*, Grace is deceitful, and beauty is vain." Is a woman's beauty really meaningless and misleading? It need not be a primary value but that does not make it worthless. No, he explained, beauty is only vain if it is built on a weak foundation. Beauty is shallow if it has nothing underneath it. But if it is added on top of the fear of God, as the rest of the verse implies, then it enhances and glorifies a woman.

Similarly, the beauty found in general culture only ennobles a Jew if it is added to a firm foundation in Torah practice and values. One can say that a Jew becomes more complete through science, literature and the best the world has to offer. But only when he is completely committed to Torah and *mitzvos*. I believe that this is a, but not the only, primary principle of Modern Orthodoxy.

Don't get me wrong. I am not calling for schools to scale back their literature or music courses to fit my personal comfort level. I am not asking them to rip pages out of their textbooks or black out disagreeable passages. I am suggesting that each individual think carefully about the influence they allow general culture to have on them. We all must think about our attitudes to—for example—pleasure, sexuality, authority, and community, and constantly measure how successful we have been at deriving our values, wherever we find them, in the spirit of Torah.

Rabbi Riskin wrote in the above-quoted article: "Torah Judaism draws its strength from *Mitzvos Ma'asiyos*, from action imperatives. But these actions must be supported by *Mitzvos She'b'lev*, Torah attitudes which give meaning to our behavior. America has spawned inverted Marranoes: Jews who act out the rituals, but have the inner responses of the secularist." We must remain independent in our fundamental beliefs about Torah, the world and our lives. Torah must be the spirit of our lives. Everything else can add to our understanding and enjoyment of the world but must not supplant any Torah values.

How Much Does Unity Cost?

Members of the Jewish community rightly strive for unity. Orthodox, Reform, Conservative... we are all Jews yet we wear denominational labels that seem like a remnant of last century.[172] We are good at getting along on the individual level; can't we unite organizationally and institutionally? We are one people yet we have different shuls and different schools. Why can't we just be Jews, no label necessary?

God desires peace within the Jewish people. The Sages tell us that there is no greater vessel for divine blessing, no more effective method of earning heavenly grace, than peace (Mishnah *Uktzin* 3:12). We are given permission to occasionally lie, based on God's example, for the sake of peace (*Yevamos* 65b). When there is Jewish unity, even if some Jews are idolators the community is safe from divine fury (*Tanchuma, Shoftim* 18). Yet, with all this admirable desire for unity, there is another type of peace that sometimes lies neglected. To be good Jews, we need to ensure the proper priority order of communal peace.

Unity requires four elements, each essential to the survival of unity and each alluded to in a famous rabbinic passage (*Avos* 1:12): "Hillel said: Be among Aharon's students: (1) love peace, (2) pursue peace, (3) love people, (4) and bring them close to Torah."

---

172. This essay originally appeared in *The Jewish Link of NJ*, April 1, 2015.

The first essential element of unity is Desire. Only people who want to unite, who strive for peace, can do so. Like a happy marriage, communal unity requires constant work to overcome the inherent divisiveness of human nature. We all see things primarily from our own perspectives. If we are not deeply committed to unity, we will quickly resign in frustration. Because the Torah tells us to strive for unity, we must all find this desire.

The second necessary component of unity is Compromise. We must pursue peace, actively attempt to work through our differences and resolve our competing needs. That can only be accomplished through compromise. No single person has all the wisdom so we have to learn to accommodate other visions of what is right.

Third is Respect, love for each other. We have to step out of our own skins to see life from each other's perspective. Only then we will be able to recognize the deep passion and conviction we each bring to our positions. Without mutual respect, we cannot sit at a table and work together in good faith. At most, we would be able to temporarily cooperate in a spirit of distrust.

The fourth essential element for unity is Common Purpose. We can only unite in pursuit of a goal. Otherwise, we are merely acting friendly, which is no small matter but still not enough. For Aharon, and for us, bringing peace to the world is inherently linked to bringing people closer to Torah. For Jews committed to the Torah, the ultimate Common Purpose is maintaining and spreading Torah faith and observance. There are other common purposes, such as combating anti-semitism and supporting Israel. We can unite under those and similar banners. But when it comes to religion, which lies at the center of our very being, we unite in support of a divinely ordained Judaism.

Rav Ya'akov Ettlinger (19th century, Germany) put the issue as follows (*Minchas Ani, Pinchas*): Do not argue that we must unite with religious reformers for the sake of peace. While peace with other Jews is very important, we must first have peace with God. I do not believe that Rav Ettlinger was arguing for erecting a communal barrier between Orthodox and Reform Jews. Rather, he was saying that we must proudly advocate for Torah views even when they become unpopular and divisive. When we join with others, it must be in pursuit of a Torah vision of the common good.

However, this position is ambiguous because Torah interpretations abound. Who can say that any particular position is not a legitimate Torah view? This is a particularly problematic question. *Havdalah*, distinguishing between sacred and profane, between right and wrong, between good and evil, forms one of our primary challenges in life. The inability to differentiate between legitimate and illegitimate Torah interpretations is a sign of a crippled critical mind. It is a paralysis of judgment that quickly and inevitably leads to religious collapse.

Rav Norman Lamm (contemporary, U.S.), in the title essay of his *Seventy Faces: Articles of Faith*,[173] writes (pp. 136-137): "A pluralism that accepts everything as co-legitimate is not pluralism, but the kind of relativism that leads to spiritual nihilism. If everything is kosher, nothing is kosher. If 'Torah' has an infinite number of faces, then it is faceless and without value or significance."

Torah scholars have the duty to teach what is and is not Torah. While the layman's instinct is usually very good at quickly discerning improper interpretations, we must ultimately defer to our experts. In order to make peace with God, we must ensure that we unite toward goals that are at least consistent with Torah and ideally advocate Torah faith and observance.

Why do we need different schools and shuls? Why must we maintain separate institutions and only join together on specific

---

173. Hoboken, NJ, 2001.

topics of mutual benefit? Because our primary goal in life is to maintain and spread Torah faith and observance. However, joining with those who advocate other goals, who even wish to undermine traditional beliefs and attitudes, is an absurd negation of the very core of our lives. We do not demand religious perfection; even idolators are welcome to join our ranks as long as they do not publicly advocate their sins. We must be willing to pay dearly for communal peace but sometimes the price can be too high.

Tzelofchad's Daughters and Open Orthodoxy

In February 2014, Rav Hershel Schachter (contemporary, U.S.) published a Hebrew responsum forbidding girls to wear *tefillin*.[174] An "Open Orthodox" critic, in an attempted rebuttal to Rav Hershel Schachter's responsum, offered a number of arguments. Elsewhere, we examined his claim that Rashi held the bar low for issuing halakhic rulings.[175] Here I would like to discuss his statement that Tzelofchad's daughters successfully requested equal inheritance rights, thereby contradicting Rav Schachter's claim that this was a Sadducee, and therefore inappropriate, endeavor.

In the English version of the critic's letter,[176] he writes:

> With apologies to Kevod HaRav, the Sadducees were not the first to complain about discrimination against women in issues of inheritance; they were preceded by hundreds of years by the daughters of Zelaphchad who complained (Num 27:4) "Why should the name of our father be lost among his family because he had no son? Give us a possession among the brothers of our father." And in the

---

174. Rav Yair Hoffman's unauthorized English translation was published on the website *The Yeshiva World*, February 11, 2014.
175. See "Rabbinic Qualifications" in this volume.
176. Published on the website *Morethodoxy*, February 21, 2014.

language of the Sifre "Their eyes saw that which Moses' eyes did not see" (that is that there are times when women can see something that even someone as great as Moses, who spoke with the Shechina "mouth to mouth," did not see.) And God consented to their words unequivocally: "Correctly have the daughters of Zelaphchad spoken." God listened to their claim ("God conceded the truth!" Avot D'Rebbe Natan Ch. 37) and changed the laws of inheritance to make them more egalitarian (relatively, as should be understood)

Surprisingly, the critic claims that Tzelofchad's daughters argued against "discrimination against women in issues of inheritance." I say surprisingly because, as we shall see, the words he subsequently quotes contradict this claim. However, he is not the first to read this passage as a response to discrimination against women.

Gunther Plaut (20th century, U.S.), in his famous Reform commentary, writes:[177]

> The projected allotment of the land causes the five daughters of Zelophehad to plead equal treatment for themselves and raises the question of inheritance by women.

As Plaut reads the text, Tzelofchad's daughters wanted equal, or at least more equal, rights for themselves in inheritance. Similarly, Reform rabbi Yoel H. Kahn (contemporary, U.S.) writes:[178]

---

177. Gunther Plaut, *The Torah: A Modern Commentary* (New York, NY, 1981), p. 1199.
178. reformjudaism.org/whence-our-inheritance, accessed January 1, 2018.

It is a story of women appealing for equal justice and, within the cultural norms of their world, receiving satisfaction—at the explicit instruction of God!

The difficulty with this reading is that the text has the women complaining about their father's rights, not their own. As the critic quotes, the daughters ask (Num. 27:4): "Why should the name of our father be lost among his family because he had no son?" Their entire request was that their father's name be continued, in this case through them due to lack of any sons. They did not complain about discrimination against women but discrimination against a man with only daughters.

From a literary perspective, the emphasis in the entire passage is on male inheritance. Robert Alter (contemporary, U.S.), in his *The Five Books of Moses* (p. 866),[179] points this out:

> The case of inheriting daughters puts a certain strain on the patriarchal system, but its patriarchal character remains firmly in place, as the reiteration of "fathers" and "sons" makes clear, and thus a limitation on the choice of husband (to which noninheriting daughters would not be subject) is imposed on these young women in order to preserve the integrity of the tribal configuration with its patriarchal definition.

This is not a case of women achieving inheritance rights but an exceptional case that allows the father's rights to continue through his daughter's sons.[180]

---

179. Robert Alter, *The Five Books of Moses* (New York, NY, 2008), p.160.
180. Jacob Milgrom, *The JPS Torah Commentary: Numbers* (Philadelphia, PA, 1990), Num. 27:8 intro, writes: "The daughter does not really inherit; she transfers the inheritance from father to grandson and thereby keeps the ancestral land in the father's line."

Perhaps the most direct treatment of this subject from a rabbinic perspective was written by Rav Elchanan Samet (contemporary, Israel), in his *Iyunim Be-Parashos Ha-Shavu'a*.[181] He attempts to address the feminist aspects of this passage from an unbiased perspective, or at least as unbiased as anyone can be. His conclusions are ably summarized by Rav Hayyim Angel (contemporary, U.S.), in the latter's *A Synagogue Companion*:[182]

> The daughters of Zelophehad were not motivated by their own rights, nor was equality of inheritance rights for women what lay at the root of their demands. In fact, their argument is deeply rooted in a patriarchal social structure.
>
> Nonetheless, at the root of their argument, and in its acceptance by God, lies a basic principle connected to the inherent equality of the sexes. The daughters of Zelophehad point out an injustice, that because of the laws of inheritance whereby only males inherit, their father's name will be eliminated from within his family. They argue that the principle of preserving a man's name should take precedence over the laws of inheritance.
>
> On a basic human level, a man who has children, whether male or female, understands that he has in fact achieved continuity. This continuity is a fact stronger than any social order that gives precedence to one sex or another.

In other words, while there is a level of some feminist theory—of equality of men and women—in this passage, it is not on the level that the critic claims. Tzelofchad's daughters do not "complain about discrimination against women in issues of inheritance."

---

181. First series, Jerusalem, 2002, vol. 2, pp. 248-261.
182. New York, 2014, p. 160.

Certainly, the Sages were concerned with the welfare of women in regards to inheritance. However, their response was not to legislate equality. In talmudic times, when the patriarchal family structure of the Bible was no longer strong enough to protect orphaned daughters financially, the Sages required the inheriting sons to provide maintenance for their sisters. And if the funds were insufficient, the daughters' claims had priority—the sons had to provide for their sisters and, if need be, collect charity to support themselves (*Kesubos* 108b).

Centuries later, when this proved insufficient, a new method was devised to ensure the financial security of orphaned daughters. Fathers were given the option to create a debt to their daughters so that they would inherit a portion of the estate (this is called a *shtar chatzi zakhar* and is discussed extensively by later authorities). Rather than legislating equality, sameness, the sages throughout the generations sought to protect the female heirs even at the expense of the men. Men and women are all created in God's image but that does not mean that their roles must be exactly the same.

Judaism and Women's Changed Status

I. Women Today

Women's roles and opportunities have changed dramatically in the past century, which has led some to call for *halakhah* to recognize this new situation. Women now have greater financial independence. They can choose from almost any occupation and even no occupation, opting to remain at home. Women often hire household help who free them from cleaning and cooking. Such a different daily existence calls for a reevaluation of women's halakhic status, some would say, acknowledging the historic changes.

Indeed, Rav Yoel Bin-Nun (contemporary, Israel) has reportedly called for such a radical rewriting of Jewish law.[183] Arguing that women's exemption from positive, time-bound commandments is based on their dependent status, Rav Bin-Nun suggests that women are now required to perform every mitzvah. The exemption no longer applies. No one has yet, to my knowledge, fully explored this argument's radical implications for halakhic egalitarianism. However, the idea of incorporating women's new status into Jewish law excites the imagination.

But is this really called for? I submit that the Talmud, as understood by its commentators, was aware of women who were financially independent and free from household duties. Such

---

183. See "The Next Frontier II", *Torah Musings*, May 5, 2010.

women existed as a minority in the ancient world and today they are more common. The status is not new, just its prevalence.[184]

II. Leaning

We see this in the laws of Pesach. The Gemara (*Pesachim* 108a) states that while women are generally exempt from leaning on their side during the *seder*, an important woman—an *ishah chashuvah*—must lean. What defines an *ishah chashuvah*? The commentaries disagree.[185]

Rashbam (12th century, France) writes that a woman is normally exempt from leaning because "of the fear (or awe) of her husband and [that] she is dependent on him." *Or Zaru'a* (13th century, Austria) similarly writes, "a woman is dependent on her husband; it is improper for her to display mastery and freedom in front of him." According to them, an independent woman would presumably be considered an *ishah chashuvah*.

Rabbenu Manoach (13th century, Provence; *Hilkhos Chametz U-Matzah* 7:8) offers other definitions of *ishah chashuvah*. One is an unmarried woman. Another is a righteous, God-fearing woman. A third is part of an explanation of why a regular woman is exempt from leaning: Women are busy preparing and serving food. Therefore, he explains, the Rabbis exempted women from leaning, just like the Torah exempted them from positive, time-bound commandments. A woman with servants, however, is an *ishah chashuvah* and is obligated to lean.

One group of Medieval authorities—Tosafos, as quoted by the *Mordekhai* and Rabbenu Yerucham (see *Beis Yosef, Orach Chaim* 472)—state that all women of their time (fourteenth-century France) reach the status of *ishah chashuvah* and must lean. This

---
184. See also Rav Aryeh Frimer, "Guarding the Treasure," *B.D.D.* 18 (April 2007), pp. 94-98.
185. What follows is based on Rav Menachem Kasher, *Haggadah Shelemah*, pp. 70-72.

raises a question of how Tosafos define *ishah chashuvah*. One is hard pressed to believe that most women in fourteenth-century France were totally independent or free from housework. I heard in the name of Rav Joseph B. Soloveitchik that Tosafos define *ishah chashuvah* as someone who has a significant role in making the family's decisions.

III. Independent Women

We see that the concept of independent women with financial means, who do not rely on or fear their husbands nor shoulder household duties, is not new. The Talmud does not clearly define its concept of an independent woman but Medieval commentaries do. And those descriptions seem quite appropriate for women's contemporary status. Even if they did not consider the possibility of independent married women, the talmudic sages knew of widows and divorcees who attained all of the qualities of an *ishah chashuvah*.

Yet neither the Talmud nor its commentaries ever suggest that an *ishah chashuvah* attains a radically new halakhic status. Rabbenu Manoach says the opposite fairly clearly. Women are exempt from leaning and from time-bound, positive commandments for the same reason. The only change for an *ishah chashuvah*, to whom this reason does not apply, is that she must lean. Her obligations to the other commandments remain unchanged.

Clemency in the Jewish Tradition

I. Why Pardon

In the United States, the President has the power to pardon someone convicted of a federal crime, freeing the individual from punishment. Similarly, many governors can pardon state crimes. This ability to grant clemency is not something that is intuitively necessary. If a court convicts and sentences a criminal, why should that work be overturned by a politician? Sometimes this is the more efficient solution to an obvious injustice, as opposed to a lengthy court procedure which would yield the same result. Other times, it is more efficient than creating new legislation, such as President Andrew Johnson's pardon for all the traitorous soldiers of the Confederacy during the Civil War.

But there is another, more troubling, reason offered for the power of pardon by Andrew Hamilton in *Federalist 7s*:[186]

> The criminal code of every country partakes so much of necessary severity, that without an easy access to exceptions in favor of unfortunate guilt, justice would wear a countenance too sanguinary and cruel.

Later, Hamilton refers to the pardoner as a "dispenser of the mercy of Government." Hamilton is not speaking about false convictions

---
186. https://en.m.wikisource.org/wiki/The_Federalist_(Dawson)/73

but about someone guilty and properly convicted. Even then, he believes that the government should have some way of showing mercy. There are degrees of guilt and someone low on the spectrum might be forgiven, in exceptional circumstances.

II. Why Not to Pardon
The Torah implicitly rejects the power to grant clemency.

> Show no pity on him; you shall purge the guilt of innocent blood from Israel (Deut. 19:13)

This verse speaks specifically about murder cases. The court is instructed to carry out its death penalty despite the obvious case for mercy. Rashi (ad loc.), based on the *Sifrei*, explains: "You shall not say: 'The first has already been killed. Why shall we kill the other one and then two Jews will be dead?'" I have heard this argument used today against capital punishment. Basically, there has been enough death why should we cause more of it?

The Torah, as expressed in this midrash quoted by Rashi, rejects this question. A convicted murderer must be punished appropriately. Ramban (ad loc.) explains the Torah's rationale: "Mercy for murderers is [causes or leads to] further bloodshed by those murderers and by other criminals." If we fail to punish criminals, we will enable their future crimes and will also remove the deterrent from other potential criminals. Mercy today yields cruelty tomorrow.

Ramban adds that this is a general rule, not restricted to capital punishments. Regarding the death penalty, with its finality, we are more likely to find reasons to delay the punishment. That is why the Torah added this prohibition against showing mercy to someone convicted of a crime punished with the death penalty.

But even for lesser crimes, we must administer the punishment despite our natural inclination toward mercy.

This might surprise some people who believe that the Sages of the Talmud added laws to make it almost impossible to convict someone. For example, witnesses must warn the criminal that what he is about to do is a crime punishable by execution and he has to respond verbally that he is doing it anyway (on this, see *Mishneh Torah, Hilkhos Sanhedrin*, ch. 12). However, traditional Jews believe that this is part of the Oral Torah, which was given together with, and as an explanation of, the Written Torah. The same Torah that commands us to execute the death penalty without mercy also greatly restricts the possibility of conviction. Those who reject this and believe (heretically, in my opinion) that the Sages invented the limitations on conviction, effectively accuse the Sages of violating a biblical prohibition by showing mercy on people who would otherwise be convicted of capital crimes.

III. Pardons Today

As we have seen, the Torah leaves no room for clemency. After conviction, the penalty must be administered without mercy. Does this mean we should oppose the pardon? Not necessarily. What follows are some thoughts from someone who has not studied American law, an amateur at best.

Man-made laws suffer from greater limitations than divine laws. The Rambam (*Moreh Nevukhim* 3:34, 41) teaches that the Torah's laws cannot account for every case, and therefore some people will suffer under the Torah (such as the historical case of an *agunah* whose husband is missing). However, man-made laws are subject to great imperfection. Clemency is a guard against poor legislation that fails to consider the potential consequences. It allows for mercy when the law overreaches.

Additionally, we have to take into account not just differences between Torah and civil legislation but also judicial process. The Torah's judicial process differs from most Western court systems in many ways. In particular, a Jewish court almost never convicts a criminal case on a biblical level. The standard for evidence is very high, as we saw above regarding the warning requirement. In such a system, clemency for the rare convict would threaten to eliminate all punishment on a biblical level. American courts, on the other hand, convict and punish criminals frequently. Clemency has a much more limited impact on such a system.

Applying these Torah values to a specific policy is unclear. However, the Torah has to be our starting point, the source of the values which we attempt to apply.

Biblical Defamation in Divorce and Politics

I. The Source of Defamation

Unsurprisingly, one of the two sources in the Torah for defamation, *hotzaʾas shem ra*, is an ugly divorce. The *Chafetz Chaim*, the classic work on Jewish speech ethics by the 19th-20th century, Polish rabbi who is now called by the book's name, distinguishes between *disparagement* (true damaging statements) and *defamation* (false damaging statements). He calls the former *lashon hara* and the latter *hotzaʾas shem ra* (*Chafetz Chaim, Lashon Hara* 1:1). While some disagree based on *Shabbos* 33b, which explicitly connects *lashon hara* with falsehood,[187] common usage now follows the *Chafetz Chaim*'s definitions and equates *lashon hara* with damaging truth and *hotzaʾas shem ra* with damaging lies.

Rabbeinu Yonah (13th century, Spain; *Shaʾarei Teshuvah* 3:112) cites two sources in the Torah for the prohibition of *hotzaʾas shem ra*. The Torah (Num. 14:37) denounces as defamers the spies sent to Israel who returned with a false negative report. And the Torah describes as defamation the actions of a man who falsely accuses his bride of infidelity in order to divorce her (Deut. 22:14). The latter case offers an interesting lesson from linguistic derivations.

---

187. See *Sedei Chemed, Lamed* no. 63, quoted in the Dirshu edition of *Chafetz Chaim*, ad loc, n. 7.

II. Description of Events

The Torah describes the husband's false accusation, in my overly literal translation: "and he placed to her *alilos devarim* and emitted on her a bad name [*hotzi aleha shem ra*]" (Deut. 22:14). "*Devarim*" means words or things. "*Alilos*" is somewhat obscure because there are so many possible parallels.

The great tenth-century Spanish grammarian Rav Menachem Ibn Saruk taught Rav Yehudah Ibn Chayuj, arguably the most important Hebrew grammarian in history. This student solved the greatest problem in Hebrew grammar, the complexity of verb formations, by discovering that Hebrew verbs fundamentally have a three-letter root. The teacher Rav Menachem's work does not operate within that understanding and therefore contains additional complexity. In his classic work, *Macheberes Menachem*, he includes *alilos* within the two-letter root *al*, which has ten different categories. The fourth category includes:

- "*nora alilah*, awesome in his doing" (Ps. 66:5)
- "*hodi'u va-ammim alilosav*, make known His doings among the peoples" (Ps. 105:1)
- "*es asher hisalalti*, what I have done [in Egypt]" (Ex. 10:2)
- "*rav ha-aliliyah*, mighty in deed" (Jer. 32:19)
- "*ve-khol ilah u-shechisah*, no occasion nor fault" (Dan. 6:5)
- "*ve-sam lah alilos devarim*" (Deut. 22:14) — the verse under discussion.

Based on the grouping of citations, Rav Menachem must have meant that words from the root "*al*" in this fourth category mean deed or action. In the case of defamation, *alilos devarim* means "words of actions," i.e., the husband presents his claim. The phrase has no connotation of falsehood or accusation, merely a presentation of facts or claims. The taint of falsehood is explained later in the verse, when it says that the man emitted on her (gave her) a bad name.

Rav Yonah Ibn Janach (11th century, Spain) studied under a different student of Rav Menachem, Rav Yitzchak Ibn Jikatilla. While Rav Yonah critiqued Rav Yehudah Ibn Chayuj's work, he accepted the basic principle of three-letter roots. In his *Sefer Ha-Shorashim* (entry: *a-l-l*), Rav Yonah defines *alilos devarim* in our verse as "causation." The husband puts forward his reasons for demanding a divorce. Rav Avraham Ibn Ezra (12th century, Spain; Deut., ad loc.) explains similarly.

III. Accusations of Infidelity

Radak (Rav David Kimchi, 13th century, Spain; *Sefer Ha-Shorashim*, *a-l-l*) defines *alilos devarim* in our verse as an explanation of the indirect cause of events. He adds a word in the local dialect, which I presume is Spanish, in Hebrew letters, אינקוי״שו, which could be read as *encausos* or *inquisos*. I am not aware of any such Spanish word, although my knowledge of thirteenth-century Spanish is lacking. F. Lebrecht, in the Latin footnotes to the 1847 edition of Radak's *Sefer Ha-Shorashim*, writes:

> Prov. *encaous, encaoussement* incusatio, accusatio (Roquef. s.v.), *encusar* accusare.

Radak seems to translate *alilos devarim* as an accusation, an explanation of the course of events describing cause and effect.

Onkelos translates *alilos devarim* into the Aramaic *taskupei milin*. Rav Dovid Tzvi Hoffmann (19th-20th century, Germany), in his commentary to Deut. 22:14 (p. 437 in the Hebrew translation), connects *taskupei* to the Ancient Greek word *sycophant*. While in contemporary English this word means an insincere flatterer, it has a very specific meaning in Greek—false accuser in court.

Rav Ya'akov Tzvi Mecklenburg (19th century, Germany; *Ha-Kesav Ve-Ha-Kabbalah*, Deut. 22:14) connects *alilos* with *ma'al*, rebellion. This word is used in relation to marital infidelity regarding the *sotah*, wayward woman (Num. 5:12). The connection between those two words seems grammatically improbable to me.

Prof. Aharon Mirsky (20th century, Israel; *Da'as Mikra*, Deut. 22:14) takes a different approach. He connects *alilos* to the rape of the concubine in Givah, which is described in Judges 19:25 as "they knew her and abused her [*va-yisalelu vah*]." Therefore, he explains *alilos devarim* as matters of infidelity. The man accused his wife of infidelity.

We have seen five different explanations of the phrase *alilos devarim*:

1. Description of events (Rav Menachem Ibn Saruk)
2. Reason for divorce (Rav Yonah Ibn Janach, Rav Avraham Ibn Ezra)
3. Accusation (Radak)
4. Marital rebellion (Rav Mecklenburg)
5. Marital infidelity (Prof. Mirsky)

According to the last two explanations, the husband's claims are outright falsehoods. Even according to Radak, his accusation is false. However, according to the first two explanations, the husband is putting forth his version of the events. He is presenting facts which lead to a false conclusion. However, he might not actually be lying. He could be stating partial truths that, through omission, paint a false picture.

She may not have been a virgin, but that does not mean that she cheated on him during their betrothal period (*eirusin*). Maybe she lost her virginity earlier or maybe she was a virgin but her husband did not see evidence of it. The Sages (*Sifrei*, ad loc.) debate whether the verses here should be taken literally and the wife's father actually presents a blood-stained dress proving the bride's virginity or he merely proves clearly in some way (that is clear as a dress) that the accusation is false (Rashi, Deut. 22:17 adopts the latter interpretation). According to the first interpretation, maybe the husband intentionally did not look at the sheet, and is claiming that he has not seen proof of her virginity. According to the second, we can speculate more easily how he can make accusations of infidelity with half-truths which the woman's father must counter with a more complete description of the events.

IV. Divorces and Politics
I find this particularly relevant in contemporary battles, particularly ugly divorces. One side can present facts that are all true and still paint a false picture. Until we hear both sides, even truth can be *hotza'as shem ra* if it fails to include the full context.

We can also see this in the other biblical source for defamation—the spies. Commentaries are puzzled how the spies sinned since their report seems accurate. Ramban (Num. 13:32) points to their final statements that the land devours its inhabitants, which was a lie. Many others try to find different lies. However, Rashi (ad loc.) explains the spies' statements in a way that is based on truth. The midrash says that God sent plagues throughout the land so people would be too busy burying their dead to notice the spies. The spies reported the fact of the plagues and drew the conclusion that the land kills its inhabitants.

According to Rashi, the spies' sin of defamation is located in their presentation of a partial truth and a false interpretation. They were obligated to present all the facts, not just those that fit their narrative. This is similar to what we find in many divorces and political battles. This common political tactic of presenting partial facts and a distorted interpretation, sadly prevalent in both traditional and social media, fits the primary biblical definition of defamation. We do ourselves a disservice by taking these accusations at face value and failing to investigate the greater context and uncover the complete picture.

EpiPen Pricing and Jewish Law

In 2016, the media drew attention to the fact that the pharmaceutical company Mylan had dramatically raised the price of EpiPens, almost 400% over the prior ten years. EpiPens quickly and easily deliver the medicine Epinephrine that can save the lives of people experiencing an allergic reaction. Because of the medical tool's easy use and immediate effect, people with strong allergies carry EpiPens with them at all times, in case of emergency. The rising cost created a growing burden on allergy sufferers. Yet the rise in retail price does not correspond to rising manufacturing costs. EpiPens are extremely cheap to make. Mylan, the company that manufactures EpiPens, took advantage of its patent to increase its profits and research budget.

What does Jewish law have to say about this? I found two responsa on a related topic.

I. Intellectual Property

The Mishnah (*Yoma* 38a) describes the actions of the Garmu family of priests during the Second Temple era. They had a secret way of cooking the showbread and would not teach it to anyone else. The Rabbis brought in other bakers from Alexandria to duplicate the Garmu method, with unsuccessful results. The Temple had to double the Garmu family's wages in order to bring them back. Initially the Rabbis decried the secretiveness of the Garmus. The

Gemara (ad loc.) says that the family responded that they knew the Temple would be destroyed and did not want someone to use their technique for idolatrous activity. The Rabbis appreciated this answer and praised the family.

Rav Yitzchak Zilberstein (contemporary, Israel; *Chashukei Chemed*, *Yoma* 84a, *Avodah Zarah* 28a) quotes the Meiri's comment to this text. The Meiri says that if the community sees a religious benefit in someone teaching knowledge or a specific skill to others but he refuses to teach, the community may fire him from his position and appoint someone else. However, if he has a good religious reason for refusing, he should remain firm in his refusal and trust that God will support him.

Rav Zilberstein deduces that, absent a religious justification to withhold the information, an expert is obligated to teach others for the benefit of the community. If you know how to heal even a non-fatal disease, you must share that knowledge. Similarly, absent a religious benefit to the community, an expert has every right to maintain his professional secrets. A chef cannot be forced to reveal his secret ingredient to the public.

Rav Osher Weiss (contemporary, Israel; *Responsa Minchas Asher* 3:126) similarly writes that we are obligated to heal people with both fatal and non-fatal illnesses. Someone can be compelled to disseminate any knowledge that can increase healing. Both Rav Weiss and Rav Zilberstein quote the following passage as proof.

II. Secret Remedies

The Gemara (*Yoma* 84b) tells the following story, which is interesting for multiple reasons:

> R. Yochanan suffered from *tzefidna* [a tooth disease that could travel through the body and prove fatal]. He went to a certain gentile lady who attended to him on Thursday

and Friday. He said: "What about tomorrow?" She replied: "You will not need treatment." He asked: "But what if I do need it?" She replied: "Swear to me that you will not reveal the remedy." He said: "To the God of Israel I will not reveal." She told him the remedy and the next day he revealed it in a public lecture. But did he not swear to her? He swore that he would not reveal it to the God of Israel, but to the people of Israel he will reveal it. But is there not a desecration of God's name? He told her from the beginning [after she revealed the secret].

Consider the implications. R. Yochanan learned a woman's unique method of healing a disease which he revealed to the public without concern for her. The Talmud Yerushalmi (*Avodah Zarah* 2:2) continues the story with two versions of the ending: either the woman committed suicide or converted to Judaism. According to the first version, R. Yochanan's disclosure of her process destroyed her medical practice, depriving her of her livelihood and her important position in society. According to the second version, she was so impressed that R. Yochanan gave away that valuable information for free, out of concern for public health, that she was inspired to convert to Judaism. Either way, and despite the important issues it raises, the talmudic passage is clear that when a medical treatment saves lives, it can be revealed despite the loss such a revelation causes its owner.

III. Public Need
Rav Zilberstein mentions briefly, and Rav Weiss at greater length, that a doctor and inventor have the right to earn a living from their discoveries, even a very generous living. However, they have no right to prevent the public from accessing the medical treatment they need. The doctors' and inventors' livelihoods cannot come at the cost of other people's lives.

As I attempt to apply this to EpiPens, I think we have to distinguish between two cases. As we mentioned, the medicine is relatively inexpensive. EpiPens are valuable because of the delivery mechanism, i.e., the method. If no one else can duplicate that method, then EpiPens must be available widely at an affordable price. If the manufacturer raises that price so high above the cost of manufacture that many people will be unable to afford the product, then others have every religious right, even an obligation, to imitate and disseminate that method as long as they stay within civil law (e.g., without violating patent law or committing corporate espionage). Public health overrides private wealth.

If viable alternatives to EpiPens are available but not preferred for non-medical reasons, then the price can be raised as high as the manufacturer wants. People can get the same medical benefit from another product so there is no public health need that overrides the manufacturer's right. It is not my place to opine on the viability of EpiPen alternatives. However, from my limited research, I believe that alternatives to EpiPens exist. Due to a combination of marketing pressures and prescription rules, doctors and consumers prefer EpiPens. However, if the alternatives are equally viable and available, then, by raising the price, the manufacturer of EpiPens is not preventing people from obtaining medical treatment. Doing so is within their rights, although they risk the loss of customers to generic alternatives.

Officiating At A Gay Marriage

A rabbi has to stand for Torah values. This is important now more than ever, when values contrary to the Torah are being promoted as the only moral option. There is no morality against the Torah.

I. Is Officiating Forbidden?

For a long time, I struggled to understand whether there exists any technical barrier to an Orthodox rabbi officiating at a gay wedding. As long as the ceremony is sufficiently different from a traditional Jewish wedding ceremony to avoid confusion, and no unnecessary blessings are recited, what prevents a rabbi from leading the proceedings and adding religious meaning to a lifecycle event that would take place anyway? This seemed to me an area of judgment, in which we have to refrain from doing something otherwise permitted for public policy reasons in order to send a message. A 2017 book has convinced me otherwise.

Homosexuality in general, and gay marriage in particular, have become generational challenges to traditional religion. The mainstream acceptance of alternative sexuality has generated questions about the fairness and truth of Judaism. Why does the Torah prevent our gay friends from settling down with a life partner? For too many people, the intangible theological answers cannot compete with a friend's visible struggles. A person's pain overrides God's word. To avoid further alienating people who struggle with this issue, many traditionalists greatly limit explicit discussions of the subject or clear statements on the matter, leaving the microphone to the radicals. We live in a confused world and the real fear of alienating people causes silence on one side, which adds to the confusion.

II. Is Accommodation Possible?
One strategy of dealing with difficult situations like these is to accommodate non-traditionalists as much as halakhically possible. Don't compromise your own integrity by violating religious laws, but enable others to fulfill as many religious dicta as possible while you walk them to the line and watch them cross it. Rabbis minister to the righteous and the wicked, as well as the majority of people who are somewhere in between. By taking part in this or other similar ceremonies, you are compromising on your teaching without compromising on your personal observance. But sometimes a lesson will not be heard so you lose nothing by refraining from teaching it.

This strategy is thoughtful but short-sighted. You see the immediate gain by adding further religious dimensions to a family but you miss the long-term loss of failing to stand with your principles. The many others who witness this ceremony see a rabbi willing to wink at non-observance, to take part in a ceremony that is obviously contrary to the Torah's teachings. If you are not willing to sacrifice for the Torah on your level, don't expect others to sacrifice on their levels either.

However, Rav Dovid Lichtenstein (contemporary, U.S.), in his book, *Headlines 2*,[188] convinced me that I was missing a factor in my halakhic evaluation of the subject. One chapter in the book

---

188. New York, NY, 2017.

discusses whether a marriage registrar may sign a gay marriage certificate. As the book's title implies, it deals with real situations reported in the news. When I read about this episode, I thought that *halakhah* would allow the woman to sign the wedding certificate. She was not enabling the couple to marry because they could go somewhere else for the registration. She was not involved in the ceremony itself when it took place. Therefore, signing the certificate should be permissible.

III. Flattery

Rav Lichtenstein raises a further consideration. The Torah prohibits "*chanufah*," loosely translated as flattery. The Mishnah (*Sotah* 41a) describes how Aggripas the king once read the Torah at the Hakhel ceremony. When he reached the verse, "You shall not appoint on you a foreign man" (Deut. 17:15), which disqualified him from the kingship, he began to cry and the Rabbis called out, "You are our brother." The Gemara (*Sotah* 41b) points to this sinful rabbinic response as a reason for the persecution of the Jewish people that accompanied the destruction of the Second Temple. This was flattery, false approval of a sin, which is itself sinful.

Rabbeinu Yonah (13th century, Spain; *Sha'arei Teshuvah* 3:188) deduces from this story that you must suffer martyrdom before approving a sin. Otherwise, how could the rabbis have been expected to stand up to a ruling monarch with the power to kill them? Tosafos (*Sotah*, ad loc.) disagree based on *Nedarim* 22a. A murderer killed someone in front of the sage Ulla and asked him if he did a good job. Ulla responded in the positive but later, full of regret, he asked R. Yochanan whether he had done the wrong thing. R. Yochanan assured Ulla that he had acted properly because he had answered approvingly in order to save his own life.

This debate revolves around a case when one's life is in danger. Absent that extenuating circumstance, all agree that you may not explicitly approve of sinful behavior.[189]

IV. Conclusion

Rav Lichtenstein proceeds to argue that signing a marriage certificate constitutes explicit approval of that marriage. If that marriage is forbidden, its approval is *chanufah*.[190] Presumably, it is similarly forbidden to sign a marriage certificate of a Jew and a gentile. One can argue that a gay marriage is not technically forbidden but I find that argument hard to support. Marriage includes marital relations, unique exceptions notwithstanding.

For this reason, officiating at such a marriage, or otherwise explicitly celebrating it, should also be forbidden as *chanufah*. Just like we neither celebrate nor officiate at an intermarriage, despite the couple's personal joy, we also may not do so at a gay marriage. The Torah demands that we stand up for our values.

---

189. Note that this does not discuss praising someone sinful for his good qualities unrelated to the sin. See *Iggeros Moshe, Orach Chaim* 2:51.

190. Rav Lichtenstein concludes some chapters with quotes from notable rabbis who discussed this issue on his radio show. On this issue, Rav Dovid Cohen said that, because of *chanufah*, you are obligated to forfeit your job rather than sign a gay marriage certificate.

May A Jew Register in a National Muslim Registry

In the complex emotional and political turmoil in the aftermath of the 2016 presidential election, there was talk of a national registry of Muslims.[191] It is not clear to me whether this was seriously under consideration by anyone. Be that as it may, some Jews expressed concern over such a registry and voiced a desire to register as a Muslim in order to undermine the database. I have strong feelings about the whole issue but wish to put all the political talk aside and discuss whether a Jew would be religiously permitted to register as a Muslim if such a registry were put in place. While such an act would probably be illegal because it contains a false claim and undermines the government's effort, we will assume for this discussion that the false claim is justified and permitted under U.S. law. We will only discuss whether a Jew may register under a different religion. The answer lies in a debate between two Holocaust survivors.

 The underlying issue arose for centuries as Jews were persecuted. For example, tax farmers often placed unfair, excessive burdens on Jews. Can a Jew dress like a gentile when the tax farmer visits in order to avoid the extra tax? Often, anti-Semitic road bandits would harm Jews—killing the men and raping

191. This essay originally appeared in *The Jewish Link of NJ*, November 23, 2016.

the women—rather than just stealing from them. Can travelers pretend to be gentiles to avoid the danger of anti-Semitic violence? Too often throughout history, religious missionaries attempted to force Jews to convert at the pain of death. Can a Jew say that he belongs to another religion in order to save his life?

I. Four Cases

Four talmudic cases serve as the basis for subsequent rulings.

1. The Gemara (*Avodah Zarah* 18b) tells of R. Meir's escape from Romans. At one point, he pretended to be a gentile by sticking his finger into non-kosher food and pretending to suck the non-kosher food off his finger. In order to save his life, he pretended to be a gentile.
2. In discussing ways to avoid an anti-Semitic tax farmer, the Gemara (*Bava Basra* 113a) says that you may not wear clothing that contains a forbidden *sha'atnez* mixture in order to avoid the extra tax. This might imply that you are allowed to dress like a gentile in order to pretend to be one, only without *sha'atnez*. However, the Rosh (12th-13th centuries, Germany-Spain; *Bava Kamma* 10:11) explains this passage differently. He says that the tax farmer exempts specifically clothes made from *sha'atnez*. According to the Rosh, you cannot pretend to be a gentile because that seems like a rejection of Judaism.
3. In Babylonia, Zoroastrian priests and their servants were exempt from taxes. The Gemara (*Nedarim* 62b) permits a Torah scholar to say that he is a "servant of the fire" in order to avoid the tax. Rashi (11th century, France; ad loc., s.v. *avda*) understands this to mean that he claims he is an idolatrous priest. The Ran (14th century, Spain ad loc., s.v. *avda*) and *Nimmukei Yosef* (14th-15th centuries, Spain; ad loc., s.v. *avda*) explain that he is claiming merely that he is a servant of an

idolatrous priest and not a priest himself. They add that the man is not as if he accepted another religion because he clearly made his statement for tax purposes.

4. The Mishnah (*Avodah Zarah* 2:1) says that a Jewish woman should not be alone with lawless gentiles because they are suspected of rape and that a Jewish man should not be alone with lawless gentiles because they are suspected of murder. The Talmud Yerushalmi (*Avodah Zarah* 2:1) asks why the Mishnah is not concerned about the murder of a woman, just rape. It answers that a woman can hide among gentile women and say that she is a gentile. A man cannot do that (because of circumcision or because of his beard and sidelocks). The Rosh (*Avodah Zarah* 2:4) finds this surprising because the woman, by saying that she is a gentile, rejects Judaism and accepts another religion. Rather, he explains, the Yerushalmi is discussing the possibility of a woman doing so against the law, not the permissibility of her actions within the law.

Practical Conclusion

Rav Yisrael Isserlein (15th century, Austria; *Terumas Ha-Deshen* 1:197) accepts the Rosh's rulings and distinguishes between financial cases and life-threatening cases. To save money, a Jew may not pretend he is a gentile. If there is a life threat, you are allowed to dress like a gentile and pretend you are not Jewish. However, you are never allowed to say that you are a gentile because saying so is equivalent to rejecting Judaism. He suggests that R. Meir, in the story above, was pretending to be a non-religious Jew, not a gentile. *Terumas Ha-Deshen* seems to disagree with the Ran and *Nimmukei Yosef* above.

Significantly, the Rema (16th century, Poland; *Shulchan Arukh, Yoreh De'ah* 177:2) rules like the *Terumas Ha-Deshen*. This ruling seems to be the final word, at least for Ashkenazim. To save lives, we can hint, imply, and feign but we cannot explicitly reject our religion by accepting another. But what constitutes a life threat and what constitutes explicitly saying that you are a gentile?

II. Details

Rav Shmuel de Modena (16th century, Greece; Responsa Maharshdam, *Yoreh De'ah* 199) was asked by conversos who had escaped—Jews who were forcibly converted to Christianity but managed to leave the country and return to Judaism: When writing to colleagues or relatives in their old country, can they use their Christian names? If they use Jewish names, their correspondence likely will not get through and they will lose contact with relatives and money from their businesses. Does using the Christian name imply an acceptance of Christianity and/or a rejection of Judaism?

Maharshdam takes a number of issues into account before ruling leniently. Among them is the difference between saying you are a gentile and writing that you are. The former is worse. Speaking allows for further questioning that can lead to saying religiously improper things out of fear of detection. Writing is a one-time event that cannot lead to further statements about identity. This seems particularly relevant to a registry in which you check off a box.

Rav Ephraim Oshry (20th century, Lithuania-U.S.) was a talented yeshiva student in Kovna before the Holocaust and answered a number of chilling halakhic questions during and after the war, which he published in multiple volumes of *Responsa Mi-Ma'amakim*. One question (vol. 4, no. 12) regards a man who purchased non-Jewish identity papers but never had to use them. Still, he wanted to know whether the purchase alone constitutes a sin, perhaps even apostasy, for which he needs to repent. Rav Oshry concludes that this does not constitute a sin and the questioner does not need to repent. However, in his answer, he notes that previous authorities generally dealt with two cases—dressing like a gentile and saying you are a gentile. Rav Oshry suggests that presenting gentile identity papers is closer to saying than to dressing because there is an action involved. You are not just letting people draw their own conclusions but presenting them with an affirmative identity statement.

Another Holocaust survivor, Rav Menashe Klein (20th century, Czechoslovakia-U.S.), takes issue with this suggestion (*Mishneh Halakhos*, vol. 9, no. 170). Rav Klein says that there is no difference between presenting gentile clothes and gentile identity papers. For example, if a Jew dresses as a priest in order to save his life, he is making a public statement greater than just handing papers to a limited number of guards. Therefore, since it is permissible, using gentile identity papers to save your life is a great mitzvah. According to Rav Oshry, the problem is *actively* declaring a gentile identity. According to Rav Klein, the problem is the verbal statement itself.

According to Maharshdam and Rav Klein, you would be able to register as a Muslim in writing. According to Rav Oshry, you would not be allowed to do so because it constitutes saying you are a gentile.

III. Islam

Additionally, we can question whether Islam falls under this prohibition. Since Islam is a strong monotheistic religion that eschews icons, perhaps its adoption by a Jew is less severe than Christianity, Zoroastrianism, or other religions. Rambam makes that distinction in his *Iggeres Ha-Shemad,* Epistle on Martyrdom. Rambam points out that the Muslim missionaries who were forcing Jews to convert on threat of death were only demanding verbal acceptance of Islam. "This compulsion imposes no action, only speech."[192] Therefore, "if anyone comes to me to ask me whether to surrender his life or acknowledge, I tell him to confess and not choose death. However, he should not continue to live in the domain of that ruler" (ibid.). Rather, Rambam counsels converting verbally to avoid penalty and fleeing the country as soon as possible, even abandoning family and property, if necessary. And someone who has the opportunity to leave and practice Judaism freely but instead stays as a secret Jew is guilty of profaning God's name (p. 33).

Even if Islam does not constitute paganism or idolatry, willingly adopting it constitutes a *chillul Hashem*. Therefore, it seems forbidden to claim to be a Muslim, just like it is forbidden to claim to be a Christian or Zoroastrian.

Based on all the above, it seems forbidden to register as a Muslim in order to show solidarity with friends and fellow citizens in the unlikely event that a registry will be established. Those Jews who wish to support Muslims should find another way to do so. It would be ironic to diminish our own religious identities in order to support other people's rights to maintain theirs. There must be a better way to accomplish the desired goal.

---

192. Tr. Abraham Halkin, *Epistles of Maimonides: Crisis and Leadership* (Philadelphia, PA, 1985), p. 30.

Counting for a Minyan

In 2017, Orthodox Jews in Lakewood, New Jersey, were arrested for allegedly deceiving the government in order to obtain benefits illegally. While we assume that people are innocent until proven guilty, we can explore the implications of this alleged crime. Specifically, I would like to discuss whether we can count for a *minyan* a man who has stolen from the government.

I. Theft, Lying, and *Chillul Hashem*

Rav Hershel Schachter (contemporary, U.S.; "Dina De'malchusa Dina" in the first issue of *The Journal of Contemporary Halacha and Society*) expresses the majority opinion that the rule of *dina de-malchusa dina*—the law of the land is the law—applies to, among other things, monetary matters in the United States. Therefore, illegally obtaining government benefits constitutes a violation of *dina de-malchusa dina* and theft from the government. A minority opinion, voiced most prominently by Rav Menashe Klein (20th century, Czechoslovakia-U.S.; *Mishneh Halakhos* 6:277), argues that this rule only applies to a king, not a democratic government.

However, Rav Klein (ibid., 6:311) rules that one is still forbidden to steal from the government. Tax money belongs to the original taxpayers for whom the government serves as a (reluctant) partnership to fund joint ventures. Someone who steals from the government steals from every taxpayer, among them righteous people and great Torah scholars. When asked whether Torah institutions can falsely obtain government benefits, Rav Klein (ibid., 12:446) responds that the Lord despises theft and wrongdoing. He quotes Rav Mendel of Rimanov (18th-19th centuries, Poland) who was asked why sometimes a boy who has studied in yeshiva for many years can abandon religion. Rav Mendel famously responded that the boy's parents must have profited improperly and fed the child food bought with stolen funds, which damaged him spiritually and led him to leave the fold. Rav Moshe Feinstein (20th century, Russia-U.S.; *Iggeros Moshe, Choshen Mishpat* 2:29) adequately sums up the issue by saying that taking undeserved benefits from the government constitutes theft, lies, and a *chillul Hashem*, and that "there is no leniency whatsoever" on this matter.

II. Counting for a *Minyan*

The Rambam (12th century, Egypt; *Pe'er Ha-Dor*, no. 71) was asked whether we can count Karaites for a *minyan*. His answer was no, but there are different versions of his explanation why. According to the majority version, we cannot count Karaites because they do not believe in the concept of *minyan*. Rav David Yosef (20th century, Israel), in his edition of *Pe'er Ha-Dor* (71 n. 4), explains that if not for this specific lack of belief, we would count Karaites in a *minyan* even though they lack a basic Jewish belief and commit sins.

The *Sefer Ha-Manhig* (12th-13th centuries, Provence; no. 79) quotes the Gemara (*Sanhedrin* 44a) that points out an important biblical term. Even though Achan sinned by taking from the remains of the destroyed city of Jericho, the Bible still says "Israel has sinned" (Josh. 7:11). This means that even though Achan sinned, he was still part of Israel. He still retained his Jewish sanctity and membership in the nation. Therefore, concludes the *Sefer Ha-Manhig*, even a sinner can be counted in a *minyan* as long as he has not been excommunicated (put in *cherem*). Regarding someone excommunicated, the Rambam (*Mishneh Torah, Hilkhos Talmud Torah* 7:4) writes that among his punishments is that he cannot be counted for a *minyan*. Similarly, the Rivash (14th century, Algeria) writes in a responsum (no. 172) that we count a sinner for a *minyan* but not someone excommunicated. This is how the *Shulchan Arukh* (*Orach Chaim* 55:11) rules.

III. Rebellious Acts
The *Chakham Tzvi* (17th-18th centuries, Amsterdam; no. 38) writes that we count in a *minyan* someone who sins occasionally but not someone who commits sins on a consistent basis. Similarly, the author of the *Or Ha-Chaim* (18th century, Italy-Jerusalem; *Pri To'ar, Yoreh De'ah* 119:8) writes that someone who does not believe in the words of the talmudic Sages cannot be counted for a *minyan*. The *Pri Megadim* (*Eshel Avraham* 55:4) distinguishes between someone who sins out of desire and someone who sins rebelliously or for other reasons. Someone who sins out of desire, because he was drawn away by temptation, can be counted for a *minyan*. Succumbing to temptation, while wrong, does not disqualify someone from a *minyan*. Sins due to rebellion or disbelief, however, are of a different kind and with different consequences, including disqualification from a *minyan*.

The Netziv (19th century, Russia; *Meishiv Davar* 1:9) compares prayer to a sacrifice. The Gemara (*Chullin* 5a) says that we accept a sacrifice from a Jewish sinner but not from an apostate or a Shabbos violator. Similarly, argues the Netziv, we include a sinner in a *minyan* but not an apostate or a Shabbos violator. Rav David Tzvi Hoffmann (19th-20th centuries, Germany; *Melamed Le-Ho'il* 1:29) writes that there is room to be lenient and count a Shabbos violator in a *minyan*. He suggests that Shabbos violators today have the status of a *tinok she-nishba*, a child who was raised among gentiles, without a traditional Jewish education. Rav Yosef Zechariah Stern (19th century, Lithuania; *Zeikher Yehosef, Orach Chaim* 21:6) expands this approach slightly. The Gemara (*Sanhedrin* 26b) says that while normally someone who commits a sin is invalid as a witness, this does not apply if the sin is something that people mistakenly think is permitted. Similarly, he suggests, someone who lives in a community in which Shabbos violation is considered normal rather than a sin should still be counted for a *minyan*.

However, Rav Yechiel Ya'akov Weinberg (20th century, Germany-Switzerland; *Seridei Eish* 1:7; 2:6 in old editions) was asked whether we can count someone intermarried for a *minyan*. He answered that someone intermarried should be excommunicated and therefore cannot be counted for a *minyan*, even though the excommunication cannot be done for technical reasons.

IV. Putting It All Together

I hesitate to draw any practical conclusions because these weighty matters need to be addressed by our leading rabbis. Preliminarily, it would seem, based on the above, that according to the *Chakham Tzvi*, people who repeatedly cheat the government, year after year, cannot be counted for a *minyan* (see also *Minchas Yitzchak* 3:65). According to the *Seridei Eish*, if the community believes that the *chillul Hashem* caused by government cheats merits excommunication, even just in theory, then those who commit this sin cannot be counted for a *minyan*. On the other hand, if—Heaven forbid—this sin is so common that people do not consider it forbidden, then people who violate it can count for a *minyan* according to the *Zeikher Yehosef*. Widespread sin is not permission but the opposite—recognition of a communal, rather than personal, spiritual illness. Additionally, Rav Moshe Feinstein (20th century, U.S.; *Iggeros Moshe, Orach Chaim* 1:23) permits counting every sinner for a *minyan*, presumably aside from someone actually excommunicated. Therefore, according to Rav Feinstein, even government cheats can count for a *minyan* despite their theft, lies, and *chillul Hashem*.

VI. Forfeiting Membership

We can try applying these principles to an entirely different kind of Jew. Can a man who is intermarried be counted for a *minyan*? The *Minchas Yitzchak* (20th century, England-Israel; 3:65) quotes the above *Chakham Tzvi* (no. 38) who writes that there are certain sins that are so rebellious that the community would excommunicate someone who commits them. Examples he gives are openly violating Shabbos and repeatedly sleeping with non-Jewish women. The *Chakham Tzvi* writes that even if the community has not excommunicated such a person, we cannot give public honor to someone who should be excommunicated because it gives the mistaken impression to people that these sins are acceptable. Therefore, the *Chakham Tzvi* concludes, we should not count them for a *minyan* or call them to the Torah (see *Mishneh Torah, Hilkhos Talmud Torah* 7:4). This means that someone who is intermarried should not be counted for a *minyan*.

Living in early twentieth-century Germany, the *Seridei Esh* (ibid.) writes similarly, that since the community must excommunicate someone who intermarries in order to teach that it is unacceptable, even if for whatever reason they cannot excommunicate him they still may not call him to the Torah.

The above *Minchas Yitzchak* raises the issue, regarding someone who violates Shabbos, that people today are not necessarily raised in tight, traditional communities and therefore do not violate Shabbos with the same intentions as in past generations—i.e., they are *tinokos she-nishbu* (captive children raised outside an observant community) and therefore not fully culpable for their violations. Therefore, there is reason to be lenient regarding someone who violates Shabbos. While the *Minchas Yitzchak* does not indicate whether he agrees with this position (which has become fairly normative), he points out that this logic does not apply to intermarriage. In 1959 Manchester, where he wrote the responsum, every Jew was raised knowing that intermarriage is absolutely unacceptable. Therefore, no one can claim that they were not adequately educated regarding this prohibition.

Similarly, the *Seridei Esh* (ibid. 11:13) writes that since not calling Shabbos violators to the Torah is an issue of public policy and communal education, it is up to the local rabbi to determine whether refusing to call someone to the Torah will teach them (and the community) a proper lesson or will serve to alienate people from the Torah. If the former, then they should not be called up. If the latter, then the rabbi is free to permit it.

VII. Today's Reality

The question, then, is whether in the year 2018 intermarriage has sadly become so common that we cannot say that every Jew is raised knowing that intermarriage is absolutely unacceptable. Perhaps there are people today who are *tinokos she-nishbu* regarding intermarriage and our failing to call them to the Torah only alienates them further. According to the above reasoning, perhaps in certain communities and outreach synagogues, where there is not an issue of appearing to condone such violations, intermarried men may be counted for a *minyan* and called to the Torah.[193] It seems that Rav Moshe Feinstein would also permit counting someone intermarried for a *minyan*, albeit for a different reason.

---

193. After writing this, I found that Rav Hershel Schachter reached a similar conclusion in a lecture: "Intermarriage on our doorstep. How do we respond?" March 10, 1999 https://www.yutorah.org/lectures/lecture.cfm/725222 at minute 36.

Women Rabbis

I. An Important Decision

In 2009, Rabbi Avi Weiss (contemporary, U.S.) ordained a woman and established Yeshivat Maharat to train more women for the rabbinate.[194] In response, the Modern Orthodox community gathered its leading Torah scholars to discuss the issue and decide whether this move was consistent with the Torah tradition as understood and accepted in the Orthodox community. The result was a 2010 resolution of the Rabbinical Council of America (RCA) rejecting the ordination and recognition of women as rabbis

As I understand it, this resolution encourages women's Torah scholarship and leadership, but also seeks to preserve traditional gender roles. Contemporary society has become increasingly gender neutral. In contrast, Judaism recognizes both theologically and practically the differences between men and women. A Jewish woman has a unique role in the family and the community. As women explore new roles in these confusing times, we as a community need to allow them room to find their paths while avoiding the temptation of adopting the secular value of gender neutrality.

---

194. This essay originally appeared in *The Jewish Link of NJ*, February 3, 2017. Some portions were added from an article published in *The Jerusalem Post*, February 10, 2018.

Four years after the 2010 resolution, as Yeshivat Maharat celebrated its first graduation, the RCA reiterated its position and expressed its regret over this "violation of our mesorah [tradition]." In October 2015, the Rabbinical Council of America issued a resolution (that I sponsored) that its members may not ordain women into the Orthodox rabbinate nor hire a woman rabbi, regardless of title. This was necessary because matters of Jewish law that affect the community need to be decided by experts, not journalists or activists. On this issue, the leading Torah scholars of the day agree that this development is unprecedented and contrary to Torah tradition.

In January 2017, after a long process of communal comment and rabbinic inquiry, the Orthodox Union (OU) issued a statement effectively adopting the above resolution, with an accompanying study of the subject by seven leading rabbis. When we face changing times and perplexing religious questions, we direct our inquiries to leading rabbis, as Jews have done for millennia. I commend the OU for following this time-honored process. The OU also opened the door for discussion with many community members, particularly women, as described in the organization's statement. To my knowledge, this remarkable process of policy setting is unprecedented in its openness. Decades ago, when *mechitzah*—the synagogue partition between the men's and women's sections—became an issue that divided the Orthodox community and eventually set the standard for Orthodoxy, the process for determining this standard was much less transparent and open. The issue of women rabbis, which is the *mechitzah* of this generation, is being handled with much more patience and openness.

In February 2018, the OU announced that it would enforce its ban on women rabbis in member synagogues. Current member synagogues that are not in compliance have three years, while all other current and new member synagogues may not have women in clergy positions.

However, I don't think *halakhah* is the only question or answer in the issue of women rabbis. There is a moral element, as well, that underlies the sensitive rabbinic response and should resonate particularly strongly within the Modern Orthodox community. Of course, we accept the rabbinic conclusion, but how do we process it? How do we incorporate this direction into our mindset?

II. Religion and Inequality

The term "Modern Orthodox" is, in a sense, self-contradictory, which makes you wonder why it has been used for so long as a description of a significant portion of the Jewish community. The "Orthodox" part refers to the community's strong commitment to traditional core beliefs and practices. The "Modern" part implies a willingness to absorb practices and values from contemporary culture. Sometimes the two complement each other but often they conflict.

As moderns, we instinctively maintain the equality of all people and uphold their freedom to choose their own paths without legal or social impediments. But this presents a challenge to Judaism, which limits certain positions to particular categories of people.

During the times of the Temples in Jerusalem, priests had different roles, privileges, and responsibilities than Levites, who in turn had different roles than Israelites. While in the absence of the Temple these large role distinctions no longer apply, Jewish life retains minor differentiations (e.g., priests are called to the Torah in synagogue first, followed by Levites and then Israelites) and, perhaps more significantly, Orthodox Jews eagerly await the Messianic Era when these ancient divisions of classes and roles will be reinstated. How are we moderns to view the different privileges and responsibilities given to some people merely because they were born to priestly parents?

The case of bastardy is even more difficult. Unlike the vague colloquial usage, in Jewish law the case is highly defined—the child of a technically-defined incestuous relationship or of a union between a married Jewish woman and a Jewish man who is not her husband. Such a person is considered a *"mamzer"* and may only marry another *"mamzer,"* which is a heartbreakingly severe disadvantage. Again, the modern notion of equality seems to argue against this rule.

III. Women's Issues
There are more examples, of course, but particularly pressing today is the question of the role of women in the Orthodox Jewish community. The amply attested tradition is that women are exempt from most time-bound positive commandments. Additionally, they are exempt from being called to testify before a religious court. These two exemptions logically lead to the exclusion of women from public roles in Jewish ritual. For example, because a woman is not obligated to hear the blowing of a shofar on Rosh Hashanah, even if she chooses to do so she cannot blow a shofar in synagogue for the benefit of others who are obligated to hear it. The same applies to leading public prayer and reading the Torah in synagogue. Her lack of obligation prevents her from performing the acts on behalf of those who are obligated.

While women were excluded from public ritual for thousands of years without much debate, the modern value of equality challenges that tradition. By what moral justification does our tradition differentiate based on gender? The challenge is particularly strong because Judaism sees moral intuitions as legitimate religious directives.

In the late 1970's and early 1980's, the Conservative Jewish movement debated exactly this issue in the context of the rabbinic ordination of women. The issue was so contentious that the final decision to ordain women led to a schism within the movement. Along the way, the Conservative debate produced three opposing views that are instructive:

IV. Three Methods of Resolution

- *Rejectionism* — an approach that openly acknowledges the conflict and allows tradition to prevail. Accepting the differentiation of gender roles, rejectionism holds that there is a profound spiritual reason for limiting the roles of women in public rituals, one that should be celebrated rather than dismissed. This is a resolution through rejection. As believers in the Divine revelation of Jewish tradition, which Orthodox Jews proudly profess, those who follow this approach reject any value that contradicts it in spirit or in law.

- *Legalism* — an approach that treats the matter merely as a regular legal inquiry: What does Jewish law say about the ordination of women? Setting aside all issues that relate to theology and ethics, legalists allow the legal texts to speak for themselves—which in practice, leads to the same answer as the rejectionists—no. This was the approach of the leading Talmudist of the Conservative movement and continues to be maintained by leading Orthodox scholars.

- *Revisionism* — an approach that redefines Jewish law to accommodate modern values. While insisting that it upholds the primacy of Jewish law, it undermines the values that inform tradition by a radical restatement of those laws. This approach has, on rare occasion, been implemented by eminent authorities in the past and has been adopted, and perhaps expanded, for the purposes of women's public participation. For example, Jewish law does not allow a woman to be called to the Torah in synagogue, but a revisionist strategy would redefine "ascending to the Torah" as merely a ceremonial rather than religious role that has the effect of preserving the form while neutralizing the restriction. This type of redefinition and expansion is done to as many areas of opportunities formerly limited to women as possible.

Each approach has its advantages and drawbacks. The rejectionist approach seems truest to tradition, but by simply denying our modern moral intuition, it fails to take seriously the tension that many people genuinely feel. The legalist approach, meanwhile, purports to have a neutral view, but only succeeds in doing implicitly what rejectionism does explicitly—ignoring the ethical questions facing religious people today.

The revisionist approach seems to resolve the tension but does so at the expense of transforming public worship into an arbitrary collection of rituals. To include women in public rituals, revisionism has to deprive those practices of their religious significance, and to allow for women's ordination, revisionism is forced to remove all aspects of communal authority from the rabbinate. In its own way, this leaves the moral dilemma intact. Additionally, there are some rituals that are immune to redefinition within the boundaries of the Orthodox legal process. Revisionism is resolution through procrastination, delaying the dilemma so that it only becomes troublesome at a later date when full egalitarianism comes face to face with a halakhic brick wall.

If none of these approaches seems satisfying, perhaps we have put the question in the wrong way. Jewish decision-making is not about choosing between absolute right and absolute wrong. It requires weighing the issues to maximize right and minimize wrong. Modern Jews face not simply a conflict between tradition and ethics, but a matrix of demands that includes ethics, customs, history, community, and education. Each of these must be weighed by its importance to Judaism. Sometimes specific values are so powerful that they override all other considerations. Some innovations are relatively unobtrusive and the "slippery slope" argument does not seem conclusive, while others are driven by an agenda whose momentum guarantees further changes in the near future. So how do we weigh all of these considerations?

V. Religious Education

In a landmark article,[195] Dr. Haym Soloveitchik (contemporary, Israel) describes a shift in practice within the Orthodox Jewish community that encompasses, but is not limited to, a trend towards stricter practice. He attributes this to a change in methods of religious instruction. Previously, religious practice had been primarily taught at home through experiencing the family's and local community's practices. With a breakdown in families and communities, religious instruction shifted to schools and books. The written law is sometimes different from how it is practiced in various locales. The new approach to education led to a centralization of religion and, to a degree, a move towards the strictest common denominator. What Dr. Soloveitchik describes was a move away from the experienced mimetic education towards the institutional education.

Many in the Modern Orthodox community object to this trend because it negates the practices they know. They were raised with a Judaism that is contradicted by the new textual standards. Those who cling dearly to their mimetic practices would want this

---

195. "Rupture and Reconstruction," *Tradition* 28:4 (Summer 1994).

value—the educational experience of Judaism as it was practiced in their youths—included in any evaluation of religious practices. In the case under discussion, it is clear that mimetic practice argues against increasing roles for women in the synagogue and the ordination of women. Such changes would do significant damage to this form of religious education.

VI. Customs

A related issue is that of continuity of communal custom. This is not the same as the value just discussed: that is individual while this is communal; and that is about education while this is about stability. There is a requirement within Jewish law to maintain the continuity of custom, as can be seen from a number of customs that are steadfastly retained—such as waiting for hours before eating dairy after a meat meal or the Ashkenazic custom to refrain from eating legumes on Passover due to their Medieval uses. This continuity of custom is important even in a case such as ours where we are discussing the absence of a practice—the lack of expanded roles for women in the community.

Women never served as ritual slaughterers, for example, although an actual prohibition was rejected in the Medieval legal literature. When the question arose of whether a woman could, in actual practice, be appointed as a slaughterer of animals, the answer given by scholars who are authoritative in the Ashkenazic tradition was no (Rema, *Yoreh De'ah* 1:1). Analogously, even if it is conceptually possible for women to serve as rabbis, communal custom—no small matter in the Jewish tradition—rejects the possibility, just as it rejects women prayer leaders and Torah readers.

VII. History and Community

The slippery-slope argument must be given its due. As a culture, Judaism embraces history as a source of inspiration and a means for studying personal and communal strategies. Over the past two centuries, radical changes in communal structure and religious practice have proven, in every case, impossible to control. The evidence seems clear that when radical innovations to ritual originate within tight legal limitations they quickly exceed those bounds.

The Orthodox response to these changes has been to maintain the consistency of ritual conservatism. Orthodoxy has refused to legitimize non-Orthodox changes to Jewish practice by giving even the appearance of adopting liberal positions. This has been confirmed in responsa by leading Modern Orthodox scholars, such as Rav David Hoffmann, Rav Yechiel Weinberg, and Rav Yitzchak Herzog, among others.

Certainly, egalitarianism is a value to be considered, but so is communal unity. There can be no question that the ordination of women would divide the Orthodox community. Whatever their reasons, the majority of Orthodox Jews will essentially excommunicate congregations and organizations led by women rabbis or allowing women to preside at Jewish rituals. Local rabbinical councils would split in half; schools would have to choose sides when making hiring decisions; family members would refuse to attend weddings where a female rabbi presides.

VIII. Putting the Pieces Together

We can now consider all of these values and how they fit together in our evaluation of the proposed innovations of the ordination of women and expansion of the leadership roles of women in religious ritual. What had initially seemed like a conflict between tradition and ethics now looks somewhat different. We have multiple values that include ethics, customs, history, community, education and other important issues, which point in different directions. Not every value has equal weight; you cannot simply add up the values on each side of the debate and follow the majority because some values are more important than others.

While we defer to halakhic scholars, in internalizing their conclusions the thinking person needs to consider each value and how important it is to him personally and to Judaism in general. Not every "slippery slope" argument is conclusive, and sometimes specific values are so powerful that they override all other considerations. Some innovations are relatively unobtrusive and don't offend other values, while others are accompanied by a momentum and agenda that all but guarantee further changes in the near future. How do we weigh all of these considerations?

This process is no simple exercise. Evaluating religious values requires careful attunement to communal trends and, more importantly, to the rhythms of Judaism, something accomplished only through extensive study and with great sensitivity. This type of values-analysis will yield confusing and occasionally contradictory results. Some areas of women's participation have different values-combinations than others. Depending on the specific practice, the measures on the scale will tip in different directions.

This type of values-analysis points to the conclusion that ordaining women and changing their roles in public ritual are not allowed, as indeed the leading rabbis have concluded. The kind of values-analysis I've been conducting does not resolve our moral problem—but that is not the point. The main outcome is not the conclusion but the process, through which we become more aware of the conflicting elements of the dilemma.

As with many issues—such as the differences between priests, Levites, and Israelites, and the case of bastardy—we sometimes live with difficult ethical dilemmas because we recognize that change would cause more damage than preserving the status quo. We understand that the moral imperative of egalitarianism does not automatically trump all other values.

Living with conflicting moral demands is difficult, but is integral to developing and maintaining awareness of the complex ethical world in which we function, and it is the only way to grow and thrive as moral beings. We use the oxymoronic term "Modern Orthodox" not because we have found a way to resolve all difficulties but because we are willing to acknowledge the importance of multiple values. And we attempt to balance their demands without negating them.

Women Leaders

The Orthodox Jewish community needs women influencers, not women rabbis.[196] So says the Rabbinical Council of America (RCA) in a 2015 resolution (which I sponsored) forbidding its members to hire women rabbis.[197] Unlike past generations, women today learn leadership skills that enable them to succeed in business and education. We in the Jewish community suffer if we sacrifice the contributions of half of our skilled population. This is especially true because men and women often have different perspectives, particularly in the Orthodox community where we sit on different sides of the *mechitzah*, the synagogue partition.

But we must define better this need for leadership before advocating radical communal change. In his book, *Lessons in Leadership: A Weekly Reading of the Jewish Bible*,[198] Rabbi Jonathan Sacks (contemporary, England) differentiates between leadership and authority. Authority means holding a position, occupying an office, wielding power. As we know, sadly too many people in authority fail to lead; they operate without imagination and inspiration. They are functionaries, perhaps fulfilling their tasks

---

196. This essay originally appeared in *Haaretz*, November 3, 2015.
197. "RCA Policy Concerning Women Rabbis" available at http://www.rabbis.org/news/article.cfm?id=105835
198. Jerusalem, 2015.

adequately but doing nothing more. In contrast, leaders wield influence, not power. They convince, inspire, offer vision.

When we say that we need female leadership, which definition are we invoking? Some people mean that we need women to fill roles in synagogues, much like rabbis do. The rabbi is the "*Mara De-Asra*," the authority in his synagogue community. This suggestion is a mistake, not only about leadership but about the Jewish community. The synagogue is the most visible symbol of Judaism but also the weakest form of religious experience. To an outside observer, the goings-on of a synagogue seem like the most exciting part of Jewish life but insiders recognize this as a misunderstanding.

The center of Judaism is in the home, in the daily life of a Jew who connects to God in small devotional acts throughout the day. Jewish worship is not just prayer but living according to Jewish law, reciting blessings, doing good to others, learning Torah. Fulfilling commandments throughout the day keeps us mindful of God and constantly expressing our relationship with our Creator. The center of the Jewish mind is in the classroom, the *beis midrash*, the sacred text. The Torah we learn inspires us; the *mitzvos* we perform connect us.

The synagogue is where we gather for a few hours each week, for some each day. Take away the synagogue and you can still have Judaism. Take away the Jewish home or text and Judaism disappears in a generation. The placement of the synagogue in the center of Judaism was a tragic mistake of the non-Orthodox movements. When we prioritize the synagogue in our thought and speech, we eclipse other aspects of Judaism, which in turn diminishes our personal religious experiences. The emphasis within Orthodox circles on women's roles in the synagogue is similarly short-sighted and inevitably self-defeating.

This focus on synagogue roles is tragically ironic in the Internet age. While our society is decentralizing, we dare not elevate the brick and mortar aspects of religion. Doing so forfeits legitimacy and surrenders Judaism's crucial advantage. Our portable homeland is the Torah, not the synagogue. Advocates for women's roles who focus on the synagogue—the rabbinate—betray a mistaken understanding of Judaism and of our times. The Internet era is the wrong time to promote authority, whether that of men or women. A shrewd investor would put his money in the decentralized influence of Torah, not synagogue life.

When it comes to Torah, women have significant room for advancement. You do not need a title to teach Torah—think of the many doctors, professors and rebbetzins who teach Torah to thousands. Nor do you need affiliation with a specific synagogue or community. Anyone who knows Torah can teach it. And with Torah, the quality of your teaching determines your influence, not your gender.

I question whether it is appropriate for me, a man, to preach about the rabbinate, which is open to me but not others. However, I speak as someone with no authority. Whatever influence I may have is unrelated to title or position but acquired solely through teaching Torah. Rabbis can exert influence inside the synagogue and beyond, acting in an age-old position of authority in the community. But today, more than ever, people are reached in many different ways and settings. Rabbis are only one of many influences on a community. Influencing through teaching Torah is the path forward for women, the road that combines tradition and progress. We need more women influencers.

When it comes to authority, we have traditions differentiating between men and women, which the RCA reiterated. Influence, however, is open to all. Rabbi Sacks points out that there are leaders "who hold no official position at all but who are consulted for advice and held up as role models. They have no power but great influence. Israel's prophets belonged to this category. So, often, did the *gedolei Yisrael*, the great sages of each generation. Neither Rashi nor the Rambam held any official position…. Wherever leadership depends on personal qualities—what Max Weber called 'charismatic authority'—and not on office or title, there is no distinction between women and men."

In this age of declining importance of authority and growing impact of influence, the emphasis on women rabbis is misguided. Authority has declined, as much as I lament that fact and hope to reverse that trend. Influence dominates today. We waste our energy when we debate texts and traditions on women rabbis because that is a conversation for a past era. Women's challenge today is to study and teach Torah, to influence minds and hearts, throughout the global community.

AFTERWORD

Over the past few hundred pages, we have discussed many aspects of leadership. It would be easy to get caught up in the seemingly bureaucratic elements—qualifications and certifications, authority and control, roles and responsibilities. While these are all important, we cannot ignore a crucial aspect of leadership.

In a 2005 address to recent ordinees, Rav Yisroel Belsky invoked the response of King Yoshiyahu (Josiah) to a momentous Torah reading (2 Kings 22).[1] Priests informed him that a Torah scroll had been found hidden in the Temple—at least one commentator suggests this was the original Torah scroll written by Moshe.[2] According to a tradition recorded in the Talmud Yerushalmi (*Sotah* 7:4),[3] the curses of the Torah in Deut. 27 were read. On reaching the final verse: "Cursed is anyone who does not uphold (*asher lo yakim*) the words of this law by observing them" (Deut. 27:26), Yoshiyahu cried out, "*Alay le-hakim*, it is on me to uphold." The king immediately embarked on a wildly successful mission to raise the spiritual level of the nation and to eradicate idolatry.

Every one of us, Rav Belsky continued, should feel "*Alay le-hakim*." To some degree, leadership is about position—having the

---

1. Published in R. Dov Brisman ed., *Natrana De-Oraisa: Kovetz Chidushei Torah* (Brooklyn, 2006), pp. 47-49.
2. See Abarbanel, ad loc.
3. Quoted in Ramban, Deut. 27:26.

right job such as king, rabbi or president of an organization. But even without that position, every person can be a leader using God-given talents and self-motivated energy. We all must find the passion to uphold the Torah, leading in our own small and large ways. Passion, commitment, a calling to improve—these are key ingredients of leadership. Wherever we are, we can use the tools available to us to transform the community.

The Mishnah (*Kiddushin* 82a), in discussing wealth, says that everything is based on your merit. Tosafos (ibid., s.v. *ela*) explain this to mean that everything is based on your *mazal*, your fortune. Ostensibly, Tosafos seem to twist the Mishnah's words to mean the exact opposite of its plain meaning. Rav Yisrael Lipschitz (*Tiferes Yisrael*, ad loc.) offers the background necessary to understand Tosafos' interpretation.

In Rav Lipschitz's formulation, *mazal* refers to the circumstances in which you are born and raised. Due to no choice of your own, you are deeply influenced by your family genetics, the time and place in which you live, your upbringing and the food you eat (as a child, when you usually have little choice). Your education and talents, the career and life options which are presented to you, to some extent the people you know—these are largely beyond your control. These are your *mazal*.

However, the sum of your circumstances (*mazal*) do not fully determine your future. Your merits play the decisive role. Even someone set up for wealth by family and talents can lose it all, whether by a bad decision or events beyond his control. Tosafos is saying that *mazal* establishes your starting point; you decide where to go based on your efforts, your prayer, the merits you achieve.

Put differently, *mazal* gives you skills, abilities and resources. Your parents raise you well, offer you opportunities for advancement in which you thrive thanks to your many talents. You achieve a certain status or certification, earn money and make connections, develop your unique abilities and traits. What do you do with that? You can remain in that *mazal* territory and continue your life dedicated to your family or you can move beyond. You are able to harness everything you have received and direct it to serving the community, to becoming a leader in your own way. You can find your role, based on your own abilities, in communal leadership. You can say "*Alay le-hakim.*"

Leaders are not necessarily rabbis or presidents of organizations. Leaders are the people who take initiative, who solve problems, who add value to the community in a variety of ways. If you are inspired by both the letter and spirit of the Torah, if you take guidance from Torah sages, you can use your talents and resources to find ways to improve people's spiritual and physical wellbeing. If you succeed, people will respect and follow you. We are all called but very few answer "*Alay le-hakim.*"

www.ingramcontent.com/pod-product-compliance
Lightning Source LLC
Chambersburg PA
CBHW030134170426
43199CB00008B/56